TODAY'S WORLD

Linda Robinson Fellag

Heinle & Heinle Publishers
An International Thomson
Publishing Company
Boston, Massachusetts, 02116, USA

ITP

The publication of *Today's World* was directed by the members of the Heinle & Heinle Global Innovations Publishing Team:

David C. Lee, Editorial Director
John F. McHugh, Market Development Director
Lisa McLaughlin, Production Services Coordinator

Also participating in the publication of this program were:

Director of Production: Elizabeth Holthaus
Publisher: Stanley J. Galek
Senior Assistant Editor: Kenneth Mattsson
Manufacturing Coordinator: Mary Beth Hennebury
Full Service Project Manager/Compositor: PC&F, Inc.
Interior Design: Maureen Lauran
Cover Design: Maureen Lauran

Manufactured in the United States of America

ISBN: 0-8384-5858-0

Heinle & Heinle Publishers is an International Thomson Publishing Company.

10 9 8 7 6 5 4 3 2 1

To Juanita "Polly" Hatcher of Navasota, Texas,
a lover of books, family, and the good life.

PHOTO CREDITS

TEXT CREDITS

WELCOME TO TAPESTRY

*E*nter the world of Tapestry! Language learning can be seen as an ever-developing tapestry woven with many threads and colors. The elements of the tapestry are related to different language skills like listening and speaking, reading and writing; the characteristics of the teachers; the desires, needs, and backgrounds of the students; and the general second language development process. When all these elements are working together harmoniously, the result is a colorful, continuously growing tapestry of language competence of which the student and the teacher can be proud.

This volume is part of the Tapestry Program for students of English as a second language (ESL) at levels from beginning to "bridge" (which follows the advanced level and prepares students to enter regular postsecondary programs along with native English speakers). Upper level materials in the Tapestry Program are also appropriate for developmental English courses—especially reading and composition courses. Tapestry levels include:

Beginning	Advanced
Low Intermediate	High Advanced
High Intermediate	Bridge

Because the Tapestry Program provides a unified theoretical and pedagogical foundation for all its components, you can optimally use all the Tapestry student books in a coordinated fashion as an entire curriculum of materials. (They will be published from 1993 to 1996 with further editions likely thereafter.) Alternatively, you can decide to use just certain Tapestry volumes, depending on your specific needs.

Tapestry is primarily designed for ESL students at postsecondary institutions in North America. Some want to learn ESL for academic or career advancement, others for social and personal reasons. Tapestry builds directly on all these motivations. Tapestry stimulates learners to do their best. It enables learners to use English naturally and to develop fluency as well as accuracy.

Tapestry Principles

The following principles underlie the instruction provided in all of the components of the Tapestry Program.

EMPOWERING LEARNERS

Language learners in Tapestry classrooms are active and increasingly responsible for developing their English language skills and related cultural abilities. This self direction leads to better, more rapid learning. Some cultures virtually train their students to be passive in the classroom, but Tapestry weans them from passivity by providing exceptionally high interest materials, colorful and motivating activities, personalized self-reflection tasks, peer tutoring and other forms of cooperative learning, and powerful learning strategies to boost self direction in learning.

The empowerment of learners creates refreshing new roles for teachers, too. The teacher serves as facilitator, co-communicator, diagnostician, guide, and helper. Teachers are set free to be more creative at the same time their students become more autonomous learners.

HELPING STUDENTS IMPROVE THEIR LEARNING STRATEGIES

Learning strategies are the behaviors or steps an individual uses to enhance his or her learning. Examples are taking notes, practicing, finding a conversation partner, analyzing words, using background knowledge, and controlling anxiety. Hundreds of such strategies have been identified. Successful language learners use language learning strategies that are most effective for them given their particular learning style, and they put them together smoothly to fit the needs of a given language task. On the other hand, the learning strategies of less successful learners are a desperate grab-bag of ill-matched techniques.

All learners need to know a wide range of learning strategies. All learners need systematic practice in choosing and applying strategies that are relevant for various learning needs. Tapestry is one of the only ESL programs that overtly weaves a comprehensive set of learning strategies into language activities in all its volumes. These learning strategies are arranged in eight broad categories throughout the Tapestry books:

Forming Concepts
Personalizing
Remembering New Material
Managing Your Learning
Understanding and Using Emotions
Overcoming Limitations
Testing Hypotheses
Learning with Others

The most useful strategies are sometimes repeated and flagged with a note, "It Works! Learning Strategy . . ." to remind students to use a learning strategy they have already encountered. This recycling reinforces the value of learning strategies and provides greater practice.

RECOGNIZING AND HANDLING LEARNING STYLES EFFECTIVELY

Learners have different learning styles (for instance, visual, auditory, hands-on; reflective, impulsive; analytic, global; extroverted, introverted; closure-oriented, open). Particularly in an ESL setting, where students come from vastly different cultural backgrounds, learning styles differences abound and can cause "style conflicts."

Unlike most language instruction materials, Tapestry provides exciting activities specifically tailored to the needs of students with a large range of learning styles. You can use any Tapestry volume with the confidence that the activities and materials are intentionally geared for many different styles. Insights from the latest educational and psychological research undergird this style-nourishing variety.

OFFERING AUTHENTIC, MEANINGFUL COMMUNICATION

Students need to encounter language that provides authentic, meaningful communication. They must be involved in real-life communication tasks that cause them to *want* and *need* to read, write, speak, and listen to English. Moreover, the tasks—to be most effective—must be arranged around themes relevant to learners.

Themes like family relationships, survival in the educational system, personal health, friendships in a new country, political changes, and protection of the environment are all valuable to ESL learners. Tapestry focuses on topics like these. In every Tapestry volume, you will see specific content drawn from very broad areas such as home life, science and technology, business, humanities, social sciences, global issues, and multiculturalism. All the themes are real and important, and they are fashioned into language tasks that students enjoy.

At the advanced level, Tapestry also includes special books each focused on a single broad theme. For instance, there are two books on business English, two on English for science and technology, and two on academic communication and study skills.

UNDERSTANDING AND VALUING DIFFERENT CULTURES

Many ESL books and programs focus completely on the "new" culture, that is, the culture which the students are entering. The implicit message is that ESL students should just learn about this target culture, and there is no need to understand their own culture better or to find out about the cultures of their international classmates. To some ESL students, this makes them feel their own culture is not valued in the new country.

Tapestry is designed to provide a clear and understandable entry into North American culture. Nevertheless, the Tapestry Program values *all* the cultures found in the ESL classroom. Tapestry students have constant opportunities to become "culturally fluent" in North American culture while they are learning English, but they also have the chance to think about the cultures of their classmates and even understand their home culture from different perspectives.

INTEGRATING THE LANGUAGE SKILLS

Communication in a language is not restricted to one skill or another. ESL students are typically expected to learn (to a greater or lesser degree) all four language skills: reading, writing, speaking, and listening. They are also expected to develop strong grammatical competence, as well as becoming socioculturally sensitive and knowing what to do when they encounter a "language barrier."

Research shows that multi-skill learning is more effective than isolated-skill learning, because related activities in several skills provide reinforcement and refresh the learner's memory. Therefore, Tapestry integrates all the skills. A given Tapestry volume might highlight one skill, such as reading, but all other skills are also included to support and strengthen overall language development.

However, many intensive ESL programs are divided into classes labeled according to one skill (Reading Comprehension Class) or at most two skills (Listening/Speaking Class or Oral Communication Class). The volumes in the Tapestry Program can easily be used to fit this traditional format, because each volume clearly identifies its highlighted or central skill(s).

Grammar is interwoven into all Tapestry volumes. However, there is also a separate reference book for students, *The Tapestry Grammar*, and a Grammar Strand composed of grammar "work-out" books at each of the levels in the Tapestry Program.

Other Features of the Tapestry Program

PILOT SITES

It is not enough to provide volumes full of appealing tasks and beautiful pictures. Users deserve to know that the materials have been pilot-tested. In many ESL series, pilot testing takes place at only a few sites or even just in the classroom of the author. In contrast, Heinle & Heinle Publishers have developed a network of Tapestry Pilot Test Sites throughout North America. At this time, there are approximately 40 such sites, although the number grows weekly. These sites try out the materials and provide suggestions for revisions. They are all actively engaged in making Tapestry the best program possible.

AN OVERALL GUIDEBOOK

To offer coherence to the entire Tapestry Program and especially to offer support for teachers who want to understand the principles and practice of Tapestry, we have written a book entitled, *The Tapestry of Language Learning. The Individual in the Communicative Classroom* (Scarcella and Oxford, published in 1992 by Heinle & Heinle).

A Last Word

We are pleased to welcome you to Tapestry! We use the Tapestry principles every day, and we hope these principles—and all the books in the Tapestry Program— provide you the same strength, confidence, and joy that they give us. We look forward to comments from both teachers and students who use any part of the Tapestry Program.

Rebecca L. Oxford
University of Alabama
Tuscaloosa, Alabama

Robin C. Scarcella
University of California at Irvine
Irvine, California

PREFACE

*T*oday's World is an integrated skills reading textbook intended for the high-advanced student in a pre-academic or partially-academic English language program.

The pedagogical basis for this book is that English learners improve their reading better by developing global cognitive and metacognitive strategies rather than discrete reading skills. At the advanced level, in particular, learning shifts from comprehension of textual language to comprehension and retention of textual *ideas*. Therefore, instruction that emphasizes critical thinking, promotes task-centered reading, and demands self-monitoring and responsibility from students most effectively produces independent readers.

Learning and reading strategies theorists provide a variety of taxonomies to define and delineate strategies to achieve these objectives. Weinstein (1992) categorizes learning strategies as rehearsal strategies, elaboration strategies, organization strategies, comprehension monitoring strategies, and affective strategies. Nist and Diehl (1991) fit these strategies into a reading and study system at the prereading, reading, organizing, and reviewing stages.

The system used in this textbook incorporates a range of strategies systems. In eight theme-based chapters, students read and study each text, applying strategies that are appropriate to each text.

READINGS

This textbook consists of eight chapters of related readings on present-day themes. Each chapter contains a variety of readings: poems, short stories, articles, essays, and related graphics. The themes are selected to engage students' interest, present opposing views, and offer international perspectives.

LEARNING GOALS

Each chapter opens with a set of learning goals designed to focus students' reading on specific content as well as develop specific learning and reading strategies. Before they begin each chapter, students rank the predicted value of a set of given learning objectives; they also add their own goals to the list. At the end of each chapter, they reassess their choices of learning objectives. This feature of the text helps students focus their reading and take responsibility for their learning.

READING JOURNAL

Throughout the text, students are required to keep a reading journal as a study tool. Many of the activities are recorded in the journal: freewriting before reading, writing in reaction to a reading, listening reports, vocabulary lists with definitions, graphic organizers, and journal entries relating to the students' personal reading habits. This feature of the text is meant to endow students with good study habits that they will carry into their later academic life.

STRATEGIES AND ACTIVITIES

In each chapter, reading strategies are organized into these categories: Preparing to Read, Comprehension, Language Study, Reactions, Reviewing, Evaluation, and Expansion.

Preparing to Read activities set the stage for the topic and language level of each text. These activities also encourage students to read for a purpose.

Comprehension checks after each reading enable the students to track their comprehension of main ideas and details in the texts. One reading per chapter also serves as a check for reading speed. Students record their comprehension and reading speed scores in Appendix I.

Language Study activities help students find textual organization and, through it, meaning. The activities also provide students with a variety of strategies for expanding their vocabulary knowledge.

Reactions activities allow students to check their understanding of the main ideas of the texts as well as to respond with their own ideas. The activities integrate the use of speaking, listening, writing, and reading.

A variety of *Reviewing* activities offer students practice in recalling important ideas from their reading. The activities foster communication and collaboration among students.

Evaluation activities allow students to self-test their comprehension of the chapter readings as a whole. Answers to chapter self-tests are included in Appendix II. In the evaluation stage, students also self-assess their reading habits and re-evaluate their learning goals.

Finally, *Expansion* projects give students opportunities to speak and write about what they have read and to read further in the subject area.

As reading theorists suggest, strategies presented at each stage of reading are modelled to students when they are first introduced. Later, students have repeated opportunities to practice each strategy. As language learning is a highly individualized endeavor, some strategies that work for some students will be ineffective for others. Instructors should try all the strategies so that each student can discover which ones work for him or her.

Appendix I contains direct instruction of techniques to facilitate reading speed and a Reading Rate/Comprehension Chart. Appendix II contains answer keys to comprehension checks in each chapter (including comprehension of timed readings), to chapter-end examinations, and to other exercises.

Acknowledgments

The author wishes to acknowledge the ESL students at Community College of Philadelphia and beyond, whose struggles to master college-level reading require us to devise more effective pedagogy. Elaine DiGiovanni and Suzanne Kalbach, ESL instructors in the English Department at CCP, also lent their pedagogical expertise and interest in reading strategies. In addition, a special thanks to Ken Mattsson, Heinle & Heinle senior assistant editor; Dave Lee, editorial director; and Rebecca Oxford and Robin Scarcella, series editors, for their faith in me and their dedication to the *Tapestry* series. Also, thanks to the following ESL professionals who gave helpful comments during the development of this text: Lida Baker, UCLA; Kim Brown, Portland State University; Arron Grow, Mississippi State University; Thomas Leverett, Southern Illinois University; Donald Linder, Hunter College; Patrick Oglesby, Duke University; Merritt Stark, Henderson State University. Finally, to my family, Fodil, Nadia, and Nora Fellag, thank you for your patience in the long hours during which this book robbed you of my company.

Linda Robinson Fellag
Community College of Philadelphia
Philadelphia, Pennsylvania

Contents

Departure

LEARNING GOALS

ACTIVITY: SETTING PERSONAL GOALS

List in order of importance (with 1 as "most valuable") the learning objectives that are significant to you. Add personal learning objectives to the list if you wish.

GOAL	RANK
1. To increase comprehension of readings	_____
2. To expand vocabulary	_____
3. To increase reading speed	_____
4. To improve study skills	_____
5. To learn more about the subjects of this chapter	_____
6. _____	_____
7. _____	_____

PREPARING TO READ

In Chapter 1 you will read three engaging stories about individuals who left their native countries and traveled to new lands. In each story, the traveler departed from his country under different conditions, at different stages in his life, and for different purposes. However, the prospect of new adventures loomed ahead for each, and one or all of the stories may remind you of your own experience of traveling to a new place. The stories are entitled:

"Truce in Heaven, Peace on Earth," from *Blue Dragon, White Tiger: A Tet Story,* by Tran Van Dinh
"I Leave South Africa," from *Kaffir Boy in America,* by Mark Mathabane
"Chinese Immigrants Tell of Darwinian Voyage," by Diana Jean Schemo

ACTIVITY: PREDICTING CONTENT

Before you read, discuss these questions in a small group:

1. Considering the titles of the readings in Chapter 1, what topics do you predict will be covered?
2. Look ahead at the photographs and other graphic material in the chapter. Read the accompanying captions. What do they suggest about the content of the chapter?

3. Look at the headings in Reading 3, "Chinese Immigrants Tell of Darwinian Voyage." What do they suggest about the topic of the reading?
4. What would you like to know about the immigrants in these stories? Make a list of your questions.

LEARNING STRATEGY

Forming Concepts: Listening for ideas about a topic enables you to better understand the topic.

ACTIVITY: LISTENING FOR IDEAS

A. With a partner, prepare for the topic of emigration by interviewing one person who has emigrated to a new place. You might choose an employee or student (outside your class) at your school, a friend, or a family member. After you have copied the following form into your study notebook, ask the person to talk about his or her trip to the new place and about his or her first reactions upon arrival. As you listen, write your notes on the form.

1. Name of Emigrant: _____

   His/Her Country of Origin: _____

   Date of Emigration: _____

   Length of Stay in New Place: _____

2. Description of Trip:

   Means of Transportation: (i.e., airplane) _____

   Length of Travel Time: _____

   Brief Description of Trip: _____

   _____

   _____

3. Arrival:

   Place of Arrival: _____

   Person's First Impressions of the New Place: _____

   _____

   _____

Threads

Commonly confused words:
emigrate: to leave for another place of residence
immigrate: to come to another place of residence

The World Almanac and Book of Facts, 1994

B. With your partner, present the information you collected from your interview to a group of classmates. Then, discuss your impressions of each of the group members' interviews.

ACTIVITY: PREVIEWING

When reading a difficult passage, it is helpful to **preview** an article in order to understand its general meaning. Previewing helps you understand the writer's goals and provides you with a general picture of what the writer thinks is significant. To preview a passage, you read the title and introduction before you read the passage. Next, you read the conclusion. Finally, you skim the entire passage quickly.

1. To begin previewing, reread the title of the first story. What is a *truce*? What might the author mean by this title?
2. Next, read the first paragraph of the story. What does this paragraph tell you about Minh, the narrator?
3. Since each reading in this textbook is preceded by a glossary of vocabulary items, look over these terms before you read.

LEARNING STRATEGY

Managing Your Learning: Becoming a more efficient, faster reader allows you to maximize your study time.

ACTIVITY: READING FASTER

Recording Your Time

Increasing your reading speed maximizes study time, but it takes regular practice. Review some common techniques for increasing your reading speed in "How to Read Faster" on page 197 of Appendix I. Practice these and other techniques in later chapters.

Begin by recording the exact times at which you start and finish reading the following passage. Then calculate your reading speed, take the comprehension test after the reading, and record your rate and comprehension score in the chart on page 200 of Appendix I.

Reading 1

AUTHOR NOTES

Tran Van Dinh was born in Hue, Vietnam, in 1923. He relates the emigration of Vietnamese "boat people" to Thailand in this excerpt from his novel, *Blue Dragon, White Tiger: A Tet Story* (1983).

Glossary
Blue Dragon   Animals, such as dragons, often figure prominently in Vietnamese stories.

Chinese Tang poet Tu Fu   a famous Chinese poet who flourished during the prosperous Tang dynasty (618–906)

Tet's eve   Tet is the term for the New Year celebration in Vietnamese and other Asian cultures.

TRUCE IN HEAVEN, PEACE ON EARTH

by Tran Van Dinh

Minh looked at the sea beyond. It was bluer than it had been on any other day of the whole journey. He imagined that a majestic Blue Dragon surged from the depths of the blue sea and with his ivory claws took all of them to the Isle of the Eastern Ocean where there would be no frontiers to cross or politics to tear people down.

The sky wasn't as clear as the day before. Isolated mountain-shaped white clouds began to appear. They brought to his memory a line by the famed Chinese Tang poet Tu Fu:

In the sky, a cloud appeared as a white cloth
Suddenly, it turned into a bluish dog.

Minh didn't see any bluish dog. The white clouds now converged to take the form of a huge attacking tiger. A cold wind blew. Minh smelt the odor of dead fish. He heard Thai voices but could not understand what they were saying. A motor-boat appeared suddenly alongside the junk, with three bronze-skinned men on board.

The tallest among them pointed a machine gun at Minh and asked loudly, "Vietnamese fleeing Communists?"

"Yes," Minh said, his teeth clenched. Before he could ask them if they were Thai Navy patrolmen, the man with the machine gun ordered his two revolver-carrying followers to jump over to Minh's boat. One fired a shot in the air. "Thai bandits!" Minh shouted.

But it was too late. The bandits lined everyone up on the deck. While the machine-gunner stood guard over the victims, his two aides searched all corners of the boat. They took one submachine gun that Don had had neither time nor the chance to use. Then all three searched the Vietnamese, who lowered their heads more in shame and anger than in fear. From the Chinese merchant they took gold ingots that were hung on his shoulders under his T-shirt. They stripped Trang of the brand new hundred-dollar bills that had been sewn so carefully under his coat, as well as removing his watch. Then the tall bandit took Xuan aside and led her down into the cabin.

Minh could hear Xuan's metallic voice screaming at the Thai bandit in Vietnamese as she struggled furiously. The attacker shouted in Thai, "Devil, stubborn woman, submit to me! You dare to try to kill me by biting my testicles? Submit or you'll soon see your ancestors in the depth of the sea!"

A deadly silence followed. About five minutes later the bandit emerged, his hands stained with blood, his face scratched, carrying Xuan's broken body. Laughing, he threw it into the blue water. He jumped back into his motorboat with his two accomplices and in a few seconds they had all disappeared into the white cloud-covered horizon.

Minh looked at the sky with imploring eyes. Indeed, the White Tiger cloud had now been transformed into an advancing bluish dog.

The sky darkened. The wind blew stronger and colder. Winter seemed to descend on the New Spring operation. Everybody wept and sobbed. For the next twelve hours, they all lay on the deck, numb with the misfortune that had befallen them. No one ate anything, no one said anything.

Late the next afternoon Trang called the passengers together.

"My friends," he said, "despite our misfortune we have reached our goal. We'll be in Chantaburi no later than five o'clock. I have told you that the Prime Minister of Thailand is an old friend of our dear friend and brother, Doctor Minh. With your approval, I shall ask him to be our representative to the Thai authorities. We can celebrate the Tet's eve in Chantaburi, but I think it would be proper that we do so on our boat, which is, according to international law, Vietnamese territory."

With the end of their journey in sight, the passengers seemed to have forgotten the nightmarish incident that had engulfed them in sorrow and despair the day before. They applauded Trang's announcement, and Minh was asked to speak.

"I shall never forget, as long as I live, our boat family. I shall do everything I can to help all of you settle in the new lands of freedom, either

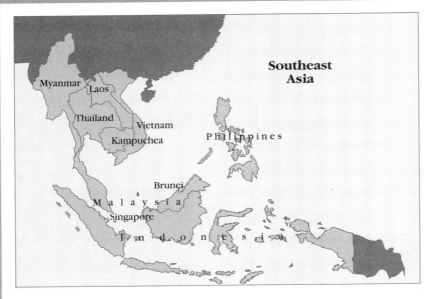

Southeast Asia

Minh picked up the receiver. "Hello, Mr. Prime Minister. Congratulations."

"Stop it, Minh. I'm still Chamni, your old friend."

"But I'm now a boat person without a country, a wandering soul, as we say in Vietnamese."

"Forget about your boat and your wandering soul. You can stay in Thailand as long as you wish, as my government's guest. Thailand is now your country. Buddha will protect you. I'll have the colonel bring you to Bangkok tonight so you can have a good rest and we can meet for breakfast tomorrow. As for your compatriot boat people, how many of them are there?"

"Nineteen, including me."

"They'll be given special consideration by the Ministry of Interior, but in the meantime they'll have to stay in a refugee camp. I'm sorry about that, but I can't change all the laws even as a Prime Minister. I have to leave for a meeting now. I'll see you tomorrow. Sleep well, my dear friend."

"Thank you and goodnight, Mr. Prime Minister."

The colonel invited Minh to have dinner with him before his trip to Bangkok by helicopter. Minh explained that because it was Tet's eve, he preferred to eat with his compatriots. The colonel quickly proposed that the whole group be invited along to a Chinese restaurant. They accepted the invitation but they had no appetite: Minh had warned them before dinner that they would be temporarily sent to a refugee camp.

in Thailand or America. Obviously, the situation here is very favorable to us because of my connection with the Prime Minister, but one always has to be careful about politics in Thailand. The Prime Minister reached power through a coup d'etat, and there could be a counter-coup at any time. When we arrive there, I'll contact the Prime Minister and see what his attitude to us will be." His short speech ended with several rounds of applause.

Early in the evening the junk lowered its anchor off Chantaburi. Operation New Spring had come to an end. A police motorboat met the refugees. In Thai Minh asked the police office to take him to the local army commander. Within half an hour, Minh and the police lieutenant were at the office of Colonel Amneuy Luksanand, commanding officer of the 25th Royal Thai Infantry Regiment. Minh explained the situation, reported the bandits' attack, and requested that he be allowed to contact the Prime Minister, his old friend Chamni. The colonel politely invited Minh to wait while he phoned Bangkok.

Minh was admiring a pot of blooming orchids when the colonel entered the living room.

"Professor, the Prime Minister is on the line. You can use the phone in my office."

Comprehension

Mark the following statements "True" or "False," based on information in "Truce in Heaven, Peace on Earth." Do not look back at the story as you mark your answers. Refer to page 202 in Appendix II for the correct answers, and then check the text, if you wish. Record your comprehension score and reading rate on page 200 of Appendix I.

_____ **1.** The narrator, Minh, was traveling by sea.

_____ **2.** Looking out on the ocean made Minh recall a Chinese poem.

_____ **3.** The gun-carrying Thais who boarded Minh's boat were Thai Navy patrolmen.

_____ **4.** The Thai men took gold and money from Minh and his fellow travelers.

_____ **5.** One of the Thai men murdered a Vietnamese man aboard the boat.

_____ **6.** The Vietnamese group called their trip "the New Spring" operation.

_____ **7.** Dr. Minh was an old friend of a Thai Army colonel.

_____ **8.** Minh and his Vietnamese companions were told they would have to stay in a Thai refugee camp.

_____ **9.** The Vietnamese boat travelers had arrived on Tet's eve.

_____ **10.** In the end, the Vietnamese group ate happily at a Chinese restaurant with the Thai army colonel.

_____ **CORRECT** × **10** = _____ %

Managing Your Learning: Annotating a text helps you focus on difficult or important parts of a reading.

ACTIVITY: ANNOTATING A TEXT

Annotating, or marking, a text is a common technique used by students to help them remember what they read. Often, readers **underline** or **highlight** key sentences for later study. Many readers also **circle** or **underline** important or unfamiliar words in a reading. Yet another useful way to mark a text is by making notes in the margins.

Reread "Truce in Heaven, Peace on Earth." This time, mark the reading by circling or underlining important or unfamiliar words or sentences; write question marks in the margins next to parts that you find difficult or confusing; and mark with asterisks the parts you think are important to remember. Be selective in the amount of information that you underline or highlight.

One paragraph of the text is marked below as an example:

** <u>With the end of their journey in sight, the passengers seemed to have forgotten the nightmarish incident</u> that had (engulfed them in sorrow and) **??** (despair) the day before. They applauded Trang's announcement, and Minh was asked to speak.

ACTIVITY: IDENTIFYING THE ORGANIZATION

Narrative

Effective readers understand the ways in which an author organizes his or her writing. When an author like Tran Van Dinh writes, he organizes his text in specific ways. Usually in the first paragraph or paragraphs, he establishes a main idea (or ideas) for his writing. Then he uses each paragraph to explain one specific part of his overall idea. Identifying the writer's organization allows you to understand the writer's main idea and its relationship to other ideas in the passage.

"Truce in Heaven, Peace on Earth" is an example of **narrative** writing. In this type of organization, the writer tells a story. Here, Dinh narrates the story of a man (similar in background to himself) who took a dangerous ocean journey from Vietnam to Thailand. Personal stories such as these are predominantly organized in narrative form, with the events following chronological order. Thus he tells each part of the story in the order in which it happened. When you read narrative writing, you will find certain features: the use of past-tense verbs, transitions that separate events in the story, and, of course, chronological order.

Read the following narrative statements, taken from a key section of "Truce in Heaven, Peace on Earth." Using numbers, place them in chronological order.

——— **1.** About five minutes later the bandit emerged, his hands stained with blood, his face scratched, carrying Xuan's broken body.

——— **2.** No one ate anything, no one said anything.

——— **3.** . . . in a few seconds they had all disappeared into the white cloud-covered horizon.

——— **4.** Then the tall bandit took Xuan aside and led her down into the cabin.

——— **5.** A motorboat appeared suddenly alongside the junk . . .

——— **6.** . . . the man with the machine gun ordered his two revolver-carrying followers to jump over to Minh's boat.

——— **7.** Then all three searched the Vietnamese, who lowered their heads more in shame and anger than in fear.

——— **8.** The bandits lined everyone up on the deck.

LANGUAGE STUDY

LEARNING STRATEGY

Personalizing: By choosing the new information you learn *yourself*, you increase your interest in learning it.

ACTIVITY: PERSONAL VOCABULARY

From "Truce in Heaven, Peace on Earth," select ten new vocabulary words that you want to learn. Write these words in a reading journal, a notebook in which you put information relevant to your reading, or put each word on a separate 3-by-5-inch or 4-by-8-inch notecard. Title one page (or your first card) "Truce in Heaven, Peace on Earth." Then make your Personal Vocabulary List. Beside each word on your list, or on each card, write the dictionary definition and the part of speech (i.e., noun, verb, adjective, adverb). If you use cards, write the word by itself on the back of the card so that you can test yourself on the definitions. Notice that in the example below, noun is abbreviated as *n*.

truce *n*.   A temporary cessation or suspension of hostilities by agreement of the opposing sides; armistice.

REACTIONS

ACTIVITY: SHARING IMPRESSIONS

"Truce in Heaven, Peace on Earth" recounts a perilous journey in which a group of Vietnamese escape to Thailand. Discuss the following questions, which relate to their experiences, in a small group.

1. When Minh described the dark sky and the clouds in the beginning of the story, what feelings do you think he experienced?
2. The Vietnamese boat people felt "shame and anger rather than fear" as the Thai bandits stole their belongings. How would you have felt in their position? What would you have done?
3. After the Thai bandits killed the Vietnamese woman, her fellow travelers reacted by not eating and not talking. How do you think the Vietnamese boat group felt at this moment?
4. When the group arrived in Thailand, Minh told them that he would try to help them in Thailand or in America. Then the group applauded. What does this part of the story tell you about the character of the boat people?
5. The Vietnamese boat adventure brings the group to Thailand on Tet's (New Year's) Eve. How do you imagine they felt about arriving on this important holiday? How would you feel if you had been in their situation on the eve of a holiday?
6. Finally, in the end of the story, when the boat people learned they would have to stay in a Thai refugee camp, they reacted by not eating their meal at a Chinese restaurant. How did they feel? What does their reaction tell you about life in a Thai refugee camp?
7. If a member of your group knows about a situation similar to the one presented in the story, ask him or her to describe it to the group.

PREPARING TO READ

ACTIVITY: PREVIEWING

The title of the next reading, written in 1978, straightforwardly tells the reader that author Mark Mathabane is South African. What do you know about South Africa today? What do you imagine about South Africa in 1978? Why do you suppose the author left his country?

LEARNING STRATEGY

Managing Your Learning: Scheduling your time wisely as you are learning a new subject helps you to avoid "cramming" your studying into a short time period.

10

"I Leave South Africa" is a lengthy text. To read texts like this, you should divide your reading assignment into manageable "chunks," or sections. One way to divide up your reading is to decide to read from one heading to another. Another real consideration is the amount of time your instructor gives you to complete the reading task. Yet another way is to skim the reading to determine logical places to divide your reading, such as after a long section of dialogue (conversation in quotation marks), as in "I Leave South Africa."

Consider your reading deadline; then divide "I Leave South Africa" into three or four chunks, and read one at a time.

Reading 2

Mark Mathabane has lived in the United States since 1978, writing not only about his South African homeland but also about his immigrant experiences. *Kaffir Boy* and *Kaffir Boy in America* are his best-known novels.

Glossary

Mandingo   various groups of people inhabiting the upper Niger River valley of western Africa

Roots   a popular novel by Alex Haley about Africans sold into slavery and transported to the United States; the television movie based on the novel

Afrikaner   an Afrikaans-speaking descendant of the Dutch settlers of South Africa

Afro   a rounded, bushy hairstyle

permanent wave, or jerry-curl   a long-lasting hair setting

Brylcreem   a brand of men's hair cream

Calvinistic   relating to the Christian religious doctrine of John Calvin, which stresses god's omnipotence

Playboy   an American magazine featuring female nudity

I LEAVE SOUTH AFRICA

by Mark Mathabane

The plane landed at Atlanta's International Airport the afternoon of September 17, 1978. I double-checked the name and description of Dr. Killion's friend who was to meet me. Shortly after the plane came to a standstill at the gate, and I was stashing Dr. Killion's letter into my totebag, I felt a tap on my shoulder, and turning met the steady and unsettling gaze of the Black Muslim.

"Are you from Africa?" he asked as he offered to help me with my luggage.

"Yes." I wondered how he could tell.

"A student?"

"Yes." We were aboard a jumbo jet, almost at the back of it. From the throng in front it was clear that it would be some time before we disembarked, so we fell into conversation. He asked if it was my first time in the United States, and I replied that it was. He spoke in a thick American accent.

"Glad to meet you, brother," he said. We shook hands. "My name is Nkwame."

"I'm Mark," I said, somewhat intimidated by his aspect.

"Mark is not African," he said coolly. "What's your African name, brother?"

"Johannes."

"That isn't an African name either."

I was startled by this. How did he know I had an African name? I hardly used it myself because it was an unwritten rule among black youths raised in the ghettos to deny their tribal identity and affiliation, and that denial applied especially to names. But I didn't want to offend this persistent stranger, so I gave it to him. "Thanyani."

"What does it stand for?"

How did he know that my name stood for something? I wondered in amazement. My worst fears were confirmed. Black Americans did indeed possess the sophistication to see through any ruse an African puts up. Then and there I decided to tell nothing but the truth.

"The wise one," I said, and quickly added, "but the interpretation is not meant to be taken literally, sir."

We were now headed out of the plane. He carried my tennis rackets.

"The wise one, heh," he mused. "You Africans sure have a way with names. You know," he went on with great warmth, "one of my nephews is named after a famous African chief. Of the Mandingo tribe, I believe. Ever since I saw 'Roots' I have always wanted to know where my homeland is."

I found this statement baffling for I thought that as an American his homeland was America. I did not know about "Roots."

"Which black college in Atlanta will you be attending, Thanyani?" he asked. "You will be attending a black college, I hope?"

Black colleges? I stared at him. My mind conjured up images of the dismal tribal schools I hated and had left behind in the ghetto. My God, did such schools exist in America?

"No, sir," I stammered. "I won't be attending school in Atlanta. I'm headed for Limestone College in South Carolina."

"Is Limestone a black college?"

"No, sir," I said hastily.

"What a pity," he sighed. "You would be better off at a black college."

I continued staring at him.

He went on. "At a black college," he said with emphasis, "you can meet with your true brothers and sisters. There's so much you can teach them about the true Africa and the struggles of our people over there. And they have a lot to teach you about being black in America. And, you know, there are lots of black colleges in the South."

I nearly fainted at this revelation. Black schools in America? Was I hearing things or what? I almost blurted out that I had attended black schools all my life and wanted to have nothing to do with them. But instead I said, "Limestone College is supposed to be a good college, too, sir. It's integrated."

"That don't mean nothing," he snapped. "Integrated schools are the worst places for black folks. I thought you Africans would have enough brains to know that this integration business in America is a fraud. It ain't good for the black mind and culture. Integration, integration," he railed. "What good has integration done the black man? We've simply become more dependent on the white devil and forgotten how to do things for ourselves. Also, no matter how integrated we become, white folks won't accept us as equals. So why should we break our backs trying to mix with them, heh? To them we will always be niggers."

I was shaken by his outburst. I longed to be gone from him, especially since he had drawn me aside in the corridor leading towards customs. The Black Muslim must have realized that I was a complete stranger to him, that his bitter tone terrified and confused me, for he quickly recollected himself and smiled.

"Well, good luck in your studies, brother," he said, handing me my rackets. "By the way, where in Africa did you say you were from? Nigeria?"

"No, South Africa."

"South what!" he said.

"South Africa," I repeated. "That place with all those terrible race problems. Where black people have no rights and are being murdered every day."

I expected my statement to shock him; instead he calmly said, "You will find a lot of South Africa in this country, brother. Keep your eyes wide open all the time. Never let down your guard or you're dead. And while you're up there in South Carolina, watch out for the Ku Klux Klan. That's their home. And don't you ever believe that integration nonsense."

He left. I wondered what he meant by his warning. I stumbled my way to customs. There was a long queue and when my turn came the white, somber-faced immigration official, with cropped reddish-brown hair, seemed transformed into an Afrikaner bureaucrat. I almost screamed. He demanded my passport. After inspecting it, he asked to see my plane ticket. I handed it to him.

"It's a one-way ticket," he said.

"Yes, sir. I couldn't afford a return ticket," I answered, wondering what could be wrong.

"Under the student visa regulations you're required to have a return ticket," he said icily. "Otherwise how will you get back home? You intend returning home after your studies, don't you?"

"Yes, sir."

"Then you ought to have a return ticket."

I remained silent.

"Do you have relatives or a guardian in America?"

I speedily handed him a letter from Stan Smith, along with several completed immigration forms indicating that he had pledged to be my legal guardian for the duration of my stay in the States. The immigration official inspected the documents, then left his cubicle and went to consult his superior. I trembled at the thought that I might be denied entry into the United States. But the one-way ticket, which created the impression that I was coming to America for good, was hardly my fault. Having had no money to purchase a ticket of my own, I had depended on the charity of white friends, and I was in no position to insist that they buy me a return ticket. The immigration official came back. He stamped my passport and welcomed me to the United States. I almost fell on my knees and kissed the hallowed ground.

"Welcome to America, Mark," a tall, lean-faced white man greeted me as I came out of customs. It was Dr. Waller.

His kind voice and smiling face, as he introduced himself and asked me if I had a good flight, raised my spirits. As we walked toward the baggage claim area I stared at everything about me with childlike wonder. I scarcely believed I had finally set foot in *the* America. I felt the difference between South Africa and America instantly. The air seemed pervaded with freedom and hope and opportunity. Every object seemed brighter, newer, more modern, fresher, the people appeared better dressed, more intelligent, richer, warmer, happier, and full of energy—despite the profound impersonality of the place.

"I would like to use the lavatory," I told Dr. Waller.

"There should be one over there." He pointed to a sign ahead which read RESTROOMS. "I'll wait for you at the newsstand over there."

When I reached the restroom, I found it had the sign MEN in black and white on it. Just before I entered I instinctively scoured the walls to see if I had missed the other more important sign: BLACKS ONLY or WHITES ONLY, but there was none. I hesitated before entering: this freedom was too new, too strange, too unreal, and called for the utmost caution. Despite what I believed about America, there still lingered in the recesses of my mind the terror I had suffered in South Africa when I had inadvertently disobeyed the racial etiquette, like that time in Pretoria when I mistakenly boarded a white bus, and Granny had to grovel before the irate redneck driver, emphatically declaring that it was an insanity "not of the normal kind" which had made me commit such a crime, and to appease him proceeded to wipe, with her lovely tribal dress, the steps where I had trod. In such moments of doubt such traumas made me mistrust my instincts. I saw a lanky black American with a mammoth Afro enter and I followed. I relieved myself next to a white man and he didn't die.

The black American washed his hands and began combing his Afro. I gazed at his hair with wonder. In South Africa blacks adored Afros and often incurred great expense cultivating that curious hairdo, in imitation of black Americans. Those who succeeded in giving their naturally crinkly, nappy, and matted hair, which they loathed, that buoyant "American" look were showered with praise and considered handsome and "glamorous," as were those who successfully gave it the permanent wave or jerry-curl, and bleached their faces with special creams which affected the pigmentation.

I remember how Uncle Pietrus, on my father's side, a tall, athletic, handsome man who earned slave wages, was never without creams such as Ambi to bleach his face, and regularly wore a meticulously combed Afro greased with Brylcreem. Many in the neighborhood considered him the paragon of manly beauty, and women were swept away by his "American" looks.

From time to time he proudly told me stories of how, in the center of Johannesburg, whites who encountered black men and women with bleached faces, Afros, or straightened hair, and clad in the latest fashion from America, often mistook them for black Americans and treated them as honorary whites. A reasonable American accent made the masquerade almost foolproof. So for many blacks there were these incentives to resemble black Americans, to adopt their mannerisms and life-styles. And the so-called Coloureds (mixed race), with their naturally lighter skin and straightened hair, not only frequently took advantage of this deception but often passed for whites. But they were rarely secure in their false identity. And in their desperation to elude discovery and humiliation at being subjected to fraudulent race-determining tests like the pencil test (where the authorities run a pencil through one's hair: if the pencil slides smoothly through, one gets classified white; if it gets tangled, that's "positive" proof of being black), they often adopted racist attitudes toward blacks more virulent than those of the most racist whites.

I had sense enough to disdain the practice of whitening one's skin. I considered it pathetic and demeaning to blacks. As for the companies which manufactured these popular creams, they are insidiously catering to a demand created by over three hundred years of white oppression and domination. During that traumatic time the black man's culture and values, trumpeted as superior, became the standards of intelligence, excellence, and beauty.

I left the bathroom and rejoined Dr. Waller at the newsstand. I found him reading a magazine.

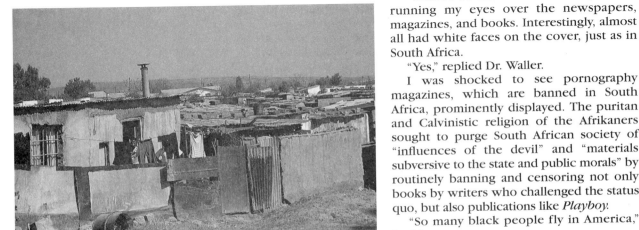

A black township in apartheid South Africa.

"There's so much to read here," I said, running my eyes over the newspapers, magazines, and books. Interestingly, almost all had white faces on the cover, just as in South Africa.

"Yes," replied Dr. Waller.

I was shocked to see pornography magazines, which are banned in South Africa, prominently displayed. The puritan and Calvinistic religion of the Afrikaners sought to purge South African society of "influences of the devil" and "materials subversive to the state and public morals" by routinely banning and censoring not only books by writers who challenged the status quo, but also publications like *Playboy*.

"So many black people fly in America," I said.

"A plane is like a car to many Americans," said Dr. Waller.

"To many of my people cars are what planes are to Americans."

At the baggage-claim area I saw black and white people constantly rubbing shoulders, animatedly, talking to one another, and no one seemed to mind. There were no ubiquitous armed policemen.

"There truly is no apartheid here," I said to myself. "This is indeed the Promised Land."

I felt so happy and relieved that for the first time the tension that went with being black in South Africa left me. I became a new person.

Comprehension

Without rereading the story, mark the following statements "True" or "False," based on information in "I Leave South Africa." Refer to page 202 in Appendix II for the correct answers, and then check the text, if you wish. Record your comprehension score and reading rate on page 200 of Appendix I.

_____ 1. Mark Mathabane, the narrator, arrived in Atlanta in 1978.

_____ 2. The Black Muslim who started a conversation with him was an African.

_____ 3. The narrator was surprised because the Black Muslim knew about African names.

_____ 4. The Black Muslim man recommended that Mathabane attend an integrated college.

_____ 5. Mathabane had trouble with customs because he had lost his passport.

_____ 6. Dr. Waller was a white man who met Mathabane after he left customs.

_____ 7. Immediately, Mathabane felt American life was worse than life in South Africa.

_____ 8. He expected to find "WHITES ONLY" and "BLACKS ONLY" bathrooms in the United States.

_____ 9. In South Africa, "the pencil test" determined whether a person was smart.

_____ 10. Another difference from South Africa that Mathabane found in the United States was pornographic magazines.

_____ **CORRECT** × **10** = _____ %

LANGUAGE STUDY

ACTIVITY: PERSONAL VOCABULARY

IT WORKS!
Learning Strategy:
Choosing What
to Learn

Choose ten new vocabulary words from "I Leave South Africa" that you want to learn. Write these words in your reading journal or on vocabulary cards. Title a page (or the first card) "I Leave South Africa." Then start your Personal Vocabulary List, writing the words along with their dictionary definition and part of speech (i.e. noun, verb, adjective, adverb). Follow the example on page 9. Then below each word and definition, copy the sentence in which the word is used in "I Leave South Africa."

ACTIVITY: READING FASTER

IT WORKS!
Learning Strategy:
Reading Faster

Clustering

One of the best techniques for speeding up your reading rate is **clustering.** Clustering means reading **groups of words** rather than one word at a time. As your eyes move from left to right across the page, they should not stop to identify each individual word. Instead, you can read more rapidly if you read words in small, logical groups. Clustering also enables you to see the logical relations between groups of words in a sentence.

Here's an example of the way you might be reading now:

I   became   a   new   person.

Here's another way you might read this line, using the clustering technique:

I became   a new person.

Notice that when you use clustering, you read *logical groups* of words together. The subject and verb (*I became*) are read together, and the article, adjective, and noun (*a new person*) are read together. Why wouldn't it make sense to group the words into clusters like this?:

I   became a new   person.

Use the clustering technique and circle the logical clusters of words in the sentences below, which come from "I Leave South Africa." Compare your clusters with a classmate's.

1. The plane landed at Atlanta's International Airport the afternoon of September 17, 1978.
2. We were aboard a jumbo jet, almost at the back of it.
3. The immigration official inspected the documents, then left his cubicle and went to consult his superior.
4. I felt the difference between South Africa and America instantly.
5. "I would like to use the lavatory," I told Dr. Waller.

REACTIONS

ACTIVITY: DRAMATIZING

In a small group, dramatize "I Leave South Africa" by acting out possible scenes in which two or more of the following characters interact: Mark Mathabane, the narrator; the Black American he meets on the plane; the white customs official; and the white professor who picks Mathabane up at the airport.

Begin by discussing the relationships among each group of actors in the story. Then create a scene in which two or more characters are interacting. Here are a few suggested scenes, although you may want to create your own.

1. Mathabane and the Black American debate whether freedom exists in the United States.
2. The customs official refuses to let Mathabane into the United States, and he must convince the official to change his mind.
3. Mathabane asks Dr. Waller which colleges in the United States are better, black or integrated.

PREPARING TO READ

ACTIVITY: PREVIEWING

The third reading, entitled "Chinese Immigrants Tell of Darwinian Voyage," appeared in the *New York Times*. Its title makes reference to scientist Charles Darwin. What is he famous for? What kind of voyage did Darwin make? Why do you think the article about Chinese immigrants bears this title?

Chinese aboard an America-bound ship in the 1800s.

Reading 3

Glossary

Darwinian   relating to the difficult, five-year Pacific Ocean voyage in which scientist Charles Darwin explored animal life

Myanmar   formerly Burma

prison blues   the blue prison uniform

"take the Fifth"   ask for protection under the Fifth Amendment to the U.S. Constitution, which deals with the rights of accused criminals

Queens   a borough of New York City

loan shark   a slang term for moneylender

Mauritius   an island country off the eastern African coast

cargo hold   a storage area beneath a ship's deck

Taoist   relating to a Chinese philosophy and religion based on the teachings of Lao-tse in the sixth century B.C.

sandbar   a sandy elevation on the ocean floor

henchmen   loyal supporters

Threads

People arrested for illegally entering the United States gained the right to a lawyer in 1992, according to a new U.S. Immigration and Naturalization Service policy.

New York Times, June 12, 1992

CHINESE IMMIGRANTS TELL OF DARWINIAN VOYAGE

by Diana Jean Schemo

BETHLEHEM, Pa., June 11, [1993]—As Chen Fuxing tells it, the Golden Venture's odyssey to America was a trial of desperation and fear. The lack of food, water, light, and space broke the 300 travelers down, and a kind of Darwinian order took shape. The weaker ones, who typically got the last scraps of a daily meal of rice and water, would argue and beg for more, with disputes erupting into brawls among the passengers. People fell sick, but without medicine others would feel helpless and leave them alone.

Mr. Chen's voyage to America began nearly two years ago. He set out from a rural village in southeastern China, where busy meant a ten-hour day on the family's rice farm. He trekked through the mountains of Myanmar and Thailand, slept in an airless cabin the size of a small bathroom with three other people on one ship, and eventually became a virtual prisoner on the Golden Venture, which the authorities say was used to transport Chinese immigrants who paid as much as $35,000 each for the voyage to America.

Unwelcomed Darkness

Mr. Chen, a 30-year-old farmer and sometime factory worker, saw a darkness on the freighter that he never connected with his quest for America. "A lot of fighting was going on," he said, and shook his head. "I think it changed many people, being on that ship."

Mr. Chen and Yi Powen, another refugee, described their journeys, mainly through interpreters, during a news conference and in separate interviews at the maximum-security Lehigh County Prison and at the medium-security Salisbury Interim Correctional Facility in Bethlehem. Wearing prison blues and matching sneakers—manufactured in China—Mr. Chen at times tried out the halting English he had taught himself before leaving China. Asked what he hoped to accomplish in America, he said. "I'll take the Fifth."

Of 60 refugees whom prison officials asked to speak at a press conference, the two came forward in the hope that their families in China would see them on television and know they were not among the half-dozen people who died when the ship ran aground off Queens last Sunday. Their accounts offered an insight into the hardships that many of the other passengers suffered during their ordeal at sea.

Mr. Yi, who is 30 and the father of two sons, occasionally forced a smile at the roomful of reporters, though at times he appeared almost in pain, tense and touching his stomach. A tea leaf farmer, Mr. Yi was one of fewer than 100 refugees who traveled on the Golden Venture from Thailand to America, stopped to pick up Mr. Chen and about 200 other refugees from their gathering point in Mombasa in Kenya.

This is the story of their flight.

Chen Fuxing left for America on Oct. 22, 1991, his older brother having borrowed $25,000 from a loan shark to pay for Mr. Chen's chance at a new life. He took nothing but the clothes he wore and $1,000 his brother gave him for the 17,000-mile journey. At the Myanmar border, he met up with a group of six refugees and a guide, crossing over the mountains and into Thailand in a month-long hike.

"Luckily, it didn't rain," he said. Along the way, some in his group fell ill, and Mr. Chen learned a cardinal rule of his unfolding voyage: See only to yourself. None of the other travelers would stop to help those who couldn't keep up, but all eight made it through the mountains. "We knew of other groups where people died, and we all managed," he said.

In Thailand, the group was brought to a warehouse—they did not know where in the country it was—and locked up with other refugees waiting for a boat. They waited more than six months for the *Najd II,* a passenger ship registered in Saudi Arabia. Nearly 300 Chinese bound for America climbed aboard the *Najd II* in August 1992, ferried to the ship on speedboats leaving from the coast near Bangkok.

The passengers were assigned four to a cabin, largely as they boarded, Mr. Chen said. Some of the rooms were passable, but in some the air hung still and stale. The cabins had no toilets. The entire ship had only three toilets for the passengers.

The ship's crew would give the passengers one meal a day—usually rice with rare additions of sardines or vegetables, and barely enough potable water for each person. They left it up to the passengers or the smugglers to dole out the portions. Despite the sense of fear, arguments quickly erupted.

Usually, people would stand on line for the food, but that meant those who could grab more in the beginning left little for those behind them. Debates over how to distribute the food quickly turned into arguments, which flared into fights.

It was never clear how it was decided which passengers would distribute the food and set the rules.

"Probably, before they left China, they were appointed by the smugglers," Mr. Chen said. "And some probably emerged once we were on the ship. They just came out so naturally, and people just followed their authority."

"It's not so strange to me, since this is our way in China," he added. "We follow authority."

Each passenger received a bottle of water a day to clean themselves. But as the voyage wore on, the bottles came one every other day, and eventually, less frequently. The passengers began to smell and wilt from hunger. Without ventilation, the odors in the cramped rooms grew more difficult to bear. In steadily growing clusters, people began leaving their cabins—giving up what limited privacy they had there—and sleeping in an open area.

Saw No Abuse

Mr. Chen said he did not see any of the sexual abuse of women that Immigration and Naturalization Service officials described in a briefing Thursday. Nor did he see whether any of the smugglers or their henchmen carried weapons on the *Najd II*.

But somehow, the passengers gained the clear impression there was friction between the smugglers and the ship's crew, and came to believe the *Najd II* would never make it to America. They did not see any open fights, he said, but had a deep sense of foreboding.

At the time, the *Najd II* was floating off Mauritius, where the government had refused to grant it permission to dock. It refueled and steamed toward Mombasa, where some 200 or so stranded Chinese waited in hotels for the smugglers to patch together the final leg of their journey.

Around the time Mr. Chen and the others were waiting in Mombasa, where they were free to swim in the ocean, walk the seaside port, and go to the movies, the smugglers finally came up with the ship that would haul them to America, a rusting freighter with an unlikely name: the *Golden Venture*. If the *Najd II* was unbearable for some, the *Golden Venture* was hell for all, a floating prison.

A Fearsome Tempest

Mr. Yi was one of 90 or so passengers who boarded the *Golden Venture* from boats off Bangkok in February. The ship passed first through Singapore and then by the Cape of Good Hope, south of Africa, where it ran into a tempest that Mr. Yi feared would kill everyone on board.

Wind gales and waves as tall as 50 feet hurled the ship from side to side. The captain said he had never seen such a storm and doubted they would survive. Experienced sailors among the passengers said the same. Panic spread through the cargo hold.

"Some people were crying, and people were praying to their different gods, to the Christian god, to Buddha, and to Pu Sa," the Taoist goddess worshipped in southern China, Mr. Yi said.

But the ship made it safely through the storm, a sign Mr. Yi, and undoubtedly many other passengers, saw as an omen that they were meant to make it to America.

It was in Kenya that all the passengers who would land on the Rockaway Sandbar Saturday night finally boarded the *Golden Venture*. When they first entered, the smugglers' representatives assigned them a small sleeping space in the cargo hold and a blanket. They were confined to this space for the entire trip, an area roughly the size of a coffin, the two men said. It was six inches on either side to the next body.

"We were ordered that this is the place we sleep and this is the place we can walk around in," Mr. Chen said. "When we needed to go to the bathroom, we could go, but we had to come straight back to our places."

But for the money and telephone numbers some of them carried, there were few belongings. Their greatest trial was boredom. One passenger, the police said, played a handheld computer game, punching the buttons long after the batteries wore out.

With only one toilet for the entire ship, the men soon resorted to relieving themselves on the upper deck. But there was no running water, and unlike the *Najd II,* the *Golden Venture* did not supply occasional bottles of water for personal hygiene.

Not Allowed on Deck

On the last day or two of the trip, as the ship floated within sight of the East Coast, the men were not allowed to go on deck, but had to relieve themselves in the cargo hold, Mr. Chen said. That produced the nauseating stench immigration officials and police described after boarding the ship in New York.

The men knew nothing of missed rendezvous with smaller boats that should have brought them to the coast, or of the mutiny aboard the *Golden Venture* that Federal officials described in court earlier this week. They knew only that at some point Saturday night, the smugglers spread the word: "We've arrived! Jump!"

"Most of us were pretty weak because of seasickness," said Mr. Yi, who said he was among the last to leave, jumping only as he saw that American agents were swarming toward the ship. "We were told as long as we set foot on American soil, we would be able to stay in this country."

The Lehigh County facilities have divided the 60 men the Immigration and Naturalization Service sent here into two groups, with those suspected of being linked to the smugglers placed in the maximum security prison.

Without the presumed henchmen, he said, the men are relaxing and speaking more freely.

Neither Mr. Chen nor Mr. Yi knew of a statement from Chinese officials that those refugees returned would be subject to "re-education," but they know their country's brutal recent history. "If we have to go back, we definitely will be punished," Mr. Yi said.

"It's taken us so much pain to get here," Mr. Chen added. "All we heard was Americans really champion human rights. We were under the impression we would get to stay."

The translator looked at Mr. Chen and said: "Somehow, in his mind, he's convinced you won't send him back to hell."

Comprehension

Without rereading the story, mark the following statements "True" or "False," based on information in "Chinese Immigrants Tell of Darwinian Voyage." Refer to page 202 in Appendix II for the correct answers, and then check the text, if you wish.

_____ **1.** Chen Fuxing's voyage to the United States began two years before his ship landed in New York.

_____ **2.** The Chinese immigrants paid as much as $350 for the voyage.

_____ **3.** Chen hiked to Thailand and waited there six months for a ship.

_____ **4.** He and other passengers traveled from Thailand on the *Najd II* in private cabins.

_____ **5.** People often fought over food aboard the ship, Chen said.

_____ **6.** Chen saw women sexually abused on board the ship.

_____ **7.** The *Najd II* dropped the Chinese passengers off in Mombasa, Kenya.

_____ **8.** Yi Powen, an immigrant who boarded the *Golden Venture* in Thailand, said the ship enjoyed good weather en route to Kenya.

_____ **9.** While aboard the *Golden Venture,* the Chinese immigrants were allowed to walk freely on the deck.

_____ **10.** After being caught by U.S. immigration officials, the immigrants said they feared punishment if they returned to China.

_____ **CORRECT** × **10** = _____ %

LANGUAGE STUDY

ACTIVITY: PERSONAL VOCABULARY

Choose ten new vocabulary words from "Chinese Immigrants Tell of Darwinian Voyage" that you want to learn. Write these words in your reading journal or on vocabulary cards along with their dictionary definition and part of speech (i.e. noun, verb, adjective, adverb). Follow the example on page 9. Then, under each word and definition, copy the sentence in which the vocabulary word appears in the passage.

IT WORKS!
Learning Strategy:
Choosing What
to Learn

REACTIONS

LEARNING STRATEGY

Forming Concepts: Connecting information from different sources helps you think critically.

ACTIVITY: CONNECTING IDEAS

In a small group, answer these questions relating to "Chinese Immigrants Tell of Darwinian Voyage."

1. Whose journey was more dangerous, that of the Vietnamese boat people in Tran Van Dinh's story or that of the Chinese who arrived aboard the *Golden Venture*? In what ways were the two voyages similar? different?
2. Who has a better justification for being admitted into the United States, the Vietnamese or the Chinese travelers? Why?

ACTIVITY: DRAMATIZING

Threads

The hardest thing to learn in life is which bridge to cross and which to burn.

David Russell

In a small group, dramatize "Chinese Immigrants Tell of Darwinian Voyage" by acting out one particular part of the travelers' dangerous journey.

Begin by discussing the story and rereading your favorite sections. You might choose to act out either a part that is reported in the story or a part that is not directly explained. After you have decided which part to act out, select group members to play the other roles. Share your drama with the class.

Here are a few suggested parts of the story that your group might choose to dramatize:

1. Chinese immigrants arrange with smugglers to travel illegally to the United States.
2. Chen Fuxing and a small group of fellow travelers struggle to follow their guide as they hike through the mountains of Thailand.
3. Chinese immigrants try to convince U.S. immigration officials to let them stay in the United States.

EVALUATION

ACTIVITY: CHAPTER SELF-TEST

Assess your general understanding of the readings in Chapter 1 by taking the following chapter self-examination. The day before you take this test, select and mark ten vocabulary items from your reading journal (or from your vocabulary cards) that you would like to learn. Write them on a separate piece of paper, and turn in this list to your instructor. Then quickly review your reading journal notes about the chapter and the readings.

On the test day, your instructor will return your list of ten words. Fill in the definitions and parts of speech of the words in Part 1. Circle the appropriate completion of each statement in Part 2. Check your answers to Part 1 in your reading journal or on your cards, and score your test. See page 202 in Appendix II for the answers to Part 2.

Part 1: Vocabulary

Vocabulary Word	Definition	Part of Speech
1. _____	_____	_____
2. _____	_____	_____
3. _____	_____	_____
4. _____	_____	_____
5. _____	_____	_____
6. _____	_____	_____
7. _____	_____	_____
8. _____	_____	_____
9. _____	_____	_____
10. _____	_____	_____

_____ **CORRECT** × **10** = _____ %

Part 2: Comprehension

1. In "Truce in Heaven, Peace on Earth," the narrator is traveling from Vietnam to Thailand in hopes of
   a. immigrating to the United States.
   b. immigrating to Thailand.
   c. a or b
2. The author tells the story in chronological order, a characteristic of which organizational pattern?
   a. comparison and contrast
   b. narrative
   c. definition
   d. all of the above
3. In "I Leave South Africa," Mark Mathabane travels to the United States in order to
   a. become a U.S. citizen.
   b. play pro tennis.
   c. study at college.
   d. write books.
4. The Black American who meets Mathabane on the plane recommends he attend a black college because Mathabane would be able to
   a. meet his "true brothers and sisters."
   b. teach them a lot about Africa.
   c. learn about black America.
   d. all of the above

5. Among the differences Mathabane sees between South Africa and the United States, he notices that
   a. there's very little reading material in the airport.
   b. blacks and whites don't talk to each other.
   c. bathrooms are used by both blacks and whites.

6. In "Chinese Immigrants Tell of Darwinian Voyage," the writer says that on the *Golden Venture*, the immigrants lacked
   a. food and water.
   b. companionship.
   c. medicine.
   d. a and b
   e. a and c

7. On the *Golden Venture*, sleeping accommodations may be described as
   a. two to a cabin.
   b. a small space on deck.
   c. private cabins.
   d. none of the above

8. Chen Fuxing and Yi Powen spoke to reporters about their journey because they wanted
   a. to practice their English.
   b. to return to China.
   c. to let their families know they weren't dead.
   d. to get special consideration from U.S. immigration officials.

9. When the Chinese immigrants arrived in New York, they left the ship by
   a. small boats.
   b. helicopters.
   c. jumping off the ship.
   d. none of the above

10. Chen Fuxing believed that the U.S. immigration officials would
    a. let him stay in the United States.
    b. send him back to China.

_____ **CORRECT** $\times$ **10** = _____ %

ACTIVITY: EVALUATING YOUR GOALS

In your reading journal, write briefly in answer to the following questions:

1. The most important skills I used in reading and responding to the readings in this chapter were _____.

2. The most valuable information I gained from this chapter was _____
   _____.

Remembering New Material: Responding to a reading through writing allows you to reflect upon new ideas and retain them longer.

ACTIVITY: WRITING

In your reading journal, write a paragraph in response to <u>one</u> of the questions that follow.

1. Have you or has someone you know well moved to a new place? Describe the trip and first impressions.
2. Compare and contrast what you (or someone you know well) expected to find in the new place with what you (or someone) did find upon arrival.
3. Choose one of the main characters of the stories in Chapter 1. From his viewpoint, describe his general impressions of the new country that he found.

Reading Further

Find an article in a magazine or newspaper (or part of a book) about a group of people who emigrated to the United States or another country. In your reading journal, write a brief summary and commentary on the reading. Give the name, author, publisher, and publication date of your reading.

Arrival

ACTIVITY: SETTING PERSONAL GOALS

As in Chapter 1, list in order of importance (with 1 as "most valuable") the learning objectives that are significant to you. Add personal learning objectives to the list if you wish.

GOAL	RANK
1. To increase comprehension of readings	_____
2. To expand vocabulary	_____
3. To increase reading speed	_____
4. To improve study skills	_____
5. To learn more about the subjects of this chapter	_____
6. _____	_____
7. _____	_____

PREPARING TO READ

In Chapter 1, you read about the lives of people in "old countries" across the globe. For many, the prospect of better lives in a new country or a new region entices them to leave the familiar cultures of their childhood and emigrate to alien lands. Their successes and failures at adapting to their new lands emerge in the readings of this chapter:

> "The Struggle to Be an All-American Girl," by Elizabeth Wong
> "How It Feels to Be Colored Me," by Zora Neale Hurston
> "Legal Alien," by Pat Mora

ACTIVITY: PREDICTING CONTENT

Discuss these questions in a small group.

1. Considering the titles of the readings in Chapter 2, what aspects of life in a new land do you think the authors will explore?
2. Which of the titles makes you think of your own experiences? Why?
3. Look ahead at the photographs and other graphic material in the chapter. Read the accompanying captions. What do they suggest about the content?

LEARNING STRATEGY

Personalizing: Relating the ideas in reading to your *own* knowledge permits you to better understand what you read.

When you read, you bring to the reading experience your own knowledge. In other words, you read from a unique perspective. Your "life history" may contain experiences that are similar to those found in a reading. Moreover, you may have studied a topic that you encounter later in a reading. Also, your culture may affect the way you read and react to ideas.

If you use your personal perspective to its fullest capacity, you can enhance your ability to comprehend *and* retain what you read. You can approach a reading more confidently by exploring what you know of it *before* you read, you can think about your personal experience *as* you read, and you can reflect on ideas in a reading in relation to your life *after* you read. All these techniques will make you a more effective reader.

ACTIVITY

In your reading journal, write for five minutes in answer to this question: "What is the most difficult aspect of living in a new country?"

ACTIVITY: LISTENING FOR IDEAS

IT WORKS! Learning Strategy: Listening

A. With a small group of classmates, find the soundtrack of the musical film *West Side Story* in a local library. Listen to the song entitled "America," which presents two perspectives on the situation of Puerto Rican immigrants in the United States. First, listen for the main idea of the song. Next, listen again, and transcribe the lyrics. Work together to identify all the words from the song. Then check your version with your instructor. Copy the following form into your journal. Listen, and then write your report about the song.

1. Title of Song: _____

   Published by: _____ Year: _____

2. Music by: _____

   Lyrics by: _____

3. Main Idea of the Song:

   _____

   _____

   _____

4. Your Impression of the Song:

   _____

   _____

   _____

B. As an alternative, you may want to view one segment of the television series, "The All-American Girl," which premiered on ABC-TV in 1994, or the Asian-American musical *Flower Drum Song*. In the series and in the movie, an Asian-American family faces the challenges of living a "bicultural" lifestyle in the United States.

View one segment of the series or one part of the film, and answer the following questions briefly: (Be prepared to present your responses to the class.)

1. Describe the parent's relationship with his or her children, who are main characters in the stories.
2. Describe one cultural issue that is raised in the particular show that you viewed.
3. What is your reaction to the Asian-American family? Whose perspective do you identify most closely with? Why?

ACTIVITY: SHARING IMPRESSIONS

Share your report on the song "America" (or on the television series or movie you watched) with some of your classmates. Present your ideas and your opinions of the song or show. Listen to your group-mates' reports, then discuss differences.

ACTIVITY: PREVIEWING

A. The authors of "The Struggle to Be an All-American Girl" and "How It Feels to Be Colored Me" both relate their feelings about being members of a minority group. With a partner, make a list of words and phrases that describe how *each of you* feels as a member of a minority in a new country.

_____

_____

_____

_____

_____

_____

_____

B. In "The Struggle to Be an All-American Girl," writer Elizabeth Wong describes her childhood attitude towards her mother. How do you expect her to behave towards her mother? Why?

Reading 1

Glossary
Nationalist Republic of China   Taiwan
kow tow   the Chinese greeting in which one touches the forehead to the ground to show respect
Little Women, Black Beauty   classic children's books
Nancy Drew   a well-known character in children's stories
chop suey   a Chinese-American noodle and vegetable/meat dish
Cinco de Mayo   Mexican independence day

THE STRUGGLE TO BE AN ALL-AMERICAN GIRL

by Elizabeth Wong

It's still there, the Chinese school on Yale Street where my brother and I used to go. Despite the new coat of paint and the high wire fence, the school I knew ten years ago remains remarkably, stoically the same. (1)

Every day at 5 p.m., instead of playing with our fourth- and fifth-grade friends or sneaking out to the empty lot to hunt ghosts and animal bones, my brother and I had to go to Chinese school. No amount of kicking, screaming, or pleading could dissuade my mother, who was solidly determined to have us learn the language of our heritage. (2)

Forcibly, she walked us the seven long, hilly blocks from our home to school, depositing our defiant tearful faces before the stern principal. My only memory of him is that he swayed on his heels like a palm tree, and he always clasped his impatient twitching hands behind his back. I recognized him as a repressed maniacal child killer, and knew that if we ever saw his hands we'd be in big trouble. (3)

We all sat in little chairs in an empty auditorium. The room smelled like Chinese medicine, an imported faraway mustiness. Like ancient mothballs or dirty closets. I hated that smell. I favored crisp new scents. Like the soft French perfume that my American teacher wore in public school. (4)

There was a stage far to the right, flanked by an American flag and the flag of the Nationalist Republic of China, which was also red, white, and blue but not as pretty. (5)

Although the emphasis at the school was mainly language—speaking, reading, writing— the lessons always began with an exercise in politeness. With the entrance of the teacher, the best student would tap a bell and everyone would get up, kowtow, and chant, "Sing san ho," the phonetic for "How are you, teacher?" (6)

Being 10 years old, I had better things to learn than ideographs copied painstakingly in lines that ran right to left from the tip of a *moc but,* a real

ink pen that had to be held in an awkward way if blotches were to be avoided. After all, I could do the multiplication tables, name the satellites of Mars, and write reports on *Little Women and Black Beauty.* Nancy Drew, my favorite book heroine, never spoke Chinese. (7)

The language was a source of embarrassment. More times than not, I had tried to disassociate myself from the nagging loud voice that followed me wherever I wandered in the nearby American supermarket outside Chinatown. The voice belonged to my grandmother, a fragile woman in her seventies who could outshout the best of the street vendors. Her humor was raunchy, her Chinese rhythmless, patternless. It was quick, it was loud, it was unbeautiful. It was not like the quiet, lilting romance of French or the gentle refinement of the American South. Chinese sounded pedestrian. Public. (8)

In Chinatown, the comings and goings of hundreds of Chinese on their daily tasks sounded chaotic and frenzied. I did not want to be thought of as mad, as talking gibberish. When I spoke English, people nodded at me, smiled sweetly, said encouraging words. Even the people in my culture would cluck and say that I'd do well in life. "My, doesn't she move her lips fast," they would say, meaning that I'd be able to keep up with the world outside Chinatown. (9)

My brother was even more fanatical than I about speaking English. He was especially hard on my mother, criticizing her, often cruelly, for her pidgin speech—smatterings of Chinese scattered like chop suey in her conversation. "It's not 'What it is,' Mom." he'd say in exasperation. "It's 'What *is* it, what *is* it, what *is* it'!" Sometimes Mom might leave out an occasional "the" or "a," or perhaps a verb of being. He would stop her in midsentence: "Say it again, Mom. Say it right." When he tripped over his own tongue, he'd blame it on her: "See, Mom, it's all your fault. You set a bad example." (10)

What infuriated my mother most was when my brother cornered her on her consonants, especially "r." My father had played a cruel joke on Mom by assigning her an American name that her tongue wouldn't allow her to say. No matter how hard she tried, "Ruth" always ended up "Luth" or "Roof." (11)

After two years of writing with a *moc but* and reciting words with multiples of meanings, I finally was granted a cultural divorce. I was permitted to stop Chinese school. (12)

I thought of myself as multicultural. I preferred tacos to egg rolls; I enjoyed Cinco de Mayo more than Chinese New Year. (13)

At last, I was one of you; I wasn't one of them. (14)

Sadly, I still am. (15)

Comprehension

Without reviewing the reading, mark the following statements "True" or "False," based on the information in "The Struggle to Be an All-American Girl." Check your answers on page 202 in Appendix II. Record your comprehension score and reading rate on page 200 of Appendix I.

_____ **1.** The author attended Chinese school every weekday morning.

_____ **2.** The author's mother forced her and her brother to attend Chinese school.

_____ **3.** The author felt the Chinese school principal was strict and authoritarian.

_____ **4.** Chinese school smelled better than American school, according to the author.

_____ **5.** Every class at Chinese school began with a language lesson.

_____ **6.** The author enjoyed learning to make Chinese ideographs with a *moc but* pen.

_____ **7.** Her favorite book heroine, Nancy Drew, was not Chinese.

_____ **8.** The author liked the sound of her grandmother speaking Chinese.

_____ **9.** The author's brother often corrected his mother's English.

_____ **10.** In the end, the author quits Chinese school.

_____ **CORRECT** × **10** = _____ %

LANGUAGE STUDY

Forming Concepts: Making guesses while reading or listening challenges you to think carefully about what people mean.

Understanding what you read does not require you to understand *every* word of a passage. The effective reader is able to guess word meaning, and thus comprehend meaning, by a variety of techniques. One way is for the reader to examine words or phrases in the sentence in which an unfamiliar word appears, or look at sentences before and after the one in which an unknown word appears. The surrounding words can often give important clues to word meaning. The following passage provides an example.

The Tortoise was a <u>voluble</u> speaker. Because he talked so much, the birds decided to make him their spokesman.

The careful reader notices key words surrounding the unfamiliar term, *voluble*. Words such as "speaker," "he talked so much," and "spokesman" suggest that *voluble* relates to speaking. In fact, the word means "talkative."

ACTIVITY

Practice using the context of surrounding words and phrases to guess the meanings of the underlined words in the following sentences, taken from "The Struggle to Be an All-American Girl." In your reading journal, write your "guess." Then, with a partner, check your guesses by looking up the words in a dictionary, and if necessary, correct the definition in your journal.

1. "No amount of kicking, screaming, or pleading could <u>dissuade</u> my mother, who was solidly determined to have us learn the language of our heritage."
2. "Forcibly, she walked us the seven long, hilly blocks from our home to school, depositing our <u>defiant</u> tearful faces before the stern principal. My only memory of him is that he <u>swayed</u> on his heels like a palm tree, and he always clasped his impatient <u>twitching</u> hands behind his back."
3. "There was a stage far to the right, <u>flanked</u> by an American flag and the flag of the Nationalist Republic of China, which was also red, white, and blue but not as pretty."
4. "My brother was especially hard on my mother, criticizing her, often cruelly, for her <u>pidgin</u> speech—<u>smatterings</u> of Chinese scattered like chop suey in her conversation."

REVIEWING

IT WORKS!
Learning Strategy:
Guessing
Meaning

When you read, you also make guesses about *ideas* as well as words or phrases. Guessing about ideas often requires you to add information to a passage that is not directly stated, much as you do when you interpret someone's speech by noting that person's behavior, tone of voice, and choice of words.

When you read, you can infer meaning by a number of clues. Word choice indicates meaning. The action or lack of action by a character in a story can show meaning that is not directly stated. In addition, you can draw conclusions from information in a reading by using your own life experience.

For example, look at the following two sentences:

Ha opened the front door <u>carefully</u> and <u>crept</u> across the hallway of her house <u>at midnight</u>.

<u>At midnight</u>, Ha <u>slammed</u> the door as she entered her house and <u>threw her heavy boots</u> in the corner of the hallway.

Considering the underlined words, what can you guess about the way Ha enters her house in the first sentence? in the second sentence?

Each sentence treats arriving home at midnight in a different way. You guess through word choice that in the first sentence, Ha is scared that someone (perhaps her parents) may hear her arrive late; in the second sentence, she has no such fear. These ideas are not directly stated; however, you can infer, or guess, them based on the information that *is* stated in each sentence.

ACTIVITY: GUESSING MEANING

With a small group, discuss the following questions. They require you to make inferences (guesses) based on the information that is provided in "The Struggle to Be an All-American Girl." Share your ideas with the group, and write down all the inferences that you and your group-mates can make.

1. In paragraph 6, the author tells how each class began with "an exercise in politeness." After rereading the paragraph and considering the words she uses, how do you think the writer feels about this part of the lesson?
2. In paragraph 7, which skills does the author consider the most valuable? Which does she consider the least valuable? Which words help you infer this?
3. The author writes in paragraph 8: "In Chinatown, the comings and goings of hundreds of Chinese on their daily tasks sounded chaotic and frenzied." Considering the words the author uses, what conclusion can you make about her attitude toward Chinese people?
4. Finally, at the end of the story, the author writes: "At last, I was one of you; I wasn't one of them. Sadly, I still am." What do these two sentences mean? Who is "you" and "them"? Why does the author choose the word "sadly"?
5. Consider the title again. What does being an "all-American girl" mean to the author?

ACTIVITY: PERSONAL VOCABULARY

Choose ten vocabulary words from the text "The Struggle to Be an All-American Girl" that you would like to learn, including, if you wish, some of the words you examined in the exercise on page 34 on guessing word meaning. Write each word, its definition, and its part of speech in your reading journal or on a vocabulary card. Follow the example on page 9 of Chapter 1. Then, in your journal or on each card, write an original sentence in which you use each word. Check your sentences with your instructor.

IT WORKS!
Learning Strategy:
Choosing What
to Learn

ACTIVITY: IDENTIFYING THE ORGANIZATION

Comparison and Contrast

As you learned in Chapter 1, identifying the organization of a reading helps you to isolate and remember ideas. An effective way to identify organization is to put ideas from a reading in a graphic form, sometimes called a **graphic organizer.** Then you can use the graphic as a study tool.

Making a graphic organizer of a reading requires two steps. First, look for a pattern of organization, such as narration, which was explained in Chapter 1. Find the dominant organizational pattern in the reading—in other words, the pattern containing the most important information. Then make a drawing, map, or chart containing the information.

"The Struggle to Be an All-American Girl" contains an important organizational pattern: **comparison and contrast.** Here, the author contrasts characteristics of Chinese and American life. Often, she presents only the Chinese side of the comparison, leaving the reader to guess the characteristics of the American side.

Remembering New Material: As you review, think of graphic ways to represent the key ideas in a reading. Then put them in your notebook.

ACTIVITY

Make a graphic organizer chart in your notebook or reading journal to explain the comparisons in the reading. Under "Characteristics" make a few notes that sum up the author's description of each basis of comparison. If the author presents no information for the American side, for instance, fill in the "Characteristics" column with your own ideas as in the example. Add other items compared in the story in the blank spaces.

Comparisons in "The Struggle to Be an All-American Girl"

Basis of Comparison	*Chinese* Characteristics	*American* Characteristics
principal	_____	_____
smells	_____	_____
_____	_____	_____
_____	_____	_____
_____	_____	_____

ACTIVITY: SHARING IMPRESSIONS

When you have finished the comparison chart, discuss it with a small group. Share your reactions to the contrasts and comparisons you found. In your view, does the author characterize *Chinese* life or *American* life more favorably? Why?

PREPARING TO READ

ACTIVITY: PREVIEWING

A. The next reading is titled "How It Feels to Be Colored Me." Why does the author use the word "colored" to describe herself? What impression does this word give you?

B. Next, read the first paragraph of the story. Discuss the meanings of the following terms, and then discuss the meaning of the sentence as a whole.

>   extenuating circumstances
>   Negro

C. Finally, read the first sentence of paragraph two. Discuss what the author may mean by the phrase "became colored." What does this sentence tell you about the author's life before and after the moment she "became colored"?

D. In this story, the author writes about Southerners and Northerners. What is the historical relationship between these two regions of the United States? Are Southerners and Northerners different? If so, in what ways?

LEARNING STRATEGY

Overcoming Limitations: Examining vocabulary *before* you read a passage enables you to more easily grasp the main idea of the reading.

When you read, you encounter many passages that contain special vocabulary. Words or phrases relating to a specific field of study, idioms, or words containing unfamiliar cultural references make reading such passages challenging.

One useful strategy for overcoming this difficulty is to examine special vocabulary items *before* you read. You can preview any special vocabulary provided by an instructor or included in a glossary (such as the ones in this textbook), or you can quickly scan the passage for unfamiliar words *before* reading. As mentioned in Chapter 1, always preview the glossary words before you read, if possible.

ACTIVITY

With a partner, use a dictionary, your experience, or your instructor's assistance to define the following special words or phrases from "How It Feels to Be Colored Me." Check the glossary to find any definitions that appear there. Write the words and definitions in your reading journal. Then, as you read, check how each word is used in the passage.

>   proscenium box   Hegira
>   first-nighter   Hudson (River)
>   sharpening my oyster knife Harlem (City)
>   Reconstruction

Reading 2

AUTHOR NOTES

Zora Neale Hurston (1903–1960) is a well-known African-American writer of short stories, drama, essays, and novels. She was born in the town described in this 1928 story and was educated at Harvard University, Barnard College, and Columbia University.

Glossary

proscenium box   the area of a theater located between the curtain and the orchestra

born first-nighter   a natural fan of the theatre who regularly attends first-night performances

Reconstruction   the period (1865–1877) in which Southern states were controlled by the federal government before being readmitted to the United States.

cane chewing   chewing sweet sugar cane

parse-me-la   a dance

Hegira   a flight to escape danger, such as Muslim prophet Mohammed's flight (A.D. 622) from Mecca to Medina

Barnard   a prestigious private college in New York state

Hudson   a river in New York state

New World Cabaret   the name of a bar with musical entertainment

Seventh Avenue, Harlem City   a major street in the New York City neighborhood that was once predominantly black

42nd Street Library   a main branch of the New York City public library

HOW IT FEELS TO BE COLORED ME

by Zora Neale Hurston

I am colored but I offer nothing in the way of extenuating circumstances except the fact that I am the only Negro in the United States whose grandfather on the mother's side was *not* an Indian chief.

I remember the very day that I became colored. Up to my thirteenth year I lived in the little Negro town of Eatonville, Florida. It is exclusively a colored town. The only white people I knew passed through the town going to or coming from Orlando. The native whites rode dusty horses, the Northern tourists chugged down the sandy village road in automobiles. The town knew the Southerners and never stopped cane chewing when they passed. But the Northerners were something else again. They were peered at cautiously from behind curtains by the timid. The more venturesome would come out of the porch to watch them go past and got just as much pleasure out of the tourists as the tourists got out of the village.

The front porch might seem a daring place for the rest of the town, but it was a gallery seat for me. My favorite place was atop the gate-post. Proscenium box for a born first-nighter. Not only did I enjoy the show, but I didn't mind the actors knowing that I liked it. I usually spoke to them in passing. I'd wave at them and when they returned my salute, I would say something like this: "Howdy-do-well-I-thank-you-where-you-goin'?" Usually automobile or the horse paused at this, and after a queer exchange of compliments, I would probably "go a piece of the way" with them, as we say in farthest Florida. If one of my family happened to come to the front in time to see me, of course negotiations would be rudely broken off. But even so, it is clear that I was the first "welcome-to-our-state" Floridian, and I hope the Miami Chamber of Commerce will please take notice.

During this period, white people differed from colored to me only in that they rode through town and never lived there. They liked to hear me "speak pieces" and sing and wanted to see me dance the parse-me-la, and gave me generously of their small silver for doing these things, which seemed strange to me for I wanted to do them so much that I needed bribing to stop. Only they didn't know it. The colored people gave no dimes. They deplored any joyful tendencies in me, but I was their Zora nevertheless. I belonged to them, to the nearby hotels, to the county—everybody's Zora.

But changes came in the family when I was thirteen, and I was sent to school in Jacksonville. I left Eatonville, the town of the oleanders, as Zora. When I disembarked from the river-boat at Jacksonville, she was no more. It seemed that I had suffered a sea change. I was not Zora of Orange County any more. I was now a little colored girl. I found it out in certain ways. In my heart as well as in the mirror, I became a fast brown—warranted not to rub nor run.

But I am not tragically colored. There is no great sorrow dammed up in my soul, nor lurking behind my eyes. I do not mind at all. I do not belong to the sobbing school of Negrohood who hold that nature somehow has given them a lowdown dirty deal and whose feelings are all hurt about it. Even in the helter-skelter skirmish that is my life, I have seen that the world is to the strong regardless of a little pigmentation more or less. No, I do not weep at the world—I am too busy sharpening my oyster knife.

Someone is always at my elbow reminding me that I am the granddaughter of slaves. It fails to register depression with me. Slavery is sixty years in the past. The operation was successful and the patient is doing well, thank you. The terrible struggle that made me an American out of a potential slave said, "On the line!" The Reconstruction said "Get set!"; and the generation before said "Go!" I am off to a flying start and I must not halt in the stretch to look behind and weep. Slavery is the price I paid for civilization, and the choice was not with me. It is a bully adventure and worth all that I have paid through my ancestors for it. No one on earth ever had a greater chance for glory. The world to be won and nothing to be lost. It is thrilling to think—to know that for any act of mine, I shall get twice as much praise or twice as much blame. It is quite exciting to hold the center of the national stage, with the spectators not knowing whether to laugh or to weep.

The position of my white neighbor is much more difficult. No brown specter pulls up a chair beside me when I sit down to eat. No dark ghost thrusts its leg against mine in bed. The game of keeping what one has is never so exciting as the game of getting.

I do not always feel colored. Even now I often achieve the unconscious Zora of Eatonville before the Hegira. I feel most colored when I am thrown against a sharp white background.

For instance at Barnard. "Beside the waters of the Hudson" I feel my race. Among the thousand white persons, I am a dark rock surged upon, and overswept, but through it all, I remain myself. When covered by the waters, I am, and the ebb but reveals me again.

Sometimes it is the other way around. A white person is set down in our midst, but the contrast is just as sharp for me. For instance, when I sit in the drafty basement that is The New World Cabaret with a white person, my color comes. We enter chatting about any little nothing that we have in common and are seated by the jazz waiters. In the abrupt way that jazz orchestras have, this one plunges into a number. It loses no time in circumlocutions, but gets right down to business. It constricts the thorax and splits the heart with its tempo and narcotic harmonies. This orchestra grows rambunctious, rears on its hind legs and attacks the tonal veil with primitive fury, rending it, clawing it until it breaks through to the jungle beyond. I follow those heathen—follow them exultingly. I dance wildly inside myself; I yell within, I whoop; I shake my assegai above my head, I hurl it true to the mark *yeeeeooww!* I am in the jungle and living in the jungle way. My face is painted red and yellow and my body is painted blue. My pulse is throbbing like a war drum. I want to slaughter something—give pain, give death to what, I do not know. But the piece ends. The men of the orchestra wipe their lips and rest their fingers. I creep back slowly to the veneer we call civilization with the last tone and find the white friend sitting motionless in his seat, smoking calmly.

"Good music they have here," he remarks, drumming the table with his fingertips.

Music. The great blobs of purple and red emotion have not touched him. He has only heard what I felt. He is far away and I see him but dimly across the ocean and the continent that have fallen between us. He is so pale with his whiteness and I am *so* colored.

At certain times I have no race, I am *me*. When I set my hat at a certain angle and saunter down Seventh Avenue, Harlem City, feeling as snooty as the lions in front of the Forty-Second Street Library, for instance. So far as my feelings are concerned, Peggy Hopkins Joyce on the Boule Mich with her gorgeous raiment, stately carriage, knees knocking together in a most aristocratic manner, has nothing on me. The cosmic Zora emerges. I belong to no race nor time. I am the eternal feminine with its string of beads.

I have no separate feeling about being an American citizen and colored. I am merely a fragment of the Great Soul that surges within the boundaries. My country, right or wrong.

Sometimes, I feel discriminated again, but it does not make me angry. It merely astonishes me. How *can* any deny themselves the pleasure of my company? It's beyond me.

But in the main, I feel like a brown bag of miscellany propped against a wall. Against a wall in company with other bags, white, red, and yellow. Pour out the contents, and there is discovered a jumble of small things priceless and worthless. A first-water diamond, an empty spool, bits of broken glass, lengths of string, a key to a door long since crumbled away, a rusty knife-blade, old shoes saved for a road that never was and never will be, a nail bent under the weight of things too heavy for any nail, a dried flower or two still a little fragrant. In your hand is the brown bag. On the ground before you is the jumble it held— so much like the jumble in the bags, could they be emptied, that all might be dumped in a single heap and the bags refilled without altering the content of any greatly. A bit of colored glass more or less would not matter. Perhaps that is how the Great Stuffer of Bags filled them in the first place—who knows?

Comprehension

Mark the following statements "True" or "False," based on the information in "How It Feels to Be Colored Me." Refer to page 202 of Appendix II for the answers.

——— **1.** Zora grew up in a small town that had only black residents.

——— **2.** When white tourists drove by, Zora hid inside her house.

——— **3.** Zora left her town at the age of 13 to study in Jacksonville.

——— **4.** Zora was depressed by the fact that she was the granddaughter of slaves.

——— **5.** Zora always felt "colored."

——— **6.** She felt "colored" at Barnard (College), where most of the people were white.

——— **7.** The jazz music in the cabaret had the same effect on Zora as it did on her white friend.

——— **8.** Sometimes Zora felt she was better than other people.

——— **9.** Zora never felt discriminated against.

——— **10.** In the end of the story, Zora described herself as a "brown bag."

——— **CORRECT** × **10** = ——— %

LANGUAGE STUDY

LEARNING STRATEGY

Forming Concepts: Especially when you read literature, open your mind to all possible meanings of the language because words may actually symbolize *other* ideas.

Especially in literary passages, writers often use colorful language to express their meaning. Writers may describe a town as "hell" or a woman's eyes as being "like pools of water." Careful readers learn to understand that writers often use interesting expressions such as these to relate their meaning.

This type of "creative" language—using words to symbolize, or represent, other ideas—is called figurative language. In the examples previously given, the word "hell" symbolizes the negative quality of the town, while "pools of water" represents the beauty of the woman's eyes.

ACTIVITY

Like many writers, Zora Neale Hurston employs figurative language in her story. In a small group, reread the last paragraph of "How It Feels to Be Colored Me." Discuss and record your group's answers to these questions:

1. The author says she feels like "a brown bag . . . propped against a wall . . . in company with other bags, white, red, and yellow." What does the word "bag" represent? Why is Zora's "bag" brown? Why are the other bags colored differently? Why are the "bags" against a wall?
2. Hurston describes the contents of the bag as "a jumble of small things priceless and worthless." What ideas do these words represent?
3. Read over the contents of the bags. Why do you think Hurston includes these items? What do some of them mean?
4. Next, the author says all the bags "might be dumped in a single heap and the bags refilled without altering the content of any greatly." What is she suggesting here? What does the word *content* [of the bags] represent?
5. Finally, Hurston writes: "Perhaps that is how the Great Stuffer of Bags filled them in the first place—who knows?" Who is "the Great Stuffer of Bags"? What does she mean by this sentence?
6. Based on this part of the story, in which she uses figurative language, how do you think Hurston feels about ethnic groups outside hers? Do you agree with her ideas?

ACTIVITY: PERSONAL VOCABULARY

IT WORKS!
Learning Strategy:
Choosing What
to Learn

Choose ten vocabulary words from the text of "How It Feels to Be Colored Me" that you would like to learn. Write each word, its definition, and its part of speech in your reading journal or on a vocabulary card. Follow the example on page 9 of Chapter 1. Then, in your journal or on each card, write an original sentence in which you use each word. Check your sentences with your instructor.

REACTIONS

ACTIVITY: CONNECTING IDEAS

IT WORKS!
Learning Strategy:
Making
Connections

In your reading journal, write a composition in which you describe how Elizabeth Wong, the author of "The Struggle to Be an All-American Girl," or Zora Neale Hurston, the author of "How It Feels to Be Colored Me," feels about being a member of her respective ethnic group.

After you have written the composition, find a classmate who wrote about the author you did *not* choose. Read each other's papers, and compare how the two authors view their ethnicity.

You may want to organize your writing into one or more paragraphs using this suggested outline:

I. Introduction
Main Idea Sentence: Write one sentence that includes the name of the author, the name of her story, and how she feels about being a member of her ethnic group.

II. Body
Give supporting details from the story that you chose: Explain two or three events in the story that *show* how the author feels about her ethnic group. Include details about this part of the story.

III. Conclusion
Restate your main idea. Then give your opinion of the author's feeling about her ethnicity.

PREPARING TO READ

ACTIVITY: PREVIEWING

The author of the next poem, "Legal Alien," writes about the perceptions of different groups of people about immigrants. What do the words "legal alien" remind you of? Considering the title she has chosen, how do you think the author believes people view immigrants?

Reading 3

AUTHOR NOTES

Pat Mora, born in El Paso, Texas, explores her Hispanic cultural background in her poetry collections, *Borders* (1986) and *Chants* (1984). "Legal Alien" is taken from *Chants*.

Glossary
Me'stan volviendo loca Spanish for "It's driving me crazy."
Anglos Anglo-Americans; an Hispanic term for "white" Americans

LEGAL ALIEN
by Pat Mora

Bi-lingual, Bi-cultural,
able to slip from "How's life?"
to *"Me'stan volviendo loca,"*
able to sit in a paneled office
drafting memos in smooth English,
able to order in fluent Spanish
at a Mexican restaurant,
American but hyphenated,
viewed by Anglos as perhaps exotic,
perhaps inferior, definitely different,
viewed by Mexicans as alien.
(their eyes say, "You may speak
Spanish but you're not like me.")
an American to Mexicans
a Mexican to Americans
a handy token
sliding back and forth
between the fringes of both worlds
by smiling
by masking the discomfort
of being pre-judged
Bi-laterally.

LANGUAGE STUDY

ACTIVITY

IT WORKS!
Learning Strategy:
Guessing
Meaning

Work with a partner to guess the meanings of the following words, taken from "Legal Alien." Check your guesses in a dictionary. If they are accurate, simply put a check under "Dictionary Definition." Write the words and their definitions in your reading journal.

	Your Definition	Dictionary Definition
1. slip (line 2)	_____	_____
2. drafting (line 5)	_____	_____
3. exotic (line 9)	_____	_____
4. fringes (line 18)	_____	_____
5. masking (line 20)	_____	_____
6. bilaterally (line 22)	_____	_____

ACTIVITY: CHAPTER SELF-TEST

Assess your general understanding of the readings in Chapter 2 by taking the following chapter self-examination.

In Part 1, define the underlined words by examining the context of the surrounding words and phrases. Write the word or words that helped you guess the meaning of the underlined word.

Circle the appropriate completion of each statement in Part 2. Check your answers to Part 1 in your journal, cards, or a dictionary, and check answers for Part 2 on page 202 in Appendix II.

Part 1: Vocabulary

1. With the entrance of the teacher, the best student would tap a bell and everyone would get up, kowtow, and <u>chant</u>, "Sing san ho," the phonetic for "How are you, teacher?"

    chant = _____

    Surrounding words that helped you: _____

2. When I spoke English, people nodded at me, smiled sweetly, said encouraging words. Even the people in my culture would <u>cluck</u> and say that I'd do well in life.

    cluck = _____

    Surrounding words that helped you: _____

3. What <u>infuriated</u> my mother most was when my brother cornered her on her consonants, especially "r." My father had played a cruel joke on Mom by assigning her an American name that her tongue wouldn't allow her to say. No matter how hard she tried, "Ruth" always ended up "Luth" or "Roof."

    infuriated = _____

    Surrounding words that helped you: _____

4. The only white people I knew passed through the town going to or coming from Orlando. The native whites rode dusty horses, the Northern tourists <u>chugged</u> down the sandy village road in automobiles.

    chugged = _____

    Surrounding words that helped you: _____

5. For instance at Barnard. "Beside the waters of the Hudson" I feel my race. Among the thousand white persons, I am a dark rock <u>surged upon</u>, and overswept, but through it all, I remain myself.

    surged upon = _____

    Surrounding words that helped you: _____

6. I dance wildly inside myself; I yell within, I <u>whoop</u>; I shake my assegai above my head, I hurl it true to the mark *yeeeeooww!* I am in the jungle and living in the jungle way.

whoop = _____

Surrounding words that helped you: _____

7. Bi-lingual, Bi-cultural,
able to <u>slip</u> from "How's life?"
to "*Me'stan volviendo loca.*"

slip = _____

Surrounding words that helped you: _____

8. . . . an American to Mexicans
a Mexican to Americans
a handy token
sliding back and forth
between the <u>fringes</u> of both worlds

fringes = _____

Surrounding words that helped you: _____

_____ **CORRECT** $\times$ **6.25** = _____ **%**

(one point each for definition and surrounding words)

Part 2: Comprehension

1. In "The Struggle to Be an All-American Girl," the author first wants to become
 a. less American and more Chinese.
 b. less Chinese and more American.
 c. equally American and Chinese.

2. The Chinese school and the Chinese language are both characterized by the writer
 a. negatively.
 b. positively.
 c. both positively and negatively.

3. In the story, the writer's English level was probably
 a. very good.
 b. very poor.
 c. average among Chinese Americans.

4. Zora Neale Hurston in "How It Feels to Be Colored Me" begins the story by describing life
 a. in the Harlem section of New York City.
 b. at Barnard College.
 c. in a small town in Florida.

5. Hurston became "colored" when she
 a. left her hometown.
 b. entered college.
 c. became a writer.

6. The end of Hurston's story shows us that she believes
   a. ethnic groups have big differences.
   b. all ethnic groups are basically the same.
   c. ethnic groups should not mix with other ethnic groups.
7. Pat Mora writes in "Legal Alien" that she
   a. is perfectly bilingual
   b. speaks Spanish well but English poorly.
   c. speaks English well but Spanish poorly.
8. Her poem tells us that Mexicans view Mexican-Americans as
   a. Mexicans.
   b. Americans.
9. According to Mora, Americans, on the other hand, see Mexican-Americans as
   a. inferior.
   b. superior.
10. When Americans or Mexicans react negatively to Mora, she
    a. shouts in anger.
    b. walks away.
    c. smiles to hide her feelings.

_____ **CORRECT** × **10** = _____ %

ACTIVITY: EVALUATING YOUR GOALS

As you did in Chapter 1, in your reading journal, write briefly in answer to the following questions:

1. The most important skills I used in reading and responding to the readings in this chapter were _____.
2. The most valuable information I gained from this chapter was _____
   _____.

Threads

Immigrants in New York City specialize in particular businesses:

gas stations (Indians)

grocery stores (Koreans and Dominican Republicans)

fried chicken restaurants (Afghans)

New York Times, Jan. 12, 1992

EXPANSION

Reading Further

The experiences of those who encountered new cultures are recorded in a vast number of books. Among them, here are a few recommendations for further reading:

Growing Up Native American, edited by Patricia Riley
The Season of Stones: Life in a Palestinian Village, by Helen Winternitz
Thousand Pieces of Gold, by Ruthanne Lum McCann
In Nueva York, by Nicholasa Mohr

Language

ACTIVITY: SETTING PERSONAL GOALS

As in the previous chapters, list in order of importance (with 1 as "most valuable") the learning objectives that are significant to you. Add personal learning objectives to the list if you wish.

GOAL   **RANK**

1. To increase comprehension of readings   _____

2. To expand vocabulary   _____

3. To increase reading speed   _____

4. To improve study skills   _____

5. To learn more about the subjects of this chapter   _____

6. _____   _____

7. _____   _____

PREPARING TO READ

In Chapters 1 and 2, you read about old and new worlds. When people move to a new culture, often the first challenge they face is communicating in a new language. At the same time, they strive to hold onto their old cultures, including their native languages. When different languages and cultures meet, which becomes the dominant one? The readings in this chapter explore this question from three different vantage points:

"The Language We Know" by Simon Ortiz
"Spanglish" by Janice Castro, with Dan Cook and Cristina Garcia
"Guardians of English" from *Hold Your Tongue: Bilingualism and the Politics of "English Only"* by James Crawford

ACTIVITY: PREDICTING CONTENT

Answer these questions in a small group.

1. What viewpoints do you expect to find in the readings in Chapter 3, considering the titles?
2. Which of the three titles appeals most to you? Why?
3. Look ahead at the photographs and other graphic material in this chapter. Read the accompanying captions. What other ideas do you expect to read about?

ACTIVITY: LISTENING FOR IDEAS

ACTIVITY: LISTENING FOR IDEAS

Listen to a TV or radio program or a song in your native language. You may want to choose a newscast or cultural program in your language if these are broadcast in your area. Copy the following form on a separate piece of paper. Listen, and then complete the report.

*IT WORKS!
Learning Strategy:
Listening*

1. Title of TV or radio program: _____

   Channel: _____   Time/Date: _____

   or

   Title of Song: _____

   Artist: _____

2. Language: _____

3. Main Idea of the Program (or Song):

   _____

   _____

   _____

4. Your Impression of the Program:

   _____

   _____

ACTIVITY: SHARING IMPRESSIONS

Share your report on a TV or radio program or song in your language with some of your classmates. Present your ideas about the main point and your opinion of the program or song. Listen to your group-mates' reports, and then discuss your reactions.

ACTIVITY: PREVIEWING

The first reading is entitled "The Language We Know." Which language do you think the writer is referring to? What do you think he will say about this language?

Reading 1

Simon Ortiz is an Acoma Indian born in 1941 at Acoma Pueblo in New Mexico. His writings include a collection of award-winning poems entitled *From Sand Creek.*

Glossary

Acoma Pueblo a tribe of Indians who founded in 1100 what is now possibly the oldest continuously inhabited settlement within the U.S. borders.

pueblo a community dwelling, sometimes as many as five stories high, built of stone or adobe by Indian tribes in the southwestern United States; Spanish for "town"

parochial religious

kiva a sacred ceremonial chamber of Pueblo Indians; Hopi for "old house"

THE LANGUAGE WE KNOW
by Simon Ortiz

I don't remember a world without language. From the time of my earliest childhood, there was language. Always language, and imagination, speculation, utters of sound. Words, beginnings of words. What would I be without language? My existence has been determined by language, not only the spoken but the unspoken, the language of speech and the language of motion. I can't remember a world without memory. Memory, immediate and far away in the past, something in the sinew, blood, ageless cell. Although I don't recall the exact moment I spoke or tried to speak, I know the feeling of something tugging at the core of the mind, something unutterable uttered into existence. It is language that brings us into being in order to know life.

A Pueblo Indian village.

My childhood was the oral tradition of the Acoma Pueblo people—Aaquumeh hano—which included my immediate family of three older sisters, two younger sisters, two younger brothers, and my mother and father. My world was our world of the Aaquumeh in McCartys, one of the two villages descended from the ageless mother pueblo of Acoma. I grew up in Deetziyamah, which is the Aaquumeh name for McCartys, which is posted at the exit off the present interstate highway in western New Mexico. I grew up within a people who farmed small garden plots and fields, who were mostly poor and not well schooled in the American system's education. The language I spoke was that of a struggling people who held ferociously to a heritage, culture, language, and land despite the odds posed them by the forces surrounding them since 1540 A.D., the advent of Euro-American colonization. When I began school in 1948 at the BIA (Bureau of Indian Affairs) day school in our village, I was armed with the basic ABC's and the phrases "Good morning, Miss Oleman" and "May I please be excused to go to the bathroom," but it was an older language that was my fundamental strength.

In my childhood, the language we all spoke was Acoma, and it was a struggle to maintain it against the outright threats of corporal punishment, ostracism, and the invocation that it would impede our progress towards Americanization. Children in school were punished and looked upon with disdain if they did not speak and learn English quickly and smoothly, and so I learned it. It has occurred to me that I learned English simply because I was forced to, as so many other Indian children were. But I know, also, there was another reason, and this was that I loved language, the sound, meaning, and magic of language. Language opened up vistas of the world around me, and it allowed me to discover knowledge that would not be possible for me to know without the use of language. Later, when I began to experiment with and explore language in poetry and fiction, I allowed that a portion of that impetus was because I had come to know English through forceful acculturation. Nevertheless, the underlying force was the beauty and poetic power of language in its many forms that instilled in me the desire to become a user of language as a writer, singer, and storyteller. Significantly, it was the Acoma language, which I don't use enough of today, that inspired me to become a writer. The concepts, values, and philosophy contained in my original language and the struggle it has faced have determined my life and vision as a writer.

In Deetziyamah, I discovered the world of the Acoma land and people firsthand through my parents, sisters and brothers, and my own perceptions, voiced through all that encompasses the oral tradition, which is ageless for any culture. It is a small village, even smaller years ago, and like other Indian communities it is wealthy with its knowledge of daily event, history, and social system, all that make up a people who have a many-dimensioned heritage. Our family lived in a two-room home (built by my grandfather some years after he and my grandmother moved with their daughters from Old Acoma), which my father added rooms to later. I remember my father's work at enlarging our home for our growing family. He was a skilled stoneworker, like many other men of an older Pueblo generation who worked with sandstone and mud mortar to build their homes and pueblos. It takes time, persistence, patience, and the belief that the walls that come to stand will do so for a long, long time, perhaps even forever. I like to think that by helping to mix mud and carry stone for my father and other elders I managed to bring that influence into my consciousness as a writer.

Both my mother and my father were good storytellers and singers (as my mother is to this day—my father died in 1978), and for their generation, which was born soon after the turn of the century, they were relatively educated in the American system. Catholic missionaries had taken both of them as children to a parochial boarding school far from Acoma, and they imparted their discipline for study and quest for education to us children when we started school. But it was their indigenous sense of gaining knowledge that was most meaningful to me. Acquiring knowledge about life was above all the most important item; it was a value that one had to have in order to be fulfilled personally and on behalf of his community. And this they insisted upon imparting through the oral tradition as they told their children about our native history and our community and culture and our "stories." These stories were common knowledge of act, event, and behavior in a close-knit pueblo. It was knowledge about how one was to make a living through work that benefited his family and everyone else.

Because we were a subsistence farming people, or at least tried to be, I learned to plant, hoe weeds, irrigate and cultivate corn, chili, pumpkins, beans. Through counsel and advice I came to know that the rain which provided water was a blessing, gift, and symbol and that it was the land which provided the knowledge that I was woven into the intricate web that was my Acoma life. In our garden and our cornfields I learned about the seasons, growth cycles of cultivated plants, what one had to think and feel about the land; and at home I became aware of how we must care for each other: all of this was encompassed in an intricate relationship which had to be maintained in order that life continue. After supper on many occasions my father would bring out his drum and sing as we, the children, danced to themes about the rain, hunting, land, and people. It was all that is contained within the language of oral tradition that made me explicitly aware of a yet unarticulated urge to write, to tell what I had learned and was learning and what it all meant to me.

My grandfather was old already when I came to know him. I was only one of his many grandchildren, but I would go with him to get wood for our households, to the garden to chop weeds, and to his sheep camp to help care for his sheep. I don't remember his exact words, but I know they were about how we must sacredly concern ourselves with the people and the holy earth. I know his words were about how we must regard ourselves and others with compassion and love; I know that his knowledge was vast, as a medicine man and an elder of his kiva, and I listened as a boy should. My grandfather represented for me a link to the past that is important for me to hold in my memory because it is not only memory but knowledge that substantiates my present existence. He and the grandmothers and grandfathers before him thought about us as they lived, confirmed in their belief of a continuing life, and they brought our present beings into existence by the beliefs they held. The consciousness of that belief is what informs my present concerns with language, poetry, and fiction.

Comprehension

Without looking back at the text, mark the following statements "True" or "False," based on information from "The Language We Know." Check your answers on page 202 of Appendix II.

_____ **1.** The author grew up in an Indian pueblo in Arizona.

_____ **2.** When he began school at the Bureau of Indian Affairs day school, he already spoke English fluently.

_____ **3.** During his childhood, it was a struggle for the author to keep his Acoma language.

_____ **4.** The only reason the author learned English was because he was forced to.

_____ **5.** Ortiz grew up in a two-room home built by his grandfather.

_____ **6.** Ortiz's parents did not speak English.

_____ **7.** His parents were both good storytellers.

_____ **8.** The "oral tradition" meant telling stories about Acoma history and culture.

_____ **9.** The author did not learn how to plant and cultivate vegetables.

_____ **10.** The author's grandfather represented an important link to the past.

_____ **CORRECT** $\times$ **10** = _____ **%**

REVIEWING

As you found in Chapter 2, you can utilize your own knowledge of a topic to help you understand a related reading. Indeed, reading or listening to stories about other people's lives can give you great insight into the universality of the human experience.

When you read, you may discover that others before you have encountered problems that you thought were only your own. Recognizing these similarities can also help you better understand what you are reading.

ACTIVITY

In "The Language We Know," the author mentions several instances that relate to his language and cultural experiences. In a small group, select one of the passages that follow. Discuss the passage, and then allow each group member to respond by relating it to his or her own experience.

A. The language I spoke was that of a struggling people who held ferociously to a heritage, culture, language, and land despite the odds posed them by the forces surrounding them . . .

B. When I began school . . . I was armed with the basic ABC's . . . but it was an older language that was my fundamental strength.

C. Children in school were punished and looked upon with disdain if they did not speak and learn English quickly and smoothly, and so I learned it.

D. Language opened up vistas of the world around me, and it allowed me to discover knowledge that would not be possible for me to know without the use of language.

ACTIVITY: ANNOTATING A TEXT

Underlining or **highlighting** are popular ways for a reader to **annotate,** or mark, a text. Typically, a reader underlines (or highlights) sentences that he or she considers worth remembering. The reader expects to return to the text at a later date and study it. Therefore, one danger of relying too much on underlining and highlighting is that the reader *postpones* remembering the material, instead of trying to remember it *while* he or she is reading. Another potential problem with underlining or highlighting is that the reader marks *too much* information. Then it is difficult to see which sentences really do contain key ideas.

Be selective when you underline or highlight. Choose only those sentences that contain main ideas or important terms.

Look again at this example, a paragraph from "Truce in Heaven, Peace on Earth" in Chapter 1:

** With the end of their journey in sight, the passengers seemed to have forgotten the nightmarish incident that had (engulfed them) **??** (in sorrow and despair) the day before. They applauded Trang's announcement, and Minh was asked to speak.

They forgot their problem.

Notice how the first sentence of the paragraph is underlined because it contains an important idea. In the margin, asterisks also alert the reader that this idea is important. The note in the right-hand margin is a comment about the idea in the paragraph. And circled words with a question mark in the right-hand margin indicates problem words. When you annotate a text, it is useful to combine underlining/highlighting with margin notes, as this example illustrates.

ACTIVITY

A. Practice using selective underlining/highlighting and margin notes (question marks for incomprehensible parts, asterisks for important ideas) by marking the paragraph that follows. Compare your annotations with a classmate's.

> In Deetziyamah, I discovered the world of the Acoma land and people firsthand through my parents, sisters and brothers, and my own perceptions, voiced through all that encompasses the oral tradition, which is ageless for any culture. It is a small village, even smaller years ago, and like other Indian communities it is wealthy with its knowledge of daily event, history, and social system, all that make up a people who have a many-dimensioned heritage. Our family lived in a two-room home (built by my grandfather some years after he and my grandmother moved with their daughters from Old Acoma), which my father added rooms to later. I remember my father's work at enlarging our home for our growing family. He was a skilled stoneworker, like many other men of an older Pueblo generation who worked with sandstone and mud mortar to build their homes and pueblos. It takes time, persistence, patience, and the belief that the walls that come to stand will do so for a long, long time, perhaps even forever. I like to think that by helping to mix mud and carry stone for my father and other elders I managed to bring that influence into my consciousness as a writer.

B. Use this technique to annotate the remainder of the "The Language We Know." When you finish, compare your annotation with a classmate's.

PREPARING TO READ

ACTIVITY: PREVIEWING

A. The article that follows, which originated in *Time* magazine, is titled "Spanglish." What does "Spanglish" mean? How do you feel about its existence?

B. Read the vocabulary list below. When you read this story, you will find some words in Spanish. If you do not speak this language, try to guess the word meanings. Even if you cannot, you can still understand the main idea of the story.

Reading 2

Glossary
six-pack   a package of six beers
Robin Williams   an American comedian and actor
Latinos   a slang term for Spanish speakers; opposite of Anglos
Miller Lite   a brand of beer

SPANGLISH

by Janice Castro, with Dan Cook and Cristina Garcia

In Manhattan a first-grader greets her visiting grandparents, happily exclaiming, "Come here, *sientate!"* Her bemused grandfather, who does not speak Spanish, nevertheless knows she is asking him to sit down. A Miami personnel officer understands what a job applicant means when he says, *"Quiero un* part time." Nor do drivers miss a beat reading a billboard alongside a Los Angeles street advertising CERVEZA—SIX-PACK!

This free-form blend of Spanish and English, known as Spanglish, is common linguistic currency where concentrations of Hispanic Americans are found in the United States. In Los Angeles, where 55 percent of the city's 3 million inhabitants speak Spanish, Spanglish is as much a part of daily life as sunglasses. Unlike the broken-English efforts of earlier immigrants from Europe, Asia, and other regions, Spanglish has become a widely accepted conversational mode used casually—even playfully—by Spanish-speaking immigrants and native-born Americans alike.

Consisting of one part Hispanicized English, one part Americanized Spanish, and more than a little fractured syntax, Spanglish is a bit like a Robin Williams comedy routine: a crackling line of cross-cultural patter straight from the melting pot. Often it enters Anglo homes and families through the children, who pick it up at school or at play with their young Hispanic contemporaries. In other cases, it comes from watching TV; many an Anglo child watching *Sesame Street* has learned *uno dos tres* almost as quickly as one two three.

Spanglish takes a variety of forms from the Southern California Anglos who bid farewell with the utterly silly *"hasta la* bye-bye" to the Cuban-American drivers in Miami who *parquean their carros.* Some Spanglish sentences are mostly Spanish, with a quick detour for an English word or two. A Latino friend may cut short a conversation by glancing at his watch and excusing himself with the explanation that he must *"ir al* supermarket."

Many of the English words transplanted in this way are simply handier than their Spanish counterparts. No matter how distasteful the subject, for example, it is still easier to say "income tax" than *impuesto sobre la renta.* At the same time, many Spanish-speaking immigrants have adopted such terms as VCR, microwave, and dishwasher for what they view as largely American phenomena. Still other English words convey a cultural context that is not implicit in the Spanish. A friend who invites you to *lonche* most likely has in mind the brisk American custom of "doing lunch" rather than the languorous afternoon break traditionally implied by *almuerzo.*

Mainstream Americans exposed to similar hybrids of German, Chinese, or Hindi might be mystified. But even Anglos who speak little or no Spanish are somewhat familiar with Spanglish. Living among them, for one thing, are 19 million Hispanics. In addition, more American high school and university students sign up for Spanish than for any other foreign language.

Only in the past ten years, though, has Spanglish begun to turn into a national slang. Its popularity has grown with the explosive increases in U.S. immigration from Latin American countries. English has increasingly collided with Spanish in retail stores, offices and classrooms, in pop music, and on street corners. Anglos whose ancestors picked up such Spanish words as *rancho, bronco, tornado,* and *incommunicado,* for instance, now freely use such Spanish words as *gracias, bueno, amigo,* and *por favor.*

Among Latinos, Spanglish conversations often flow easily from Spanish into several sentences of English and back.

Spanglish is a sort of code for Latinos: the speakers know Spanish, but their hybrid language reflects the American culture in which they live. Many lean to shorter, clipped phrases in place of the longer, more graceful expressions their parents used. Says Leonel de la Cuesta, an assistant professor of modern languages at Florida International University in Miami: "In the United States, time is money, and that is showing up in Spanglish as an economy of language." Conversational examples: *taipiar* (type) and *winshi-wiper* (windshield wiper) replace *escribir a maquina* and *limpiaparabrisas.*

Major advertisers, eager to tap the estimated $134 billion in spending power wielded by Spanish-speaking Americans, have ventured into Spanglish to promote their products. In some cases, attempts to sprinkle Spanish through commercials have produced embarrassing gaffes. A Braniff airlines ad that sought to tell Spanish-speaking audiences they could settle back *en* (in) luxuriant *cuero* (leather) seats, for example, inadvertently said they could fly without clothes *(encuero).* A fractured translation of the Miller Lite slogan told readers the beer was "Filling, and less delicious." Similar blunders are often made by Anglos trying to impress Spanish-speaking pals. But if Latinos are amused by mangled Spanglish, they also recognize these goofs as a sort of friendly acceptance. As they might put it, *no problema.*

Comprehension

Mark the following statements "True" or "False," based on the information in "Spanglish." Do not refer to the article until you have checked your answers on page 202 of Appendix II. Record your reading speed and comprehension score on page 200 of Appendix I.

_____ **1.** Spanglish is a blend of Spanish and English.

_____ **2.** Spanglish is used in areas of the United States where concentrations of Hispanic Americans are found.

_____ **3.** Spanglish is not a widely accepted conversational mode.

_____ **4.** Spanish speakers sometimes use English words because English words are handier.

_____ **5.** Even Anglos who speak little or no Spanish are familiar with Spanglish.

_____ **6.** In the past 50 years, Spanglish has turned into a national slang.

_____ **7.** Spanglish conversations never flow back and forth from Spanish and English.

_____ **8.** Advertisers who use Spanglish to promote their products rarely make mistakes in Spanish.

_____ **CORRECT** × **12.5** = _____ %

LANGUAGE STUDY

ACTIVITY: GUESSING MEANING

If your native language is not Spanish, find all the Spanish words in the article and write in the margins of "Spanglish" the definitions provided in the story. For Spanish words that are not defined in the story, try to guess their meanings from the contexts of the sentences. Write your definitions in the margin of the story.

Check your guesses with a Spanish-speaking member of the class or with your instructor.

*IT WORKS!
Learning Strategy:
Guessing
Meaning*

ACTIVITY: READING FASTER

Clustering

The **clustering** technique—reading "clusters" of words—can improve your reading rate. Remember to fix your eyes on logical groups of words rather than reading one word at a time. The first few sentences of "Spanglish" have been clustered below as examples. Try to read the cluster in each column in one glance.

IT WORKS!
Learning Strategy:
Reading
Faster

> In Manhattan
> a first-grader greets
> her visiting grandparents,
> happily exclaiming,
> "Come here, *sientate!*"
> Her bemused grandfather,
> who does not speak
> Spanish,
> nevertheless knows
> she is asking him
> to sit down.

ACTIVITY

Time yourself again as you use the clustering technique to reread "Spanglish." Record your new time in the Reading Rate and Comprehension Chart on page 200 in Appendix I.

REVIEWING

ACTIVITY: IDENTIFYING THE ORGANIZATION

Introduction

An important element in the organization of a reading is the **introduction.** In longer readings, such as those in this textbook, introductions may extend to several paragraphs. The paragraph(s) at the beginning of the reading not only introduce the reader to the topic but they often contain the **thesis statement,** or main idea sentence, of the reading.

Reread the first paragraph of "The Language We Know":

> I don't remember a world without language. From the time of my earliest childhood, there was language. Always language, and imagination, speculation, utters of sound. Words, beginnings of words. What would I be without language? My existence has been determined by language, not only the spoken but the unspoken, the language of speech and the language of motion. I can't remember a world without memory. Memory, immediate and far away in the past, something in the sinew, blood, ageless cell. Although I don't recall the exact moment I spoke or tried to speak, I know the feeling of something tugging at the core of the mind, something unutterable uttered into existence. It is language that brings us into being in order to know life.

Which subject does this paragraph introduce the reader to? Which sentence do you think is the thesis statement of this paragraph?

Clearly, this paragraph introduces the subject of "language." Here, the reader also learns that the story will be presented from a personal point of view, since the writer uses "my" and "I." You may think that the main idea is expressed in the last sentence: "It is language that brings us into being in order to know life." Others may decide that the second sentence expresses the main idea.

As you examine the organization in readings, you will discover that the thesis statement can occur in various places in the introductory paragraph(s).

ACTIVITY

Reread the first paragraphs of "Spanglish." With a partner, discuss which paragraph(s) constitute the introduction, which ideas are introduced in the paragraph(s), and which sentence may be the thesis statement. Compare your ideas with those of your instructor and other classmates.

REACTIONS

ACTIVITY: SHARING IMPRESSIONS

Spanglish has become a national slang because 19 million Hispanics live in the United States, according to the authors of the article of "Spanglish." The authors mention several situations in which Spanish is used as easily as English in parts of the United States with concentrations of Spanish-speakers.

ACTIVITY

Using the chart that follows, put a check mark below the language—either English or your native language—you believe is appropriate in each situation. In a small group, discuss these situations and others in which you think one language or the other is more acceptable.

Situation	English?	Your Language?
applying for a job	___	___
billboard advertisements	___	___
talking in class	___	___
talking to store customers	___	___
talking to co-workers	___	___
music	___	___
on street corners	___	___
_____	___	___
_____	___	___
_____	___	___
_____	___	___

Black South African sits on a "Whites Only" bench.

ACTIVITY: PREVIEWING

"Guardians of English" is an excerpt from a book entitled *Hold Your Tongue: Bilingualism and the Politics of "English Only."* What does he title "Guardians of English" tell you about the content of this reading? Who do you think are the "guardians"? Do you agree with their attitude?

Reading 3

Glossary

Beverly Hills   an expensive Los Angeles neighborhood

Lions Club International   an international charitable organization

Dadaist   relating to the European art and literary movement (1916–1923) that sought to abolish traditional cultural and art forms

Senator S. I. Hayakawa   a U.S. senator

apartheid   the policy of racial separation used in South Africa until 1994

Canciones de mi Padre   Spanish for "songs of my father"

GUARDIANS OF ENGLISH

by James Crawford

For Mayor Barry Hatch, it was the ultimate act of cultural aggression. In barely a decade his hometown of Monterey Park, just east of Los Angeles, had become the Chinese Beverly Hills, home to thousands of affluent immigrants from Taiwan and Hong Kong. The newcomers bought out American businesses and restocked the shelves with Asian goods. Soon they were opening banks as well as ginseng shops, developing high-density malls and condominiums, and crowding the streets with new Mercedes. As longtime residents sold out, or were pushed out by rising rents, Anglo-Americans found themselves outnumbered by Asians, many of whom seemed to have little use for the English language. Not only was the din of Mandarin and Cantonese heard in shops and restaurants, but signs with Chinese characters began to sprout everywhere, emblems of the changing social order.

Now, in the fall of 1988, Taiwan had the nerve to send foreign aid. The Lions Club International of Taipei announced a donation of ten thousand volumes— in Chinese, naturally—to the Monterey Park public library. It was a very Asian gesture. A Chinese American member of the city council, Judy Chu, had happened to meet the club's president, and he asked her what the Lions could do to express and reinforce the closeness they felt with their sister city, which many have begun to call "Little Taipei." Chu suggested a gift to the library, then struggling to meet the needs of Chinese readers. "But little did we dream it would be ten thousand books!" she recalls. "All kinds: a lot of children's books, cultural works, back issues of magazines. At least two thousand of the volumes were bilingual. Which I thought was terrific because any English-speaking person could read them and understand a little more about Chinese culture. And there were things like a Chinese translation of 'Peanuts,' books that would help Chinese people enjoy themselves and acculturate themselves to this country." If accepted, the gift would more than double the library's well-thumbed holdings in Chinese, one-half of which were normally checked out at a given time.

While local Chinese were ecstatic, Mayor Hatch was livid. In the Taiwanese largess he saw yet another intrusion by arrogant guests who insisted on rearranging the furniture, imposing their own tastes, remaking Monterey Park to suit themselves. Hatch is a large white-haired man who teaches civics at a junior high school in nearby Bell Gardens. Punctuating his convictions with a made fist, he likes to stress what he calls "pro-America" values. But with his students increasingly Latino and Asian, and his school increasingly bilingual, Hatch feels besieged by alien cultures. "You know, I'm in the trenches with these people," he says. "We're allowing them to come in not only by hundreds and thousands, but by millions. And not only are we accepting their separate identity, their history, their loyalties, but *their language*—which is the first and most emotional issue a man has."

Though Barry Hatch once served as a Mormon missionary in Hong Kong and still claims fluency in Cantonese, in Monterey Park he has brooked no concessions to linguistic minorities. On his motion in mid-1988, the council voted to abolish the city's independent library board, then headed by a Chinese-American. Meanwhile he pressed to limit expenditures for non-English-language materials. At one budget hearing he lectured the city librarian: "This is the United States of America, and nobody likes to walk into a public building and feel like they are in a foreign land." Suddenly, with the Taiwanese Lions' donation, Hatch felt outmaneuvered.

If the Chinese wanted to keep the books, he announced, they should construct their own building rather than "encroach on space" for English-language volumes. "We built this little library with our own tax money," he explained. "We spend over a million dollars a year on it. It is an American library, paid for by American taxpayers, for the American public, and I don't see any need to turn it into a cultural center for any foreign group of people." Offended by the mayor's remarks, the Lions considered withdrawing their gift but thought better of it after hearing from library supporters and leaders of the Chinese community. Ultimately, Hatch was powerless to block delivery of the books. All he could do was boycott a dedication ceremony and refuse to sign certificates of appreciation to the donors. The expanded Chinese section has since become one of the most popular in the library.

Looking back, Hatch still contends that the Taiwanese had more in mind than a token of goodwill. "You've got to realize the attitude of these people," he says. "They're not coming to join; they're coming to conquer. They have to raise their little flag, and it's not always on a pole. They want Southern California to be an Asian part of the country. These people work in devious manners. And language is one of the most important tools they can use. *Language is the key that opens the door to taking this country and breaking it apart.*" Indeed, language became the fault line along which ethnic divisions grew in Monterey Park, a rift fostered in no small measure by Barry Hatch. The rhetoric of Chinese exclusion, long couched in racial terms, now assumed a more respectable form: the "legal protection of English."

"English is under attack," warns a new movement of civic activists. Two decades ago this idea would have struck most Americans as bizarre: the histrionics of literati, or perhaps a Dadaist charade. But in the uneasy eighties it attracted mass support. "Defend our common language!" became the rallying cry. No one had to ask, "From whom?"

Immigration to the United States has increased noticeably in recent years, and more important, its source countries have changed. In 1965, Congress abolished the national-origins quota system, a racially restrictive policy that long favored northwestern Europeans and virtually excluded Asians. As late as the 1950s, Europe was still supplying more than half of all immigrants to the United States. By the 1980s the Third World was providing 85 percent of them, not counting the undocumented. These newcomers were far less familiar, racially and culturally, and so was their speech. After half a century of decline, minority tongues were suddenly more audible and, to many Americans, more dissonant as well.

In 1981, for the first time, Congress entertained a proposal to designate English as the official language of the United States. The sponsor was Senator S. I. Hayakawa of California, a Canadian immigrant of Japanese ancestry who believed that concessions to linguistic minorities had gone too far. "English has long been the main unifying force of the American people," he asserted. "But now prolonged bilingual education in public schools and multilingual ballots threaten to divide us along language lines." A semanticist by profession, Hayakawa was best known for his college text, *Language in Thought and Action,* which explores a wide range of obstacles to effective communication. Oddly, the book never mentions bilingualism, a problem that seems to have escaped the author's notice until he entered politics.

On retiring from the Senate, in 1983 Hayakawa helped to found U.S. English, a Washington lobby to promote his constitutional English Language Amendment and similar measures at the state level. He served as the group's "honorary chairman" until his death in 1992. Started on a shoestring, U.S. English claimed 400,000 dues-paying members by decade's end. Over that time it raised and spent approximately $28 million on campaigns to "preserve the status" of English—or, more precisely, to limit public uses of other languages. Whether such restrictions are intended to encompass all or selected government programs, schools, broadcast media, workplaces, business advertising, and other domains have remained matters of dispute. Proponents have issued contradictory statements. Some have pressed merely to give English legal recognition, while others have sought to outlaw all public services in other tongues, up to and including 911 operators, and to crack down on private sector bilingualism as well.

The new guardians of English achieved few tangible changes in language policy during the 1980s. They did succeed, however, in placing a polarizing issue on the national agenda, a debate—conducted almost entirely in English—that produced misunderstanding and mistrust on all sides. Throughout the country language differences became a lightning rod for ethnic tensions:

- In Elizabeth, New Jersey, a city whose residents are 30 percent Hispanic, the mayor instituted a "Speak-English-Only" rule for city workers while performing their duties, except when other languages were needed to communicate with members of the public. He insisted it was "discourteous for City employees to converse in other than English in front of other City employees."
- A San Diego grand jury denounced schooling in languages other than English as "un-American." It asserted that "bilingual education promotes a type of cultural apartheid in that it encourages a dual society."

- Koreans in Philadelphia secured the city's permission to purchase and erect street signs in their native language. Posted in a racially mixed neighborhood, the signs soon became targets for vandalism and angry protests and had to be removed. Local German Americans, betraying an ignorance of their own history, objected that their ancestors had never enjoyed such advantages.
- A cooperative apartment building in Broward County, Florida, voted to restrict residency to persons able to speak and read the English language. "We screen everyone for the protection of our tenants," explained the co-op's president. "We don't want undesirables living here. And if we can't communicate with people, it creates a real burden."
- At a concert near Boston, when Linda Ronstadt and a mariachi band performed music from her recent album, *Canciones de mi Padre,* some members of the audience began to chant: "Sing in English." As Ronstadt continued to sing in Spanish, two hundred fans walked out.
- Responding to complaints from African-American constituents about Korean, Arab, and Hispanic merchants, an alderman in Chicago proposed that anyone seeking a retail grocer's license should have to pass an English-proficiency test. "If you don't know English, you can't understand the laws," he said. "You have to know more than Mexican."

Comprehension

Mark the following statements "True" or "False," based on information in "Guardians of English." Check your answers on page 202 of Appendix II, then reread the story, if necessary, to confirm the answers.

_____ **1.** Barry Hatch was the mayor of Los Angeles.

_____ **2.** Thousands of poor immigrants from Taiwan and Hong Kong had come to live in his town.

_____ **3.** The Lions Club of Taipei wanted to donate 15,000 books to the town library.

_____ **4.** Some of the books were bilingual, so that English readers could learn about Chinese culture and Chinese could learn about American culture.

_____ **5.** The local library had some Chinese books that were rarely checked out by townspeople.

_____ **6.** Hatch did not want to accept the books because he could not understand Chinese himself.

_____ **7.** In the end, the town received the books anyway.

_____ **8.** In the 1980s, most immigrants to the United States came from Europe.

_____ **9.** In 1981, Congress passed a law designating English as the official language of the United States.

_____ **10.** Some members of the U.S. English organization want no public services to be provided in languages other than English.

_____ **CORRECT** × 10 = _____ %

Threads

Idioms in Translation:

English: Go fly a kite!
Spanish: Go fry asparagus!

English: It's Greek to me!
French: It's Chinese!

The World Almanac and Book of Facts, 1994

ACTIVITY: ANNOTATING A TEXT

Reread "Guardians of English," annotating the text in the margins and selectively underlining or highlighting key ideas.

Consider which sentence may be the thesis statement of the essay and which other sentences contain the most important information. Then compare your annotations with those of other classmates. Discuss with your class the thesis statement and other important ideas in the reading.

ACTIVITY: IDENTIFYING THE ORGANIZATION

Argumentation

Reread the first pages of "Guardians of English," in which the writer presents the story of Mayor Barry Hatch's conflict with Chinese-speaking residents of his town, Monterey Park, California. In this section, Hatch presents arguments for "English only," while city council president Judy Chu argues against "English only" by advocating the shipment of 10,000 Chinese books to the local library.

Here, the organizational pattern of **argumentation** is used. Although the mayor apparently became emotional about the issue of the dominance of English, argumentation does not really mean arguing. It is the presentation of logical arguments in favor of and against a controversial issue, presented either in speech or writing.

ACTIVITY

In your reading journal, title a chart "English only," and place "PRO" and "CON" columns beneath the title. In "Guardians of English" find the major arguments for and against this issue. Write these briefly, in your own words, in the chart.

Compare your chart with a classmates'.

"ENGLISH ONLY"	
PRO	**CON**
_____	_____
_____	_____
_____	_____
_____	_____
_____	_____
_____	_____
_____	_____
_____	_____

LANGUAGE STUDY

LEARNING STRATEGY

**Forming Concepts: Recognizing common word parts expands
your vocabulary by enabling you to guess the meanings of
unfamiliar words.**

The study of word parts—the beginnings (prefixes), middles (roots), and endings (suffixes)—that are found in many English words is an effective way to expand your vocabulary. Each of these parts has a specific meaning, so together they provide clues to a particular word's meaning.

Many such word parts exist in English words, but not all English words have them. As you study each type of word part, you will begin to recognize that word parts don't always have the same spelling from word to word, and the important word roots do not always occur in the middle of a word. However, so many important word parts exist that you should attempt to learn them, preferably in small groups at a time.

Threads

One researcher
suggests that learning
30 key word parts will
enable you to
understand the
meaning of about
14,000 words.

ACTIVITIES

A. Examine this partial list of common prefixes along with their meanings. The right-hand column of the chart lists the name of a story and the paragraph number in which a word containing the prefix appears. Copy the chart into your reading journal. In the readings in this chapter, find at least one sample word that contains each prefix and complete the chart. One sample is provided for you.

COMMON PREFIXES			
Prefix	**Meaning**	**Sample Word**	**Story/Paragraph Number**
un	not	*unutterable*	"The Language We Know"/1
inter	between		"The Language We Know"/2
sub	under		"The Language We Know"/6
trans	across, over		"Spanglish"/5
counter	against, opposite		"Spanglish"/5
bi	two		"Guardians of English"/2
dis	apart, away, not		"Guardians of English"/7
mis	wrong		"Guardians of English"/9

B. Define each of the sample words in the chart. Discuss with a classmate how the word part, in this case the prefix, provides a clue to the word meaning. Write your definitions in your reading journal.

C. With a partner, find five words from the article "Spanglish" that contain the root "span." List the words in your journal. Define the words, and discuss their similarities in meaning.

67

LEARNING STRATEGY

Personalizing: By role-playing, you perceive a subject more deeply because you become part of it.

ACTIVITY: DRAMATIZING

The story "Guardians of English" contains many examples of conflicts that have arisen between the users of English and other languages in the United States. In a small group, choose one of the situations presented on pages 64–65.

Choose one or more group members to assume the roles of the "English only" proponents, and one or more to assume the roles of immigrants who want to use their own languages. Then act out a situation in which the groups confront each other to discuss the conflict. Make inferences (or guesses) about what might happen. Present your dramatization to the class. Here's one suggestion:

In the first situation, involving a "Speak-English-Only" rule in Elizabeth, New Jersey, one group member could portray the mayor, some group members could portray Spanish-speaking city employees, and others could be non-Spanish-speaking employees.

PREPARING TO READ

ACTIVITY: PREDICTING CONTENT

In a group, discuss which languages (other than English) you think are the most widely spoken in the United States. Which non-English languages do you think are gaining the most speakers? Which do you think are losing the most speakers? Finally, which **five** U.S. states do you think have the most non-English speaking residents? Write your group members' predictions in the boxes that follow. Then consult the chart on page 69 to check your answers.

NON-ENGLISH LANGUAGES IN THE UNITED STATES		
Most Widely Spoken	**Gaining Most Speakers**	**Losing Most Speakers**
_____	_____	_____
_____	_____	_____
_____	_____	_____
_____	_____	_____
_____	_____	_____

Comprehension

Based on the information in the preceding chart, mark the following statements T (True), F (False) or I (Insufficient Information). You may consult the chart as you answer. Check your answers on page 202 of Appendix II, and then reread the chart, if necessary, to confirm the answers.

_____ 1. Chinese is the fifth most widely spoken language in the United States.

_____ 2. More people speak Spanish in the United States than any other non-English language.

_____ 3. Nearly two million French speakers live in the United States.

_____ 4. Greek is the fastest shrinking non-English language spoken in the United States.

_____ 5. The fastest growing non-English language group in the United States comes from Cambodia.

_____ 6. Two languages of India are among the five fastest growing in the United States.

_____ 7. California and New York are among the top states with non-English speakers.

_____ 8. Texas has the most non-English speaking people in the United States.

_____ 9. About 90 to 95 percent of Florida's residents speak English at home.

_____ 10. The information in this chart came from the Census Bureau.

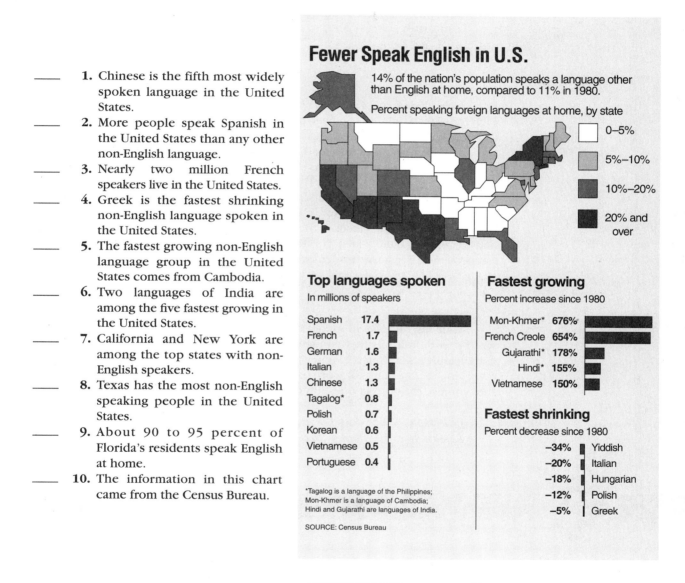

Fewer Speak English in U.S.

14% of the nation's population speaks a language other than English at home, compared to 11% in 1980.

Percent speaking foreign languages at home, by state

- 0–5%
- 5%–10%
- 10%–20%
- 20% and over

Top languages spoken

In millions of speakers

Spanish	17.4
French	1.7
German	1.6
Italian	1.3
Chinese	1.3
Tagalog*	0.8
Polish	0.7
Korean	0.6
Vietnamese	0.5
Portuguese	0.4

*Tagalog is a language of the Philippines; Mon-Khmer is a language of Cambodia; Hindi and Gujarathi are languages of India.

SOURCE: Census Bureau

Fastest growing

Percent increase since 1980

Mon-Khmer*	676%
French Creole	654%
Gujarathi*	178%
Hindi*	155%
Vietnamese	150%

Fastest shrinking

Percent decrease since 1980

–34%	Yiddish
–20%	Italian
–18%	Hungarian
–12%	Polish
–5%	Greek

_____ **CORRECT** × **10** = _____ %

LEARNING STRATEGY

Managing Your Learning: "Microteaching," or peer teaching, is an effective tool for studying *and* enhancing your communicative skills.

Effective studying requires a variety of strategies. One useful method is to teach each other material that you have just learned. "Microteaching" means one-on-one teaching between two classmates. (The prefix "micro" means "small.") Successful students often practice this method when preparing for examinations since it allows them to isolate and focus on the material that they expect to find on the test.

In microteaching, one student asks another to recall important information from reading material or lectures. If the "student" does not give the "teacher" the correct answer to the question, the "teacher" may help the "student" by providing him or her with clues. Then the "teacher" will often repeat the questions that the "student" failed to answer to ensure that he or she remembers the material.

ACTIVITY

Your instructor will model this method for you using the vocabulary and word part definitions that you studied earlier in the chapter. After you become comfortable as a "microteacher" or "microstudent," practice the method by reviewing the meanings of word parts and sample word definitions on page 67. Be sure you use the correct question form, as the sample question below illustrates:

> *QUESTION*   *What does the prefix "bi" mean?*
> *RESPONSE*   *"Bi" means "two."*

EVALUATION

ACTIVITY: CHAPTER SELF-TEST

Assess your general understanding of the readings in Chapter 3 by taking the following chapter self-examination. In Part 1, define the word parts that you studied in this chapter as well as words that contain these parts. Circle the appropriate completion of each statement in Part 2. Check your answers to Part 1 in your reading journal or on your cards, and score your test. See page 202 in Appendix II for the answers to Part 2.

Part 1: Vocabulary

Word Part	Meaning	Sample Word	Definition
un	_____	unutterable	_____
inter	_____	interstate	_____
sub	_____	subsistence	_____
trans	_____	transplanted	_____
counter	_____	counterparts	_____
bi	_____	bilingual	_____
dis	_____	dissonant	_____
mis	_____	mistrust	_____

_____ **CORRECT** $\times$ **6.25** = _____ %

(One point each for word part definition and sample word definition)

Part 2: Comprehension

1. In "The Language We Know," the author writes about the influence of his native language on his present occupation, which is
   a. a farmer.
   b. a writer.
   c. a government agent.

2. The author writes: "Language opened up vistas of the world around me." Here, the language he refers to is
   a. English.
   b. Acoma.

3. The "stories" that Ortiz's parents told him were
   a. about Indian history.
   b. about his community.
   c. part of the close-knit Indian society.
   d. all of the above

4. Spanglish is used in cities where the inhabitants
   a. speak only English.
   b. speak only Spanish.
   c. speak either English or Spanish.

5. According to the authors of "Spanglish," among foreign languages studied by college students in the United States, Spanish is
   a. number one.
   b. number two.
   c. the least popular.

6. In "Guardians of English," the changing ethnic population of Monterey Park was evidenced by the presence of
   a. Chinese product shops.
   b. Chinese languages spoken in restaurants.
   c. Chinese characters on street signs.
   d. all of the above

7. Mayor Barry Hatch's profession was
  a. librarian.
  b. teacher.
  c. store owner.
8. Hatch believed that Asians in Southern California wanted
  a. to conquer the country.
  b. to join the country.
9. In 1965, Congress abolished the national-origins quota system, which had up to that time favored
  a. Asian immigrants.
  b. northwestern European immigrants.
  c. Hispanic immigrants.
10. The U.S. English organization has sought
  a. to "preserve the status" of English.
  b. to limit public uses of other languages.
  c. both of the above

_____ **CORRECT** $\times$ **10** = _____ %

ACTIVITY: EVALUATING YOUR GOALS

As in the previous chapters, write brief answers in your reading journal to the following questions:

1. The most important skills I used in reading and responding to the readings in this chapter were _____.

2. The most valuable information I gained from this chapter was _____
_____.

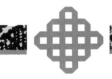

EXPANSION

Reading Further

ACTIVITY

With a partner, go to the local library and find one book *in English* that relates to your native language or another language besides English that you are interested in. A book in which the author relates the experience of using his or her native language in a new language environment might be a good choice. Or you might select a book in which someone relates the experience of learning a new language.

Using the following outline as a guide, present a short oral report about the book to your class.

I. Introduction
   A. Present the title of the book. (Also give author, publisher, publication date)
   B. Tell which language the author writes about and what his or her general experience with the language was.
II. One Interesting Part of the Book
   A. From the table of contents, read one interesting chapter from the book.
   B. Introduce and explain the main idea of this part of the book.
III. Your Opinion
   A. Conclude by giving your opinion of the book and the author's experience with the language he or she writes about.
   B. You may also want to compare the author's experience with your own.

Tribes

ACTIVITY: SETTING PERSONAL GOALS

As in the previous chapters, list in order of importance (with 1 as "most valuable") the learning objectives that are significant to you. Add personal learning objectives to the list if you wish.

GOAL   **RANK**

1. To increase comprehension of readings   _____

2. To expand vocabulary   _____

3. To increase reading speed   _____

4. To improve study skills   _____

5. To learn more about the subjects of this chapter   _____

6. _____ _____

7. _____ _____

PREPARING TO READ

Nationalism, the strong feeling of belonging to one's national group, is spreading across the globe, igniting wars and dividing states into autonomous or independence-seeking nations in Asia, Eastern Europe, Africa, the Americas, and beyond.

As leaders and everyday people face these political dilemmas, commentators such as Fodil Fellag approach the issue of nation versus state from a tribal viewpoint. In the following articles, he and other observers write about the political choices that lie ahead:

> "People, Not States, Make Nations" by Jason W. Clay
> "The Concept of Tribe" by Fodil Fellag
> "Is There an American Tribe?" by Lewis H. Lapham

ACTIVITY: PREDICTING CONTENT

Discuss the following questions in a small group.

1. Considering the titles of the readings in Chapter 4, what topics do you predict will be covered?
2. What is a *tribe*? What do you know about tribes?
3. Look ahead at the photographs and other graphic material in Chapter 4. Read the accompanying captions. What do they suggest about the content?
4. What would you like to know about tribal life? Make a list of your questions.

Threads

Fighting between predominantly Christian Armenia and Moslem Azerbaijan continued in 1993 over control of Nagomo-Karabakh, Azerbaijan, where mostly Armenians live.

The World Almanac and Book of Facts, 1994

ACTIVITY FOR IDEAS

Prepare for the topic of tribes by listening to a television or radio program about one ethnic or religious minority group in the United States or elsewhere in the world. You might choose a news program containing a report on a religious or ethnic minority or a public television documentary that depicts life in a tribal or "modern" culture. Copy the following form into your journal. Listen to the program and write your report.

1. Title of Television/Radio Program: _____

Date: _____   Channel: _____

2. Main Point of the Program:

_____

_____

3. Your Impression of the Program:

_____

_____

IT WORKS!
Learning Strategy:
Listening

ACTIVITY: SHARING IMPRESSIONS

With a small group of classmates, present your report and share your impressions of the television or radio program you heard. Discuss the following questions before you make your presentation: (Follow the outline of the report to organize your talk. Divide the speaking responsibilities among group members.)

1. Did you enjoy the program you heard? Why or why not?
2. What was your reaction to the program?
3. Was any information in the program surprising to you? If so, explain it to your group and ask for their reactions.

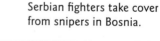

Serbian fighters take cover from snipers in Bosnia.

ACTIVITY: PREVIEWING

The title of the first reading is "People, Not States, Make Nations." Discuss with a partner the different meanings of the words "state" and "nation." Make a list of synonyms. As you look over the list, consider these questions: What is the main difference in meaning between the two words? How are they commonly used? Share your ideas with the class.

Reading 1

Glossary
Cold War   the political tension and rivalry between the Western and Eastern bloc nations
non-aligned states   nations not aligned with either the West or the East
League of Iroquois   a confederation of North American Indian tribes

PEOPLE, NOT STATES, MAKE NATIONS

by Jason W. Clay

Eastern Europe's revolts and the unraveling of Yugoslavia and the Soviet Union last year [in 1993] are part of a worldwide call to redefine the relationship of the *state* to the *nations* within them.

There are about five thousand nations in the world today. What makes each a nation is that its people share a language, culture, territorial base, and political organization and history. The Kayapo Indians are but one nation within the state called Brazil. The Penan people of Sarawak are but one nation within the state called Malaysia. To the people of nations, group identity matters more than state affiliation. The five thousand nations have existed for hundreds, even thousands of years. The majority of the world's 190 states have been around only since World War II. Very few nations have ever been given a choice when they were made part of a state.

Most of the shooting wars in the world today are being fought between nations and the states that claim to represent them. With very few exceptions, these wars are not about the independence of nations, but rather their level of autonomy: who controls the rights to resources (land, water, minerals, trees), who provides local security, who determines the policies that affect language, laws, and cultural and religious rights.

Nearly all the international debt accumulated by African states, and nearly half of all other Third World debt, comes from the purchase of weapons by states to fight their own citizens. Most of the world's 12 million refugees are the offspring of such conflicts, as are most of the 100 million internally displaced people who have been uprooted from their homelands. Most of the world's famine victims are nation peoples who are being starved by states that attempt to assimilate them while appropriating their food supplies. Most of the destructive colonization, resettlement, and villagization programs are sponsored by states, in the name of progress, in order to bring nation peoples to their knees.

A vicious circle forms. The appropriation of a nation's resources leads to conflict, conflict leads to weapons purchases, weapons purchases lead to debt, and debt leads to the appropriation of more resources—and the cycle intensifies.

As the Cold War ends, new relationships will evolve, not only between the states of the West and those of Eastern Europe, but also among their allies and non-aligned states throughout the globe. With Third World countries no longer looked on as proxies in an ideological war, the United States and other Western powers are pulling back on aid. That means cutting the umbilical cords of Third World elites. The consequent weakening of their power may unleash more struggle between states and nations within them who sense an opportunity to win more control over their futures.

Yet it is clearer now than in recent decades that cultural identity is alive and well. In Africa, for example, to justify dictatorships and one-party rule, local elites and foreign interests have long proclaimed the evils of tribalism. Lately, some self-described "liberators for life" have apparently concluded that they can survive only by opening up their political systems. Dictators throughout Africa have recently moved to allow opposition parties and elections. But simply allowing tribes to form political parties won't necessarily defuse pressures, because it won't change the fact that these are nations within states. There has been intriguing talk in Uganda of a confederation of tribes, based on the League of Iroquois, where local power would be left to the tribes and state politics would be decided by a joint council in which each tribe, regardless of size, has an equal vote. Under such a system, larger tribes are likely to resent not being able to wield proportional power. Yet this idea does address the vulnerability of small nations, which insist that they have the right to exist, as long as they do not deny others those same rights.

If nations and states are to find a peaceful coexistence, a system of decentralized federalism will have to evolve. By this I mean a political system that is built from the bottom up, one that gives autonomy and power to nation peoples, who in turn empower the state to act on their behalf.

Beyond this guiding principle there is no one model. Weak states with strong nations may break themselves into new states. Newly independent nations, after trying to make a go of it for a while, may decide it is to their advantage to be part of a larger political unit. Many nations may use independence as a negotiating stance and settle for more local control within a state. To date, because the political processes in most states are not open, the only way nations have been able to push for their rights is to take them by force. The next 20 years are likely to be bloody if the world cannot find a new and better way to answer the demands of its now emboldened nations.

Comprehension

Without looking back at the reading, mark the following statements "True" or "False." Check your comprehension with the answer key on page 202 of Appendix II. Record your score and your reading speed in the chart on page 200 of Appendix I.

_____ **1.** Nations have existed for a longer time than states have.

_____ **2.** The Kayapos of Brazil are an example of a state.

_____ **3.** Most of the wars today involve states versus other states.

_____ **4.** Famines can result from nations fighting their own citizens.

_____ **5.** There are about 12 million refugees today.

_____ **6.** Many of these refugees leave their homelands because of conflicts between states and nations.

_____ **7.** If tribes are allowed to form political parties, they will not fight state governments.

_____ **8.** States must find ways to give power to their nation peoples to avoid wars.

_____ **9.** Up to now, most states have been willing to give up power to the nation peoples.

_____ **10.** The author thinks more nation-state fighting may occur in the future.

_____ **CORRECT** × **10** = _____ %

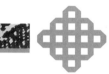 

REVIEWING

LEARNING STRATEGY

Remembering New Material: Confirming or discounting your predictions in reading helps you remember new ideas.

As you discovered in Chapters 2 and 3, you read more effectively if you utilize your prior knowledge about a topic before, as, and after you read. Relating these new ideas to your own experience allows you to make permanent "connections" in your brain that will help you remember the ideas.

An especially practical way to accomplish this is to predict ideas before reading and then "test" your guesses by reading and reflecting on the ideas in the reading. Often you will find you are able to build on your own prior knowledge.

ACTIVITY

In "People, Not States, Make Nations," you read definitions of the terms "states" and "nations." Before you read, you listed synonyms for each word and discussed the differences in meaning between the two terms.

Scan (read quickly) the first section of the reading, in which the author gives his definitions. Compare them with those on your pre-reading list. With classmates, discuss how the author's definitions contrast with your own.

In your reading journal, write the author's definitions of each word.

Forming Concepts: Identifying main ideas enables you to gain a clear understanding of reading material.

ACTIVITY: IDENTIFYING THE ORGANIZATION

Main Idea

The main idea of a reading is its central message: its thesis, main point, or central thought. If you can grasp the main idea of a reading, you will also understand the writer's reason for writing the text. Moreover, you will recognize that the rest of the reading logically develops, explains, or proves this point.

If you examine again the reading "The Concept of Tribe," for example, you can determine the main idea by first asking: "What is the topic of this reading?" If you answer, "tribes," then you have identified the topic. The next question to ask is: "What in particular does the reading *say* about 'tribes'?" The answer to this question is the main idea of the reading.

How do you find the main idea? In longer readings such as "Tribal Wisdom," the main idea may appear in various places: at the beginning of the first paragraph, in the middle of the first paragraph, in the end of the first paragraph, or in a later paragraph near the beginning of the reading. In any case, the main idea sentence will usually appear near the beginning of the reading. And it should contain both the topic and what in particular the writer *says* about the topic.

For example, read the following paragraphs, which are the two first paragraphs from "Spanglish" (page 57), and consider these questions: What is the topic? Which sentence contains the main idea (what the writer says about the topic)?

In Manhattan a first-grader greets her visiting grandparents, happily exclaiming, "Come here, *sientate!*" Her bemused grandfather, who does not speak Spanish, nevertheless knows she is asking him to sit down. A Miami personnel officer understands what a job applicant means when he says, *"Quiero un* part time." Nor do drivers miss a beat reading a billboard alongside a Los Angeles street advertising CERVEZA—SIX-PACK!

This free-form blend of Spanish and English, known as Spanglish, is common linguistic currency where concentrations of Hispanic Americans are found in the United States. In Los Angeles, where 55 percent of the city's 3 million inhabitants speak Spanish, Spanglish is as much a part of daily life as sunglasses. Unlike the broken-English efforts of earlier immigrants from Europe, Asia and other regions, Spanglish has become a widely accepted conversational mode used casually—even playfully—by Spanish-speaking immigrants and native-born Americans alike.

Most likely, you identified the topic as "Spanglish." Notice that the main idea sentence does not occur in the first paragraph (which instead presents an example of Spanglish). The first sentence of the second paragraph, in fact, contains the main idea: Spanglish is becoming more popular.

As you continue to read, you will recognize the variety of places where writers place their main idea sentences. Finding the main idea sentence will enable you to be better informed as you read the rest of the passage.

ACTIVITY

Work with a partner to identify the topic and the main idea of "People, Not States, Make Nations." Write the topic and the main idea sentence in your reading journal, and compare your choices with those of other classmates.

ACTIVITIES

A. The following is a list of three important textual patterns found in "People, Not States, Make Nations." As in previous chapters, you have found that these patterns are common in many types of reading texts. With a classmate, find <u>at least one</u> paragraph that uses each type of organizational pattern. Be prepared to explain briefly the main ideas in each paragraph you find and how it uses a particular organizational pattern.

Organization Pattern	Paragraph Number(s)	Main Idea in Pattern
Definition	_____	_____
Comparison/Contrast	_____	_____
Cause/Effect	_____	_____

IT WORKS!
Learning Strategy:
Using
Graphics

B. Make a graphic organizer to represent one of the organizational patterns used in one paragraph in the reading. You may use one of the graphics that follow as a model:

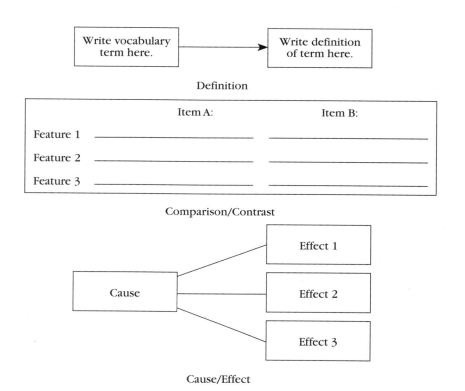

Definition

Comparison/Contrast

Cause/Effect

Key terms are vocabulary items that relate to the subject of the reading. In academic reading, you need to remember definitions of key terms that you find in readings and lectures so you can recognize and use them in examinations and later courses.

LEARNING STRATEGY

Remembering New Material: Isolating and defining key terms ensures that they will stick in your mind.

ACTIVITY

In "People, Not States, Make Nations," the main subject areas are political science and sociology. The author defines several key terms relating to political science. With a partner, define the following key terms; then list them and their definitions in your reading journal.

1. nation
2. state
3. resources
4. colonization

5. allies
6. non-aligned states
7. dictatorship
8. decentralized federalism

 **PREPARING TO READ**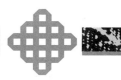

ACTIVITY: PREVIEWING

A. What does the title "The Concept of Tribe" suggest about the factual content and the opinion that will be presented? What is your impression of tribal living? Discuss these questions with a classmate.

B. Look at the following words:

backwardness   sacred territory   in communion with environment
savageness   aggressiveness

Fellag uses these words to describe the concept of "tribe." Define each term, and discuss with a classmate whether you think these words apply to the modern view of "tribe." Share your ideas with the class.

**Forming Concepts: Asking questions about a topic *before*
you read helps you to focus on finding specific information
in a passage.**

Readings in newspapers, magazines, or college textbooks often contain
headings that divide the passage into logical sections. Effective readers use
headings in a number of ways: to preview a reading, to divide the reading into
"chunks" to read at one sitting; and to formulate questions about the subject.

This third reading technique involves transforming a heading in the text into
a question. The good reader can then read that section of the text purposefully,
looking for the answer to that question.

Here's an example of how questioning can be used:

The first heading of "The Concept of Tribe" is "A Different View of Tribes."

You might construct a question about this section by using one of these
word groups (and any others you might think of):

> Why is (are) . . .?
> How do (did) . . .?
> When did . . .?
> Why did . . .?
> What is (are) . . .?
> What does (do) . . .?

Which of these word groups might be used to construct a question about the
section? A useful question could be:

> What is the different view of tribes?
> How is it different?

Constructing questions based on headings allows you to focus your reading
on finding the answers to the questions. Then the questions can serve as practical
study tools.

ACTIVITY: READING IN "CHUNKS"

Since the second reading is a lengthy text, it contains headings to show how
the subject of "The Concept of Tribe" is organized. Read the headings, and for
each, write one question in your reading journal that will help you to focus on
important answers in the reading. Keep the questions in mind as you read,
thinking about how the text answers each question.

Reading 2

AUTHOR NOTES

Author Fodil Fellag grew up in a semi-tribal system as a child in the mountains of Kabylie in Algeria before moving to the modern city of Algiers. He emigrated to the United States in 1979.

Glossary
epithet   term used to characterize a person or thing
introspective   self-examining
pejorative   downgrading
erroneous   mistaken

THE CONCEPT OF TRIBE
by Fodil Fellag

As a child growing up in French-occupied Algeria, the word tribe was used as an insult and an attempt to humiliate us Arab or Berber natives. For example, my father's identification papers referred to his place of birth as part of the Izeghfawen tribe. At the time, like the young students of French origin, I was an avid reader of adventure novels and comic books. Almost invariably, in all these reading materials, the word tribe was used in a derogatory manner. I do not recall ever reading of English tribes, or French tribes, or Swiss tribes, etc. The word tribe was simply not used in connection with peoples of European origin.

I was enraged that my father, who was a good man in all ways, could speak four languages, and had traveled through half the world, would be called a tribesman. This word to me connoted backwardness and ignorance, in fact, savageness, and I considered my people anything but savage. As I was entering adolescence, Algeria became independent of France in 1962, and I no longer had to grapple with the imposition of that stigmatizing epithet.

A Different View of Tribes

Interestingly, soon afterwards in Europe and the United States, the post-World War II generations started becoming very dissatisfied with the basic premises of their societies. These new generations saw their elders as "robots" programmed to produce and consume products of the industrial establishment. In an introspective search, many of them went to the four corners of the Earth looking for wisdom, for "the meaning of it all." Naturally, being disgusted with their overindustrialized societies, they sought out those societies most different from their own and least industrialized or exposed to modern industrial progress. And soon the concept of tribe was looked at in a different manner, no longer a pejorative one. In fact, great wisdom was found in the tribal systems.

Look, for example, at how the Amazonian Indians have lived in communion with their environment, allowing it to regenerate itself. To many disillusioned Westerners these "tribesmen" looked quite happy and they did not have to torture themselves with questions about their identity, or importance on earth. Would it not be nice if some of that wisdom could be borrowed? Why not have tribes in the United States? Or maybe tribes already did exist in the United States, only they had not been recognized as such?

A Multiplicity of Groups

And so by the mid-1990s, the American society seemed to have splintered into many groups defined by race, sex, or other attributes, and the fissures seemed to be getting larger and larger. On top of the federal political system, another one has been superimposing itself, that of the minority sub-group. And some are referring to their groups without any embarrassment, and perhaps even a bit fashionably, as tribes. Some tribal characteristics, such as loyalty to the group first, are cultivated and proudly demonstrated.

As an immigrant, I was surprised at this state of affairs when I landed in this country in 1979. I already knew a great deal about the African American and Native American movements long before coming here, but nothing had prepared me for the great multiplicity of social groups who thought of themselves as distinct from the rest. I had learned about the different classes in the United States but always in terms of income level. I had thought there was an African American culture, a Native American culture and then everyone else. It would not have been so startling if these groups had been organized around a community of interests, in a purely rational strategy to defend those interests, pressure groups as it were. Rather, I started to realize that these sub-groups involved something deeper, the sense of identity.

People define themselves by the group they belong to. On the surface these elements (self-sense and group loyalty) would appear to be tribal characteristics, but, in my opinion, they are nothing more than fads—conscious, artificial creations which are being maintained by the efforts of the groups' leaders. These groups came into existence as a way to bargain with the "majority establishment" for a solution to their real or imagined grievances. Nowadays, even after they have obtained the rights they were claiming, many are continuing the "fight" on frivolous terms.

Real Tribal Life

In traditional tribes, the members do not choose to come together to belong to the same group. They are born into the group and the question of whether they belong is never even asked. To them, it is taken for granted to such an extent that they may never ponder that concept once in their lifetime. Witness the great number of human groups who refer to themselves simply by the word "people" (or "free people") and give every other group they know a distinctive name. The members all or almost all know each other personally, and leaders are chosen for or impose themselves by their personal qualities which every member knows directly, not through a "campaign" of information. They do not obey an anonymous central authority. The loyalty towards the group is strong to the point of risking one's life for it if necessary, and often (at least in the past) that necessity did present itself.

They live in a territory which is sacred to them. In a modern, non-tribal, society anyone can go anywhere, buy or rent property and live there. The only person they have to deal with is the owner of the property. Not so in a real tribe: any newcomer must be approved by the whole group.

The Attraction to Tribes

There are, of course, many other differences between tribal and non-tribal societies, but I suspect that what seemed attractive to the modern American in the concept is on the one hand an idealistic (and erroneous) view of the tribesman at peace with himself and his environment, and on the other hand the notion of aggressiveness, a little touch of toughness, the idea that "you don't mess with me. I'm bad." It is true that people who live in tribes do not normally have a problem of identity. They usually think they know exactly who and what they are, and the purpose of their existence on Earth is provided to them through their mythology. However, it is mostly because such quests for identity are a great luxury that only the affluent of this world can afford, those who have liberated themselves from the tyranny of the natural elements.

To most of the people who would qualify as tribesmen today, life is a precarious wresting of survival from the forces of nature. They are always at the mercy of a drought, storm, earthquake, or epidemic. All energies are channeled for survival and there is little chance or inclination for pondering the big questions of the universe. So I find it strange and a bit amusing when I hear modern Westerners marvel at the virtues and wisdom of tribal systems. All through history, peoples who were less industrially advanced have tried to emulate the technologically advanced ones, never the other way around. When some groups resisted the intrusion of technology in their lives, it has been not because they found it harmful or undesirable in itself, but because it seemed too overwhelmingly complicated for them to master successfully. Consciously or subconsciously, they felt that if they became dependent upon it to satisfy their needs, they would become subjugated to the people who master it. Tribes are not organized according to some consciously, deliberately devised, and decided upon plan or human will, but are the result of historical circumstances and evolution: the people simply did what they had to do to subsist in a harsh nature. The irresistible attraction of material progress inevitably undermines the foundations of tribal organization.

As for the element of aggression towards outsiders and solidarity with insiders, I am not certain that it is to be admired. The underlying premise is that outside the group there are only enemies or potential enemies; any neighboring tribe (even if you are not presently at war with them) may only be a circumstantial friend, and you should always be prepared for a fight against them at any time.

In my native village, perched on the mountains overlooking the Mediterranean sea, and which until a few decades ago had kept some vestiges of a tribal system, I remember a time when one could commit almost any crime in the cities of North Africa or Europe and not ever be judged for it back in the village. He could find a sanctuary there any time he wished to come back, and as long as he did not commit any crime in the village itself, would be left in peace. I remember an old dictum which said in essence: "Help your fellow villager whether he is right or wrong." This situation can be seen even today to some extent in the mountains of Sicily, Corsica, and some other Mediterranean parts. For my part, I am happy it is no longer quite the case in my little native village, for I consider that all people are equal.

Put Tribalism to Rest

Today, as an immigrant in the United States, I refuse to be assimilated into any particular group defined along any other lines except personal traits. I consider that I am here as a guest and I have been treated wonderfully by everyone I have come in contact with. I spent more than 15 years in Texas and although I look and sound foreign, I have had no more "aggravation" than the average native Texan has. In fact I am surprised when my native Texan friends tell me about someone having been rude or uncivil to them, for it seems such things never happen to me, and I do discuss politics and religion! I have no sense of needing to be compartmentalized and mobilized into a particular group in order to "get my rights." Truth is, if I ever felt that need arising, I think I would rather go back where I came from.

Tribal instincts are better discussed and put to rest than expounded. Reinforcing them can only lead to harm of one kind or another. The United States is composed of normal human beings, not supermen and superwomen, and although it might sound far-fetched today, chaos could arise from a strengthening of sub-group solidarity. What is happening in the former Yugoslavia was unimaginable a decade ago. Who knows how strong the cement that keeps America together is and how much erosion it can sustain before structural damage occurs?

A tribe by definition is a human group which lacks a central power. Recently, the federal building in Oklahoma City was bombed, almost certainly the act of armed militias who reject the authority of the central government. Could this be the first result of a drift towards tribalization in the country?

Comprehension

After you have read the entire "Tribal Wisdom" text, mark the following statements as "True" or "False" based on the information in the reading. Or, check your comprehension "chunk" by "chunk" by referring to the page numbers given. Do not refer back to the reading until after you have tested yourself.

Pages 85–86

_____ 1. The word "tribe" was used in a positive way in Algeria when the author was a child.

_____ 2. The word "tribe" was not used to describe European people, according to the author.

_____ 3. After World War II, Europeans and Americans looked favorably at their own industrialized societies, the author says.

_____ 4. When he emigrated here, the author was not surprised to find that many different subgroups existed in the United States.

Page 86–87

_____ 5. Members do not choose to join traditional tribes; they are born into tribes.

_____ 6. The leader of a tribe is a member whom the other members know, not an anonymous central authority.

_____ 7. According to the author, tribe members are at the mercy of their environment.

Pages 87–88

_____ 8. Tribal aggression is not admirable, the author believes.

_____ 9. In the author's formerly tribal village, a tribe member would not be allowed to return to the village if he or she committed a crime elsewhere.

_____ 10. According to the author, the Oklahoma City bombing may signal a drift toward tribalization in the United States.

_____ **CORRECT** × **10** = _____ %

ACTIVITY: SHARING IMPRESSIONS

Fodil Fellag's text compares "modern" societies with tribal societies. Important characteristics of each group, which he presents in "The Concept of Tribe," are stated in the Comprehension check on the previous page.

In a small group, review the Comprehension statements, rewording false statements so that they reflect the ideas presented in Fellag's text. Discuss your reactions to each of the points. Make a list in your reading journal of your own opinions in support of or counter to each of the points. Then write a sentence in answer to this question: According to Fellag, which type of society is better, "modern" or tribal?

Share your group's impressions with the rest of the class.

LEARNING STRATEGY

Forming Concepts: In a debate, when you know how your opponents think, you can counter their arguments better.

ACTIVITY: DEBATING AN ISSUE

In a small group, take the position of Group A or Group B, as assigned by your instructor. Read the descriptions of both sides' positions below. In your group, discuss both positions. Write down a list of points that you will present in support of your position. Make notes about each point. Predict what the other group will argue in response to each of your points.

Choose one group member to announce your group and its position. Divide your points among the group members. In a panel discussion, present your points to the class. An opposing group will then present its points. Be prepared to respond to comments and questions to your group from the audience.

Group A. Imagine that you are a leader of a state government that has had years of conflict with a tribal minority nation within the state. You must negotiate with the leaders of the nation to find ways in which the state can control the nation yet still allow the nation to exert some control over its own governance. The tribal nation wants to retain control of its land. However, you would like to use this land for other purposes. What conditions will you offer to the nation peoples? Could you offer to provide them with extra services or benefits that might entice them to reach a compromise with you?

Group B. Imagine that you are a leader of a minority tribal people in a large state. Your tribe risks destruction by the state, which wants you to give up your fertile land. You and your supporters must convince your peace-loving tribe members to wage war against the state instead of retreat to a more remote, but less fertile, part of the country.

Threads

Civil war intensified in 1994 in the central African state of Rwanda, where 90% of the population are Hutu tribes members and 9% are Tutsi tribes members.

The World Almanac and Book of Facts, 1994

ACTIVITY: LISTENING FOR IDEAS

IT WORKS!
Learning Strategy:
Listening

As each group presents its points, take notes. Use the form provided. Decide which group is the winner of the panel discussion.

Panel Discussion Notes and Evaluation

Group A	*Group B*
Main Points	Main Points
1. _____	1. _____
2. _____	2. _____
3. _____	3. _____
4. _____	4. _____
COMMENTS:	
	Winning Group (circle one): **A** or **B**

LANGUAGE STUDY

ACTIVITY

In your reading journal, make a list of ten key terms from "The Concept of Tribe" that you think relate directly to the subject of anthropology, the study of man. Compare your list with classmates. Identify the part of speech (e.g., noun, verb) of each term. Define the terms and place them on vocabulary cards, if you wish.

IT WORKS!
Learning Strategy:
Key Terms

In Chapter 3 you practiced using word parts to unlock the meaning of unfamiliar words. The readings in Chapter 4 also contain many terms that can be analyzed in terms of key word parts.

For example, look at these terms from "People, Not States, Make Nations" page 78:

<u>dis</u>placed (paragraph 4)
<u>un</u>leash (paragraph 6)

IT WORKS!
Learning Strategy:
Word Parts

Each word contains a common prefix that you studied in Chapter 3. What does each of the prefixes mean? How does it help you define the new word?

Many words in this reading contain other common prefixes. Studying these will benefit you in future reading.

ACTIVITIES

A. Study the prefix chart that follows. Copy it into your reading journal. With a partner, find each of the vocabulary words listed in "People, Not States, Make Nations." Some prefixes are found in more than one vocabulary word in the passage.

Define each term in your journal. Write the part of speech (noun, adjective, adverb, verb) beside each word.

More Common Prefixes

Prefix	Meaning	Sample Word(s)	Paragraph Number(s)
re	again	_____	1, 4
auto	self, same	_____	3, 8
de	away, from	_____	4, 7, 8
co	together	_____	8

B. With a partner, scan "The Concept of Tribe" for words that contain the prefixes listed below. Make a chart of the prefixes, their meanings, and sample words.

over   non   under

ACTIVITY: IDENTIFYING THE ORGANIZATION

In "The Concept of Tribe," the author uses the organizational pattern of comparison and contrast in discussing tribal societies and modern societies. With a partner, scan the reading to find sections in which the author compares and/or contrasts particular aspects of the two types of societies.

Using the following headings, design a chart in your reading journal in which you make notes about particular aspects of the two types of societies the author compares. Two societal aspects are provided for you:

Comparisons in "The Concept of Tribe"

Basis of Comparison	*Tribal Societies* Characteristics	*Modern Societies* Characteristics
movement of people	_____	people can go anywhere they want
_____	_____	_____
_____	_____	_____
leaders of people	known by all tribe members	_____

Health Care workers from the Greater New York Hospital Association rally for more funding.

ACTIVITY: PREVIEWING

The title of the third reading consists of a question and an answer: "Is There an American Tribe? If There Is Not, We Are All Weakened." Consider the author's query and response. What does the question mean? Do you agree with the answer?

Reading 3

Glossary

the canon of preferred texts here, a list (canon) of literary selections for educational purposes

pick at the scab to scratch the scab (hard brown covering) over a sore, which may inhibit healing

guilds organizations, especially work-related groups such as unions

Cole Porter (1891–1964) an American composer

mongrel mixed breed, as in "mongrel dog"

IS THERE AN AMERICAN TRIBE?
IF THERE IS NOT, WE ARE ALL WEAKENED

by Lewis H. Lapham

Were I to believe what I read in the papers, I would find it easy to think that I no longer can identify myself simply as an American. As a plain American I have neither voice nor authentic proofs of existence. I acquire a presence only as a female American, a white American, an old American, a rich American, a black American, a gay American, a poor American, a native American, a dead American. The subordination of the noun to the adjectives makes a mockery of both the American premise and the democratic spirit.

These days, the news is full of arguments in the arenas of cultural opinion that echo the same bitter refrain. The ceaseless quarrels about the canon of preferred texts pick at the scab of the same questions. Who and what is an American? How and where do we find an identity that is something other than a fright mask? When using the collective national pronoun ("we the people," "we happy few," etc.) whom do we invite into the club of the we?

Do we really believe that the American achieves visible and specific meaning only by reason of his or her association with the political guilds of race, gender, age, ancestry, or social class?

That assumption is as elitist as the view that only a woman endowed with an income of $1 million a year can truly appreciate the beauty of money and the music of Cole Porter. Comparable theories of grace encourage the belief that only black people can know or teach black history, that no white man can play jazz piano, that blondes have a better time, and that Jews can't play basketball.

America was founded on precisely the opposite premise. We were always about becoming, not being, about the prospects for the future, not about the inheritance of the past. The man who rests his case on his color makes a claim to special privilege not unlike the divine right of kings. The pretensions might buttress the cathedrals of our self-esteem, but they run counter to the lessons of our history.

The American equation rests on the habit of holding our fellow citizens in thoughtful regard not because they are exceptional (or famous, or beautiful, or rich) but simply because they are our fellow citizens. If we abandon the sense of mutual respect, we abandon the premise as well as the machinery of the American enterprise.

Among all the nations of the earth, America is the one that has come most triumphantly to terms with the mixtures of blood and race, and maybe it is another of history's ironic jokes that we should wish to repudiate our talent for assimilation at precisely the moment in time when so many other nations in the world (in Africa and Western Europe as well as the Soviet Union) look to the promise of the American example. The jumble of confused or mistaken identities that was the story of nineteenth-century America has become the story of a late-twentieth-century world defined by a vast migration of people across seven continents and as many oceans. Why, then, do we lose confidence in ourselves and grow fearful of our mongrel freedoms?

Comprehension

Check your understanding of the reading by marking the following statements "True" or "False." Do not refer to the reading before the test. Check your answers on page 202 in Appendix II.

_____ **1.** The reading asks what an American is.

_____ **2.** The reading supplies a clear definition of what an American is.

_____ **3.** America is a country that has always looked to its past, according to the author.

_____ **4.** America was founded on the idea that only blacks can play jazz and Jews can't play basketball, the author says.

_____ **5.** Being an American means that you respect someone because he or she is rich or famous, the author believes.

_____ **6.** The reading suggests that Americans need to respect each other.

_____ **7.** According to the author, America has done a good job of mixing its races and classes in the past.

_____ **8.** The author believes that all Americans should join to form an American tribe.

_____ **CORRECT** × **12.5** = _____ %

LANGUAGE STUDY

ACTIVITY

With a partner, scan "Is There an American Tribe?" for words that contain any of the common prefixes listed on page 67 or page 91. Write the definitions and parts of speech of these words in your reading journal.

REACTIONS

ACTIVITY: CONNECTING IDEAS

Look back at the three readings in Chapter 4, "Tribes." Each of these articles presents a different perspective on the coexistence of nations (which can be called "tribes") and states (most often "modern" societies).

In a small group, discuss the viewpoints expressed about nations and states. Which of the author's views do you agree with? Which do you disagree with? Why? Share your opinions with the class.

REVIEWING

ACTIVITY: MICROTEACHING

As you did in Chapter 3, work with a partner to ask and answer questions about the readings in Chapter 4. Focus on these areas of study:

1. Review the questions you wrote based on the headings in "Tribal Wisdom."
2. Review all the vocabulary words you studied in key terms, word parts, and guessing meaning exercises for all three readings.

EVALUATION

ACTIVITY: CHAPTER SELF-TEST

Assess your general understanding of the readings in Chapter 4 by taking the following chapter self-examination. The day before you take this test, select ten vocabulary items from your reading journal (or from your vocabulary cards) on key terms, word parts, and guessing meaning. Write them on a separate piece of paper, and turn this list in to your instructor. Then quickly review your reading journal notes about the chapter and the readings.

On the test day, your instructor will return your vocabulary list. Fill in the definitions and parts of speech of your ten personal vocabulary words in Part 1. Circle the appropriate completion of each statement in Part 2. Check your answers to Part 1 in your reading journal or on your cards, and score your test. See page 202 in Appendix II for the answers to Part 2.

Part 1: Vocabulary

Vocabulary Word	Definition	Part of Speech
1. _____	_____	_____
2. _____	_____	_____
3. _____	_____	_____
4. _____	_____	_____
5. _____	_____	_____
6. _____	_____	_____
7. _____	_____	_____
8. _____	_____	_____
9. _____	_____	_____
10. _____	_____	_____

_____ **CORRECT** $\times$ **10** = _____ %

Part 2: Comprehension

1. In "People, Not States, Make Nations," the author writes that the Kayapos of Brazil and the Penan people of Sarawak, Malaysia, are examples of
   a. nations.
   b. states.
2. The author says that wars between nations and states involve the issue of
   a. rights to control of resources.
   b. who provides local security.
   c. language and other cultural issues.
   d. all of the above
3. For nations and states to coexist peacefully, the author says, political systems
   a. must give autonomy and power to the states.
   b. must give autonomy and power to the nations.
4. In "The Concept of Tribe," Fellag uses words like "in communion with their environment" and "aggressiveness" to describe
   a. tribal societies.
   b. modern, non-tribal societies.
   c. both tribal and non-tribal societies.
5. According to the author Westerners have, at different times,
   a. called tribal societies savage and backward.
   b. hand a romantic view of tribal life.
   c. both a. and b.
6. In traditional tribal societies, Fellag suggests, members
   a. are born into the group.
   b. do not know the other tribe members.
   c. move freely from one place to another.

7. According to the author, a strengthening of subgroups in the U.S. could result in
   a. structural damage to United States society.
   b. a situation similar to the former Yugoslavia.
   c. both **a.** and **b.**
8. In "Is There an American Tribe?" the author says newspapers identify him as
   a. a plain American.
   b. belonging to a particular subgroup of American.
9. According to the author of this reading, America was founded on the idea that
   a. only a rich woman can appreciate Cole Porter music.
   b. only a black person can teach black history.
   c. no white man can play jazz piano.
   d. none of the above
10. He believes that among all the nations of the Earth, America is the one that
    a. has best come to terms with its mixture of races.
    b. has the most problems with its mixed-race population.

_____ **CORRECT** × **10** = _____ %

LEARNING STRATEGY

Managing Your Learning: Evaluating your learning progress at different stages allows you to pinpoint your strengths and weaknesses.

ACTIVITY

Reading requires you to use a complex set of skills. One way to focus on your strengths and weaknesses is to analyze how you read difficult texts. Answer the following questions in your reading journal to help you assess your reading habits and adjust your goals accordingly. Consult your instructor for suggestions.

1. Which reading in Chapter 4 was most difficult for you? Why?
2. Identify one paragraph from your most difficult reading. Explain which words or phrases make the ideas hard to comprehend. Explain briefly the methods you used to understand the passage. Did you translate? Did you use a dictionary? Did you break difficult sentences down into sections?

ACTIVITY: EVALUATING YOUR GOALS

A. Re-evaluate the learning objectives that you have identified as most significant to you in this and previous chapters. Change the ranking of your goals if you now think some are more valuable than others. Add new personal learning objectives to the list if you wish.

GOAL   **RANK**

1. To increase comprehension of readings   _____
2. To expand vocabulary   _____
3. To increase reading speed   _____
4. To improve study skills   _____
5. To learn more about the subjects of this chapter   _____
6. _____   _____
7. _____   _____

B. In your reading journal, write briefly in answer to the following questions:

1. The most important skills I used in reading and responding to the readings in this chapter were _____.

2. The most valuable information I gained from this chapter was _____
_____.

EXPANSION

ACTIVITY: SHARING IMPRESSIONS

In a small group, discuss the following questions. Then, share your impressions with the class.

1. Is your native culture a traditional society, a modern one, or a mixture of both? Explain.
2. Compare and contrast one aspect of your native culture with the same aspect in U.S. society.
3. Would you rather live in a traditional society, a modern society, or in a society that has both traditional and modern characteristics? Describe the "ideal" society for you.

Reading Further

Read about a tribe or nation of people in the United States or another country. Find an article from a magazine or newspaper, or read part of a book. In your reading journal, write a brief summary and commentary on the reading. Give the name, author, publisher, and publication date of your reading.

Challenges

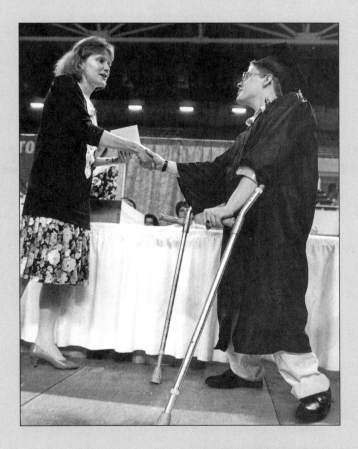

LEARNING GOALS

ACTIVITY: SETTING PERSONAL GOALS

As in the previous chapters, list in order of importance (with 1 as "most valuable") the learning objectives that are significant to you. Add personal learning objectives to the list if you wish.

GOAL	RANK
1. To increase comprehension of readings	_____
2. To expand vocabulary	_____
3. To increase reading speed	_____
4. To improve study skills	_____
5. To learn more about the subjects of this chapter	_____
6. _____	_____
7. _____	_____

PREPARING TO READ

In Chapter 5, you will read personal accounts of three individuals living with disabilities: Each of the main characters meets the daily challenges of surviving with physical handicaps. As you might expect, each has a slightly different attitude toward his or her situation. However, all the following real-life stories reveal the strength and determination of individuals struggling in a world ill-suited for those with different physical abilities.

"On Being a Cripple," from *Plaintext,* by Nancy Mairs
"Welfare Hell," from *Don't Worry, He Won't Get Far on Foot,* by John Callahan
"Blind Commuter" by Douglas Martin

ACTIVITY: PREDICTING CONTENT

Discuss these questions in a small group:

1. Considering the titles of the readings in Chapter 5, what topics do you predict will be covered?
2. What do the words *disabled* and *handicapped* mean?

3. Look ahead at the photographs and other graphic material in the chapter. Read the accompanying captions. What do they suggest about the content of the chapter?

4. What would you like to know about the lives of the main characters in these stories? Make a list of your questions.

ACTIVITY: LISTENING FOR IDEAS

In a small group, prepare yourself for the experiences of people with physical handicaps by viewing a recent movie whose main character(s) have physical disabilities. Suggested films are *The Scent of a Woman* and *Wild Hearts Can't Be Broken* (blindness), or *Coming Home* and *The Secret Garden* (wheelchair-bound characters) or *Children of a Lesser God* (deafness). Copy the following form into your journal or onto a separate piece of paper. View the movie and then fill out the following report.

IT WORKS!
Learning Strategy:
Listening

1. Title of Film: _____

   Date: _____

2. Main Characters: _____

   Physically Disabled Character: _____

3. Brief Summary of the Film:

   _____

   _____

4. Problems Character Faces with Physical Disability:

   _____

   _____

5. Your Impression of the Film:

   _____

   _____

   _____

ACTIVITY: SHARING IMPRESSIONS

Share your report on your film with classmates. Present the summary, a description of the physical disability portrayed, and your impressions. Listen to your classmates' reports, then discuss differences.

ACTIVITY: PREVIEWING

A. The first reading is entitled "On Being a Cripple." What is a *cripple*? How does this word make you feel? What do you think will be the writer's attitude about being a cripple?

B. Because this American writer gives a personal account of her life as a cripple, she includes many culturally related details. She refers to cultural items—American hobbies, places, food, American and British personalities and movies—that may be unfamiliar to you. Before you read, review the following list of culturally related vocabulary. With some of your classmates, guess the word meanings.

George Orwell
mirrored balls (on a dance floor)
Tab Hunter and Johnny Mathis
the Rolling Stones, Creedence Clearwater Revival and Cream
Pollyanna
Scrabble
Amaretto
Marx Brothers
Cape Cod
Toll House cookies

ACTIVITY: READING IN "CHUNKS"

*IT WORKS!
Learning Strategy:
Scheduling
Study Time*

"On Being a Cripple" is a lengthy text, so take into account your reading deadline and read it in three or four manageable chunks.

Reading 1

Glossary
Lindisfarne Gospel   religious texts originating from an ancient Celtic monastery on the British island of Lindisfarne
in extremis   Latin for "in the extreme" or "at the point of death"

ON BEING A CRIPPLE
by Nancy Mairs

> To escape is nothing. Not to escape is nothing.
> —Louise Bogan

1   The other day I was thinking of writing an essay on being a cripple. I was thinking hard in one of the stalls of the women's room in my office building, as I was shoving my shirt into my jeans and tugging up my zipper. Preoccupied, I flushed, picked up my book bag, took my cane down from the hook, and unlatched the door. So many movements unbalanced me, and as I pulled the door open I fell over backward, landing fully clothed on the toilet seat with my legs splayed in front of me: the old beetle-on-its-back routine. Saturday afternoon, the building deserted, I was free to laugh aloud as I wriggled back to

my feet, my voice bouncing off the yellowish tiles from all directions. Had anyone been there with me, I'd have been still and faint and hot with chagrin. I decided that it was high time to write the essay.

2   First, the matter of semantics. I am a cripple. I choose this word to name me. I choose from among several possibilities, the most common of which are "handicapped" and "disabled." I made the choice a number of years ago, without thinking, unaware of my motives for doing so. Even now, I'm not sure what those motives are, but I recognize that they are complex and not entirely flattering. People—crippled or not—wince at the word "cripple," as they do not at "handicapped" or "disabled." Perhaps I want them to wince. I want them to see me as a tough customer, one to whom the fates/gods/viruses have not been kind, but who can face the brutal truth of her existence squarely. As a cripple, I swagger.

3   But, to be fair to myself, a certain amount of honesty underlines my choice. "Cripple" seems to me a clean word, straightforward and precise. It has an honorable history, having made its first appearance in the Lindisfarne Gospel in the tenth century. As a lover of words, I like the accuracy with which it describes my condition: I have lost the full use of my limbs. "Disabled," by contrast, suggests any incapacity, physical or mental. And I certainly don't like "handicapped," which implies that I have deliberately been put at a disadvantage, by whom I can't imagine (my God is not a Handicapper General), in order to equalize chances in the great race of life. These words seem to me to be moving away from my condition, to be widening the gap between word and reality. Most remote is the recently coined euphemism "differently abled," which partakes of the same semantic hopefulness that transformed countries from "undeveloped" to "underdeveloped," then to "less developed," and finally to "developing" nations. People have continued to starve in those countries during the shift. Some realities do not obey the dictates of language.

4   Mine is one of them. Whatever you call me, I remain crippled. But I don't care what you call me, so long as it isn't "differently abled," which strikes me as pure verbal garbage designed, by its ability to describe anyone, to describe no one. I subscribe to George Orwell's thesis that "the slovenliness of our language makes it easier for us to have foolish thoughts." And I refuse to participate in the degeneration of the language to the extent that I deny that I have lost anything in the course of this calamitous disease; I refuse to pretend that the only differences between you and me are the various ordinary ones that distinguish any one person from another. But call me "disabled" or "handicapped" if you like. I have long since grown accustomed to them; and if they are vague, at least they hint at the truth. Moreover, I use them myself. Society is no readier to accept crippledness than to accept death, war, sex, sweat, or wrinkles. I would never refer to another person as a cripple. It is the word I use to name only myself.

5   I haven't always been crippled, a fact for which I am soundly grateful. To be whole of limb is, I know from experience, infinitely more pleasant and useful than to be crippled; and if that knowledge leaves me open to bitterness at my loss, the physical soundness I once enjoyed (though I did not enjoy it half enough) is well worth the occasional stab of regret. Though never any good at sports, I was a normally active child and young adult. I climbed trees, played hopscotch, jumped rope, skated, swam, rode my bicycle, sailed. I despised team sports, spending some of the wretchedest afternoons of my life, sweaty and humiliated, behind a field-hockey stick and under a basketball hoop. I tramped alone for miles along the bridle paths that webbed the woods behind the house I grew up in. I swayed through countless dim hours in the arms of one man or another under the scattered shot of light from mirrored balls, and gyrated through countless more as Tab Hunter and Johnny Mathis gave way to the Rolling Stones, Creedence Clearwater Revival, Cream. I walked down the aisle. I pushed baby carriages, changed tires in the rain, marched for peace.

6   When I was twenty-eight I started to trip and drop things. What at first seemed my natural clumsiness soon became too pronounced to shrug off. I consulted a neurologist, who told me that I had a brain tumor. A battery of tests, increasingly disagreeable, revealed no tumor. About a year and a half later I developed a blurred spot in one eye. I had, at last, the episodes "disseminated in space and time" requisite for a diagnosis: multiple sclerosis. I have never been sorry for the doctor's initial misdiagnosis, however. For almost a week, until the negative results of the tests were in, I thought I was going to die right away. Every day for the past nearly ten years, then, has been a kind of gift. I accept all gifts.

7   Multiple sclerosis is a chronic degenerative disease of the central nervous system, in which the myelin that sheathes the nerves is somehow eaten away and scar tissue forms in its place, interrupting the nerves' signals. During its course, which is unpredictable and uncontrollable, one may lose vision, hearing, speech, the ability to walk, control of bladder and/or bowels, strength in any or all extremities, sensitivity to touch, vibration, and/or pain, potency, coordination of movements—the list of possibilities is lengthy and, yes, horrifying. One may also lose one's sense of humor. That's the easiest to lose and the hardest to survive without.

8   In the past ten years, I have sustained some of these losses. Characteristic of MS are sudden attacks, called exacerbations, followed by remissions, and these I have not had. Instead, my disease has been slowly progressive. My left leg is now so weak that I walk with the aid of a brace and a cane; and for distances I use an Amigo, a variation on the electric wheelchair that looks rather like an electrified kiddie car. I no longer have much use of my left hand. Now my right side is weakening as well. I still have the blurred spot in my right eye. Overall, though, I've been lucky so far. My world has, of necessity, been circumscribed by my losses, but the terrain left me has been ample enough for me to continue many of the activities that absorb me: writing, teaching, raising children and cats and plants and snakes, reading, speaking publicly about MS and depression, even playing bridge with people patient and honorable enough to let me scatter cards every which way without sneaking a peek.

9   Lest I begin to sound like Pollyanna, however, let me say that I don't like having MS. I hate it. My life holds realities—harsh ones, some of them—that no right-minded human being ought to accept without grumbling. One of them is fatigue. I know of no one with MS who does not complain of bone-weariness; in a disease that presents an astonishing variety of symptoms, fatigue seems to be a common factor. I wake up in the morning feeling the way most people do at the end of a bad day, and I take it from there. As a result, I spend a lot of time *in extremis* and, impatient with limitation, I tend to ignore my fatigue until my body breaks down in some way and forces rest. Then I miss picnics, dinner parties, poetry readings, the brief visits of old friends from out of town. The offspring of a puritanical tradition of exceptional venerability, I cannot view these lapses without shame. My life often seems a series of small failures to do as I ought.

10   I lead, on the whole, an ordinary life, probably rather like the one I would have led had I not had MS. I am lucky that my predilections were already solitary, sedentary, and bookish—unlike the world-famous French cellist I have read about, or the young woman I talked with one long afternoon who wanted only to be a jockey. I had just begun graduate school when I found out something was wrong with me, and I have remained, interminably, a graduate student. Perhaps I would not have if I'd thought I had the stamina to return to a full-time job as a technical editor; but I've enjoyed my studies.

11   In addition to studying, I teach writing courses. I also teach medical students how to give neurological examinations. I pick up freelance editing jobs here and there. I have raised a foster son and sent him into the world, where he has made me two grandbabies, and I am still escorting my daughter and son through adolescence. I go to Mass every Saturday. I am a superb, if messy, cook. I am also an enthusiastic laundress, capable of sorting a hamper full of clothes into five subtly differentiated piles, but a terrible housekeeper. I can do italic writing and, in an emergency, bathe an oil-soaked cat. I play a fiendish game of Scrabble. When I have the time and the money, I like to sit on my front steps with my husband, drinking Amaretto and smoking a cigar, as we imagine our counterparts in Leningrad and make sure that the sun gets down once more behind the sharp childish scrawl of the Tucson Mountains.

12   This lively plenty has its bleak counterpart, of course, in all the things I can no longer do. I will never run again, except in dreams, and one day I may have to write that I will never walk again. I like to go camping, but I can't follow George and the children along the trails that wander out of a campsite through the desert or into the mountains. In fact, even on the level I've learned never to check the weather or try to hold a coherent conversation: I need all my attention for my wayward feet. Of late, I have begun to catch myself wondering how people can propel themselves without canes. With only one usable hand, I have to select my clothing with care not so much for style as for ease of ingress and egress, and even so, dressing can be laborious. I can no longer do fine stitchery, pick up babies, play the piano, braid my hair. I am immobilized by acute attacks of depression, which may or may not be physiologically related to MS but are certainly its logical concomitant.

13   These two elements, the plenty and the privation, are never pure, nor are the delight and wretchedness that accompany them. Almost every pickle that I get into as a result of my weakness and clumsiness—and I get into plenty—is funny as well as maddening and sometimes painful. I recall one May afternoon when a friend and I were going out for a drink after finishing up at school. As we were climbing into opposites sides of my car, chatting, I tripped and fell, flat and hard, onto the asphalt parking lot, my abrupt departure interrupting him in mid-sentence. "Where'd you go?" he called as he came around the back of the car to find me hauling myself up by the door frame. "Are you all right?" Yes, I told him, I was fine, just a bit rattly, and we drove off to find a shady patio and some beer. When I got home an hour or so later, my daughter greeted me with "What have you done to yourself?" I looked down. One elbow of my white turtleneck with the green froggies, one knee of my white trousers, one white kneesock were blood-soaked. We peeled off the clothes and inspected the damage, which was nasty enough but not alarming. That part wasn't funny: The abrasions took a long time to heal, and one got a little infected. Even so, when I think of my friend talking earnestly, suddenly, to the hot thin air while I dropped from his view as though through a trap door, I find the image as silly as something from a Marx Brothers movie.

14   I may find it easier than other cripples to amuse myself because I live propped by the acceptance and the assistance and, sometimes, the amusement of those around me. Grocery clerks tear my checks out of my checkbook for me, and sales clerks find chairs to put into dressing rooms when I want to try on clothes. The people I work with make sure I teach at times when I am least likely to be fatigued, in places I can get to, with the materials I need. My students, with one anonymous exception (in an end-of-the-semester evaluation), have been unperturbed by my disability. Some even like it. One was immensely cheered by the information that I paint my own fingernails; she

decided, she told me, that if I could go to such trouble over fine details, she could keep on writing essays. I suppose I became some sort of bright-fingered muse. She wrote good essays, too.

15   The most important struts in the framework of my existence, of course, are my husband and children. Dismayingly few marriages survive the MS test, and why should they? Most twenty-two- and nineteen-year-olds, like George and me, can vow in clear conscience, after a childhood of chickenpox and summer colds, to keep one another in sickness and in health so long as they both shall live. Not many are equipped for catastrophe: the dismay, the depression, the extra work, the boredom that a degenerative disease can insinuate into a relationship. And our society, with its emphasis on fun and its association of fun with physical performance, offers little encouragement for a whole spouse to stay with a crippled partner. Children experience similar stresses when faced with a crippled parent, and they are more helpless, since parents and children can't usually get divorced. They hate, of course, to be different from the peers, and the child whose mother is tacking down the aisle of a school auditorium packed with proud parents like a Cape Cod dinghy in a stiff breeze jolly well stands out in a crowd. Deprived of legal divorce, the child can at least deny the mother's disability, even her existence, forgetting to tell her about recitals and PTA meetings, refusing to accompany her to stores or church or the movies, never inviting friends to the house. Many do.

16   But I've been limping along for ten years now, and so far George and the children are still at my left elbow, holding tight. Anne and Matthew vacuum floors and dust furniture and haul trash and rake up dog droppings and button my cuffs and bake lasagna and Toll House cookies with just enough grumbling so I know that they don't have brain fever. And far from hiding me, they're forever dragging me by racks of fancy clothes or through teeming school corridors, or welcoming gaggles of friends while I'm wandering through the house in Anne's filmy pink babydoll pajamas. George generally calls before he brings someone home, but he does just as many dumb thankless chores as the children. And they all yell at me, laugh at some of my jokes, write me funny letters when we're apart—in short, treat me as an ordinary human being for whom they have some use. I think they like me. Unless they're faking . . .

17   Faking. There's the rub. Tugging at the fringes of my consciousness always is the terror that people are kind to me only because I'm a cripple. My mother almost shattered me once, with that instinct mothers have—blind, I think, in this case, but unerring nonetheless—for striking blows along the fault-lines of their children's hearts, by telling me, in an attack of selfishness, "We all have to make allowances for you, of course, because of the way you are." From the distance of a couple of years I have to admit that I haven't any idea just what she meant, and I'm not sure that she knew either. I was awfully angry. But at the time, as the words thudded home, I felt my worst fear, suddenly realized. I could bear being called selfish; I am. But I couldn't bear the corroboration that those around me were doing in fact what I'd always suspected them of doing, professing fondness while silently putting up with me because of the way I am. A cripple. I've been a little cracked ever since.

18   Along with this fear that people are secretly accepting shoddy goods comes a relentless pressure to please—to prove myself worth the burdens I impose, I guess, or to build a substantial account of goodwill against which I may write drafts in times of need. Part of the pressure arises from social expectations. In our society, anyone who deviates from the norm had better find some way to compensate. Like fat people, who are expected to be jolly, cripples must bear their lot meekly and cheerfully. A grumpy cripple isn't playing by the rules. And most of the pressure is self-generated. Early on I vowed that, if I had to have MS, by God I was going to do it well. This is a class act, ladies and gentlemen. No tears, no recriminations, no faint-heartedness.

Comprehension

Without looking back at the text, mark the following statements "True" or "False," based on information from "On Being a Cripple." Check your answers on page 202 of Appendix II.

Pages 102–103

_____ **1.** In the beginning of the story, the author describes how she fell down the stairs.

_____ **2.** The writer calls herself a "cripple" because she says the word is precise and straightforward.

_____ **3.** The narrator of the story has always been a cripple.

Pages 104–105

_____ **4.** Multiple sclerosis (MS) is a disease of the central nervous system.

_____ **5.** MS sufferers may lose their vision, hearing and speech.

_____ **6.** The writer uses a brace, cane and wheelchair to move around.

_____ **7.** The writer is unemployed.

Pages 105–106

_____ **8.** Her husband and children do not help her with the housework.

_____ **9.** Her children do not invite friends to their house because they are ashamed of their crippled mother.

_____ **10.** The author says society expects cripples to be cheerful.

_____ **CORRECT** × **10** = _____ %

LANGUAGE STUDY

LEARNING STRATEGY

Forming Concepts: Discovering the meaning of culturally related terms not only helps you understand the *language* but also the new *culture*.

Readings of a personal nature, such as "On Being a Cripple" and "Welfare Hell" (the second reading in this chapter), invariably contain references to the writer's culture. Studying these terms will facilitate your understanding of *language* as well as *culture*.

Cultural terms may appear over and over in writing and speech, so learning them will foster your comprehension of the language in general. In addition, it will enable you to better understand the background and values of people in whose new culture you may be living.

ACTIVITY

In the previewing section you examined a list of cultural terms used in the first reading. With some of your classmates, find each of the terms in the reading. Write the terms and their definitions in your reading journal after considering the following questions:

1. Did you know any of these terms before reading?
2. Can you understand each part of the reading without knowing the meaning of the cultural term? Can you guess the meaning from the context (surrounding words)?
3. What do these cultural terms tell you about Americans and American culture?

LEARNING STRATEGY

Understanding and Using Emotions: Recognizing the emotions of others helps you to interpret their messages.

Writers often express their emotions in the words and details they choose. In the stories in this chapter, the reader can discern the writer's *tone,* or attitude, toward being physically handicapped by carefully observing the words and details the writer includes. Understanding the writer's *tone* helps you to interpret his or her meaning.

Look at these sentences from "On Being a Cripple":

To be whole of limb is, I know from experience, infinitely <u>more pleasant and useful</u> than to be crippled . . .

I am a <u>superb</u>, if messy, cook. I am also an <u>enthusiastic</u> laundress, <u>capable of</u> sorting a hamper full of clothes into five <u>subtly differentiated</u> piles . . .

In the first sentence, examine the way the writer uses the more positive expression: "more pleasant and useful" to compare being "whole of limb" with being disabled. Here, she doesn't focus on the negative aspect of being disabled but rather on the positive aspect of not being disabled. Therefore, her tone is *positive,* even *cheerful.*

In the second example, look at the underlined words. Each word stresses the strong capabilities of the writer to perform difficult tasks. Again, her tone is *positive.*

ACTIVITY: RECOGNIZING TONE

Reread paragraphs 1 and 13 of "Of Being a Cripple." (These paragraphs recount two accidents that the writer has.) How would you describe the writer's *tone* or attitude toward each of these incidents? What part of her writing helps you determine her tone?

ACTIVITY: IDENTIFYING THE ORGANIZATION

Definition

Definition is a common type of organizational pattern in many types of readings: magazine and newspaper articles as well as academic textbooks and essays.

Good readers recognize that several common structures are used in a sentence or sentences to provide definitions. For example, the writer may state the definition directly in sentences like these, using a key word to introduce the definition:

George Orwell (1903–1950) *was* an English writer of novels and essays. Superb *means* excellent.

Certain punctuation used with certain grammatical structures also signals definition. In particular, commas or long dashes appearing after a defined vocabulary term may set off the word's definition. Or structures containing a general term (often plus "which" or "who") and details, may be used to define the target word. Conversely, definitions may be presented *before* the target word, using similar structures. In these sentences, which of the definitions are contained within the punctuation marks? Which appears outside the punctuation marks?

George Orwell, *an American writer,* authored an essay entitled "The Politics of the English Language."

"Handicapped"—*which is a commonly used term for physically disabled people*—implies that these people are inferior to nonhandicapped people, according to Nancy Mairs.

One popular almond-flavored liqueur, called Amaretto, is a favorite of the author's.

Recognizing punctuation and structure signals for definition enables you to focus on areas in a reading with important definitions.

ACTIVITY

A. "On Being a Cripple" contains several sections that define terms that are important to the reading. With a partner, find the sections that define the following terms, and mark the text to indicate where those terms and definitions appear.

After you have finished, compare your method of annotating the text with other classmates. Did you highlight? underline? make margin notes, such as asterisks?

1. multiple sclerosis
2. Amigo
3. exacerbations

B. With your partner, reread paragraphs two through four of the essay. How does the author explain the following terms? Does she adequately define them?

1. cripple
2. handicapped
3. disabled
4. differently abled

ACTIVITY: DRAMATIZING

With a partner, discuss the problems a person might face if he or she had a particular physical disability. Then role-play a certain situation that would dramatically illustrate the challenges of the physical disabled. You might choose to be a blind, deaf, or wheelchair-bound person. Your partner might serve as your "attendant," assisting you through difficult situations.

Choose one situation in which a person with this physical handicap would be especially challenged: for example, a blind person taking an examination in a classroom or a wheelchair-bound student entering a crowded classroom.

Dramatize the situation for a small group of classmates.

Threads

The Americans with Disabilities Act of 1990 requires handicapped access to public buildings and prohibits hiring discrimination against disabled people.

PREPARING TO READ

ACTIVITY: PREVIEWING

A. "Welfare Hell" is the title of the second reading. Why do you imagine the writer chose this title? What type of "welfare" is the writer referring to? How could *welfare* be *hell* for a physically disabled person?

B. John Callahan's story contains many idioms, or common expressions. Look at the following list containing idioms from the first part of his reading. With a partner, define those you know in your reading journal. Ask other classmates about the idioms you are unsure about.

(to) bleed the system
(to) drum up some business
to get paid under the table
in some sticky situation
being shined on
to be kowtowed to
high profile
bummed a cigarette
guilt trip

Reading 2

AUTHOR NOTES

John Callahan is a well-published artist whose cartoons humorously explore the problems of the physically handicapped in such magazines as *The New Yorker.* Examples are included on pages 110 and 113. Callahan's essay comes from his book, *Don't Worry, He Won't Get Far on Foot.*

Glossary
Tender Vittles   a brand of cat food
The New Yorker, Penthouse   names of magazines
IRS   the abbreviation for Internal Revenue Service, the U.S. government tax-collecting agency
liberals   persons with liberal political views
Birkenstocks   a brand of shoes
Reagan   the former U.S. president Ronald Reagan
contraband   illegal
Cuisinarts   food-processing appliances
moxie   the ability to face difficulty with spirit, energy
medieval   referring to the Middle Ages; also, out-of-date

WELFARE HELL
by John Callahan

1   A welfare client is supposed to cheat. Everybody expects it. Faced with sharing a dinner of Tender Vittles with the cat, many quadriplegics I know bleed the system for a few extra dollars. They tell their attendants that they are getting two hundred dollars less than the real entitlement and pocket the difference. They tell the caseworker that they are paying a hundred dollars more for rent. Or they say they are broke and get a voucher for government cheese.

2   I am a recovering alcoholic. I have opted to live a life of rigorous honesty. So instead, I go out and drum up some business and draw cartoons. I even tell welfare how much I make! Oh, I'm tempted to get paid under the table. But even if I yielded to that temptation, outfits like *The New Yorker* and *Penthouse* are not going to get involved in some sticky situation. They keep my records according to my Social Security number, and that information goes right into the IRS computer. Very high-profile and un-pauperlike. As a welfare client I'm expected to genuflect before the caseworker. Deep down, caseworkers know that they are being shined on and made fools of by many of their clients, and they expect to be kowtowed to as compensation.

3   I'm not being contemptuous. Most caseworkers begin as college-educated liberals with high ideals. But after a few years in a system that practically mandates dishonesty, they become like the one I shall call "Suzanne," a slightly overweight cop in Birkenstocks.

4   Not long after Christmas last year, Suzanne came to my apartment on one of her bimonthly inspections and saw some new posters on the wall. "Where'd you get the money for those?" she wanted to know.

5   "Friends and family."

6   "Well, you better write it down, by god. You better report it. You have to report any donations or gifts."

7   This was my cue to grovel. Instead, I talked back. "I bummed a cigarette from someone on the street the other day. Do I have to report that?"

8   "Well I'm sorry, but I don't make the rules, Mr. Callahan."

9   Suzanne tries to guilt-trip me about repairs to my wheelchair, which is always breaking down because welfare won't spend the money to maintain it properly. "You know, Mr. Callahan, I've heard that you put a lot more miles on that wheelchair than the average quadriplegic."

10 Of course I do. I'm an active worker, not a nursing-home vegetable. I live near downtown, so I can get around in a wheelchair. I wonder what she'd think if her legs suddenly gave out and she had to crawl to work.

11 Spending cuts during the Reagan administration dealt malnutrition and misery to a lot of people, not just me. But people with spinal cord injuries felt the cuts in a unique way: The government stopped taking care of our chairs.

12 My last chair never fit. I was forced to sit in a twisted position that led to lots of medical complications. But they refused to replace it. Each time it broke down and I called Suzanne, I had to endure a little lecture. Finally, she'd say, "Well, if I can find time today, I'll call the medical worker."

13 Suzanne then started the red tape flowing. She was supposed to notify the medical worker, who made an assessment. Then the medical worker called the wheelchair repair companies to get the cheapest bid. Then the medical worker alerted the main welfare office at the Oregon state capital. They pondered the matter for days while I lay in bed, immobilized. Finally, if I was lucky, they called back and approved the repair.

14 When welfare learned I was making money on my cartoons, Suzanne started "visiting" every other week instead of every other month. She poked into every corner in search of contraband Cuisinarts, unregistered girlfriends, or illegal aliens serving as butlers and maids. She never found anything, but there was always a thick pile of forms and affidavits to fill out at the end of each visit, accounting for every penny.

15 "Mr. Callahan, you've simply got to understand the gravity of the situation. Your cartoon earnings could cause your benefits to be terminated!"

16 "How do I avoid that?"

17 "I'm not sure . . . but it doesn't look good for you."

18 "Well, who do I speak to about the regulations on this?"

19 Suzanne didn't know. One day I simply called her superior and asked if he could tell me where to start. "Well, Mr. Callahan, we have reason to believe that you are a bit of a shady character. I'm fairly certain your benefits will be terminated."

20 There is no provision in the law for a gradual shift away from welfare. I am a free-lancer who is slowly building up his market. It's impossible to jump off welfare and suddenly be making two thousand dollars a month, even if I could solve the health insurance problem. But I would love to be able to pay for some of my services and not have to go through a humiliating rigmarole every time I need a spare part.

21 Like any bureaucracy with complicated rules, welfare constantly creates and eliminates "exceptions" to those rules. Quads often have strained kidneys and need extra protein. So an exception allowed me to keep a little more money to supplement my diet. Then came a note that the exception had been cut off retroactively. I owed welfare for meat and cheese I'd bought with my own money and already eaten. I volunteered to come over to the office and throw up, but they wanted cash.

22 One day after those benefits were cut off, Suzanne pinched the spare tire around my middle and said, "Well, it sure looks like your attendant's feeding you pretty well. You don't look like you're starving to death." My diet is mainly

cheap carbohydrates because that's all I can afford, plus it is very hard for a quadriplegic, especially in his 30s or older, to find ways to burn calories and stay trim. Such insensitivity is typical.

23   Absurd as it may seem, my success as a cartoonist makes me feel like a renegade, a culprit. When a check comes in from a magazine I look at it, and part of me says, "Way to go, Callahan! You're getting published!" But the other half of me says, "Watch out! You're cheating the system. You're cheating welfare. You shouldn't have this money. Better put it in an envelope and run it right down to Suzanne."

24   I know I am lucky to live in a country where I do get some help from the government. I want to distinguish sharply between the professional and courteous treatment I have always received from Social Security and my problems with the inadequately funded and state-administered welfare program. The plain fact is, though, that until recently, when I began to be perceived as something of a minor media threat, welfare treated me like a bum.

25   So I have had to make conscious efforts to build up my self-esteem, to tell myself that I am a good person, that I am trying, that I am as good as the average guy working down at the 7-Eleven or over at IBM. I want to get ahead. I have the talent, the desire, and the moxie to do it. I have twice the drive of the average able-bodied person I know. What I am being told by the welfare system is no, we won't let you do it.

26   There needs to be some ombudsman or legal resource for all welfare clients, because the system so easily lends itself to abuse by the givers as well as by the recipients. Welfare sent Suzanne to snoop around in my apartment the other day because I was using a larger than usual amount of urological supplies. I was, indeed: The hole that has been surgically cut in the wall of my abdomen had changed size and the connection to my urine bag was leaking.

27   The implication of her visit was that I was cheating. What did they think I was up to, selling urine bags to Greeks as wineskins?

28   While she was taking notes, my phone rang and Suzanne answered it. The caller was a state senator, which rattled Suzanne a little. Would I sit on the governor's advisory board and try to do something about the thousands of welfare clients who, like me, could earn part or all of their own livings if they were allowed to do so, one step at a time?

29   Hell, yes, I would! I'd sit on an emery board if I could help change some of these medieval rules that have given me gray hair and a heart murmur! Someday quadriplegics will thrive under a new system based on incentive and encouragement. They will be free to develop their talents without guilt or fear—or just hold a good, steady job.

"I'll have what I'm having."

Comprehension

Mark the following statements "True" or "False," based on information from "Welfare Hell." Do not look back at the text as you answer. Check your answers on page 202 of Appendix II.

_____ 1. Callahan says that everybody expects welfare recipients to cheat the government system.

_____ 2. Callahan cheats on his welfare.

_____ 3. The caseworker, Suzanne, notices Callahan's new posters because she likes them.

_____ 4. Callahan complains that during the Reagan Administration the government stopped taking care of quadraplegics' wheelchairs.

_____ 5. When she learned that Callahan was making money on his cartoons, Suzanne was very happy.

_____ 6. Suzanne warned Callahan that his welfare benefits might be cut because of his cartoon earnings.

_____ 7. Callahan says he would love to be able to pay for some of his expenses.

_____ 8. The writer reports that when his extra benefits to pay for increased protein were cut, the government demanded he pay back the money.

_____ 9. Callahan said the welfare system treated him "like a bum" until he became well-known in the media.

_____ 10. Callahan doesn't want the government system to encourage handicapped people to get jobs.

_____ **CORRECT** $\times$ **10** = _____ %

LANGUAGE STUDY

IT WORKS!
Learning Strategy:
Recognizing
Emotions

In "Welfare Hell," John Callahan displays different **tones,** or attitudes, toward his subject: the problems that quadriplegics have with the welfare system.

Look at each of the sentences below, and choose a word or two that might describe the writer's tone:

I know I am lucky to live in a country where I do get some help from the government.

Spending cuts during the Reagan administration dealt malnutrition and misery to a lot of people, not just me.

In the first sentence, the writer's tone might be described as: *positive, optimistic,* or *grateful.* However, in the second sentence, the writer's attitude changes to *serious* or even *angry.*

ACTIVITY: RECOGNIZING TONE

Identify the writer's tone in each of the sentences that follow by marking each as **P** (positive), **A** (angry), or **H** (humorous). (Some passages may contain more than one tone.) Then compare your answers with a classmate's.

_____ 1. A welfare client is supposed to cheat. Everybody expects it. Faced with sharing a dinner of Tender Vittles with the cat, many quadriplegics I know bleed the system for a few extra dollars.

_____ 2. When welfare learned I was making money on my cartoons, Suzanne started "visiting" every other week instead of every other month. She poked into every corner in search of contraband Cuisinarts, unregistered girlfriends, or illegal aliens serving as butlers and maids.

_____ 3. I owed welfare for meat and cheese I'd bought with my own money and already eaten. I volunteered to come over to the office and throw up, but they wanted cash.

_____ 4. I want to get ahead. I have the talent, the desire, and the moxie to do it.

LEARNING STRATEGY

Overcoming Limitations: Learning idioms makes you feel more confident and comfortable in using a language.

"Welfare Hell" contains many idioms, or common expressions, partially because the writer's tone is often humorous or angry. To relate his situation as a quadriplegic humorously, he uses idioms to "lighten up" what might otherwise seem a depressing topic. Also, he uses idioms to show his anger towards the welfare system.

Idioms are commonly used in speech as well as writing, but since idioms are culture-specific, learning them takes time and practice. However, the benefit is that when you use them correctly, you not only understand native English speakers and writers better, but you also become a confident, self-assured speaker and writer of English.

ACTIVITIES

A. Make a list of the idioms in "Welfare Hell" in your reading journal. Begin by copying the terms you previewed on page 110. With a partner, write the idiom and its definition. Then add the following idioms from the reading to your list. (In parentheses are the numbers of the paragraphs where they are found in the reading.) Discuss the meanings with other classmates and your instructor.

1. vegetable (10)
2. gave out (10)
3. red tape (13)
4. gravity of the situation (15)
5. shady character (19)
6. spare tire (22)
7. up to (25)
8. given me gray hair(27)

B. Define and record in your journal or on vocabulary cards the following idioms from "On Being a Cripple."

1. tough customer (2)
2. whole of limb (5)
3. pickle that I get into (12)
4. jolly well (14)
5. There's the rub. (16)
6. cracked (16)
7. a class act (17)

REACTIONS

ACTIVITY: WRITING

IT WORKS!
Learning Strategy:
Responding
in Writing

Callahan's "Welfare Hell" raises many questions about a government's responsibility towards its disabled citizens. In your reading journal, write a paragraph in which you answer one of the questions that follow.

1. How much financial support should physically disabled citizens receive?
2. What kind of housing should the government provide?
3. What type of job training would be appropriate? (Specify the disabled group.)
4. What system should be used for monitoring the welfare recipients?

PREPARING TO READ

ACTIVITY: PREVIEWING

The third reading is entitled "Blind Commuter." How do you imagine a *blind* person might *commute*? Where would he commute to?

Reading 3

Glossary
cheerleader   one who cheers on sports players at a school game, such as football
walkup   a multistory building with no elevator

BLIND COMMUTER

by Douglas Martin

You could feel sorry for Alberto Torres, who is blind. The last thing he remembers seeing was his daughter, Lauren, being born 13 years ago. Then the world went blank; he can only imagine what his only child looks like as a cheerleader and honor student. (1)

Total darkness came as a result of an inflammation of his optic nerve—a condition that was unrelated to the retinal disease that had obscured his vision since birth. "I went to sleep and woke up with nothing," he said. (2)

Bad luck is no stranger to this warm and thoughtful 37-year-old man. His mother died of cancer when he was 4, and Mr. Torres's ailing father had to give him up to foster care when he was 11. He later worked for 19 years in a workshop assembling mops and other household goods, mind-numbing stuff. (3)

Earlier this month, Alberto Torres's wife, Idalia, who had just been laid off from her job as a receptionist, had a radical mastectomy and now faces a year of chemotherapy and radiation treatments. Things seemed always to go from almost unbelievably bad to worse. Even Mr. Torres' good luck has a dark side: Five years ago, his beloved seeing-eye dog, Gambler, got him out of the path of a truck. Mr. Torres was unharmed, Gambler died. (4)

But know this and know it well: Mr. Torres does not feel sorry for himself. "These are just little bumps you have to go over in your life," he said. (5)

At 5 A.M. on a recent morning, we caught up with Mr. Torres at the Nassau Avenue subway stop in Greenpoint, Brooklyn, where he lives in a third-floor walkup. He had been up since 3, feeding Greg, his new dog, making coffee, getting ready. "When you're blind, it takes a little longer to do things," he said. (6)

Mr. Torres was beginning the labyrinthine two-hour trip to his job developing film in the X-ray department of the emergency room of the Bronx Municipal Hospital Center. He would take the G train to Queens Plaza where he would walk up a set of stairs and down another to the Manhattan-bound R train. He would then ride the R to 59th Street where he would walk upstairs to switch to the No. 6. (7)

At one point along the journey, he might chat with a stranger. At another, someone would pat Greg, calling him by name. People offered assistance, even seats. (8)

At 125th Street, Mr. Torres would transfer to the No. 4 by crossing the platform. At 149th Street, he would descend to the No. 2. He would take that to East 180th Street where he invariably waits interminably for his final train, the Dyre Avenue shuttle to Pelham Parkway. Then he and Greg would walk 20 minutes to the hospital. (9)

"They shouldn't make any special provisions for me," Mr. Torres said. "It's a job, and I should be on time." (10)

It was a hard job to come by. Before he got the job, Mr. Torres was determined to escape the workshop run by the Lighthouse, an organization dedicated to rehabilitate the visually impaired, and to try to make it on his own. He wanted a job developing X-ray film, something that everyone must do in the dark. The Lighthouse called many hospitals, to no avail, even though they offered to pay his first three months' salary and provide training. (11)

117

The Lighthouse people would have much preferred something closer to his home. But they believed he could handle the arduous trip, as well as the work. "Our philosophy here is that blind people can do just about anything besides drive buses," said Marianne Melley, who tries to help place blind people in jobs. (12)

And that, as it turned out, was also the thinking about disabled people at the Bronx hospital. "We find what a person can do rather than what he can't do," said Noel McFarlane, the hospital's associate executive director. (13)

"The point is that it works," Pamela Brier, executive director, said. (14)

One day a while ago marked the first anniversary of Mr. Torres's hiring. He will likely develop 150 or so X-rays, his usual output, to celebrate. The cards with names and other data will be folded on the upper right-hand corner so he can photograph them right-side-up. That is the only concession to blindness. (15)

Mr. Torres works by himself in a small, chemical-scented darkroom. He cannot wear protective gloves, because he needs to feel. It is exacting work, and, since this is an emergency room, lives can be at stake. His immediate supervisor, Alcides Santambrosio, says he trusts him 100 percent. (16)

Mr. Torres makes $20,000 a year. He could be pocketing more than $12,000 from disability payments. But his motivation transcends money. "If I start feeling like a victim, that makes me bitter," he said. "And why be bitter? That makes you go into a hole and stay there." (17)

"I'm not doing anything out of the ordinary," insisted Mr. Torres as he briskly completed the task. (18)

Comprehension

Mark the following statements "True" or "False," based on information from "Blind Commuter." Do not look back at the text as you answer. Check your answers on page 203 of Appendix II. Record your reading speed and comprehension score on page 200 of Appendix I.

_____ **1.** Albert Torres became blind at birth.

_____ **2.** One night he went to bed sighted and woke up blind.

_____ **3.** Mr. Torres' mother died when he was 11.

_____ **4.** Mr. Torres feels sorry for himself.

_____ **5.** Mr. Torres wakes up at 6 a.m.

_____ **6.** It takes him two hours to get to work.

_____ **7.** Mr. Torres works at the Lighthouse, an organization that helps blind people.

_____ **8.** The Lighthouse organization believes that blind people can do almost anything except drive buses.

_____ **9.** Mr. Torres earns $12,000 per year.

_____ **10.** He says he doesn't want to feel like a victim, because it will make him feel better.

_____ **CORRECT** × **10** = _____ %

LANGUAGE STUDY

ACTIVITY: IDENTIFYING THE ORGANIZATION

"Blind Commuter," the story of a blind New Yorker, presents readers with the causes and effects of Alberto Torres's blindness. Identifying the sections of the reading that contain **causes** and **effects** helps you to isolate important information.

To do this, copy the following chart into your reading journal. Work with a partner to identify which particular causes and effects of blindness appear in the paragraphs listed. Briefly write the causes and effects beside each paragraph number (in parentheses).

Causes and Effects of Blindness (from "Blind Commuter")

Causes of Blindness	Effects of Blindness
(2) _____ _____ _____ _____ _____	(1) _____ (6) _____ (8) _____ (11) _____ (15) _____ par. 16 _____

ACTIVITY: PERSONAL VOCABULARY

Choose ten vocabulary words from "Blind Commuter" that you would like to learn. Write each word, its definition, and its part of speech in your reading journal or on a vocabulary card. Then, in your journal or on each card, write an original sentence in which you use each word. Check your sentences with your instructor.

ACTIVITY: READING FASTER

Key Words

Increasing your reading rate should be a continuous process. As you practice the techniques of clustering and scanning that you have tried in previous chapters, you will become more comfortable with using them.

Another way to speed up your reading is by reading only **key words,** or words that contain the most information. Here's an example:

<u>I saw</u> a big, brown <u>dog</u> in the <u>forest</u>.

Using this technique, the speedy reader can focus only on those words that contain the most meaning and skip over less meaningful words—for example, those that are not underlined in the sentence above. Of course, using this technique means that you lose some of the meaning of what you read. But it certainly speeds up the process.

ACTIVITY

A. In the sentences that follow, underline the key words—the words that contain the most information. Then compare your sentence with a classmate's.

1. At 5 A.M. on a recent morning, we caught up with Mr. Torres at the Nassau Avenue subway stop in Greenpoint, Brooklyn, where he lives in a third-floor walkup.
2. Mr. Torres was beginning the labyrinthine two-hour trip to his job developing film in the X-ray department of the emergency room of the Bronx Municipal Hospital Center.
3. Before he got the job, Mr. Torres was determined to escape the workshop run by the Lighthouse, an organization dedicated to rehabilitate the visually impaired, and to try to make it on his own.
4. "Our philosophy here is that blind people can do just about anything besides drive buses," said Marianne Melley, who tries to help place blind people in jobs.

B. Reread "Blind Commuter" and practice the "key word" reading technique.

REACTIONS

ACTIVITY: SHARING IMPRESSIONS

In a small group, consider the plight of either quadriplegics or blind people in society, drawing upon your own experience as well as the information in the three readings in this chapter.

Discuss the questions on page 116 about "Welfare Hell" that you answered in your reading journal. As a group, organize a panel discussion in which each group member presents his or her ideas about one or more of those questions. Choose a panel leader who will introduce the topic and speakers.

Present your discussion to your class.

REVIEWING

LEARNING STRATEGY

Managing Your Learning: Using concept cards to record important ideas or words is a useful way to learn.

Effective readers use a variety of techniques to study and remember new information. Reading journals and vocabulary cards are two methods for recording ideas and vocabulary on a certain reading or topic.

In language learning, 3-by-5-inch or 5-by-7-inch white index cards are also commonly used for studying important ideas in reading. Students write the target idea on one side of the card and definitions, synonyms, or pictures to help them remember the meaning on the other side. Here's an example:

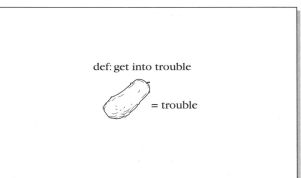

ACTIVITY

Select ten important ideas or vocabulary items from the text and from exercises on cultural terms, idioms, and personal vocabulary that you worked on in the chapter. For each item, make a concept card, using an index card. Write the target word or phrase on one side and the definition, a synonym, or an associative drawing on the other side.

Study both sides of each card until you can look at one side and recall the associated item on the other side.

EVALUATION

ACTIVITY: CHAPTER SELF-TEST

Assess your general understanding of the readings in Chapter 5 by taking the following chapter self-examination. The day before you take this test, write your concept card or journal words on a separate piece of paper, and give the list to your instructor. Then quickly review your reading journal notes about the chapter and the readings.

On the test day, your instructor will return your vocabulary list so that you can fill in the definitions of your ten personal vocabulary words or phrases in Part 1. Circle the appropriate completion of each statement in Part 2. Check your answers to Part 1 in your reading journal or on your cards, and score your test. See page 203 in Appendix II for the answers to Part 2.

Part 1: Vocabulary

Vocabulary Word or Phrase	Definition
1. _____	_____
2. _____	_____
3. _____	_____
4. _____	_____
5. _____	_____
6. _____	_____
7. _____	_____
8. _____	_____
9. _____	_____
10. _____	_____

_____ **CORRECT** $\times$ **10** = _____ **%**

Part 2: Comprehension

1. The author of "On Being a Cripple" believes the WORST word someone can use to describe a handicapped person is
   a. a cripple.
   b. differently abled.
   c. disabled.
2. In her childhood, the author of this story says she was
   a. confined to a wheelchair.
   b. ill most of the time.
   c. normally active.

3. In "On Being a Cripple," Mairs learned that she had multiple sclerosis when
   a. her vision became blurred.
   b. she couldn't hear.
   c. she could no longer play the piano.
4. According to John Callahan in "Welfare Hell," many quadriplegics
   a. are honest about their welfare payments.
   b. tell caseworkers that their rent is $100 higher than it really is.
   c. tell the government that they are broke when they are not.
   d. b and c
5. When Callahan's wheelchair breaks,
   a. his caseworker, Suzanne, drives him places in her car.
   b. the government repairs his chair after a long process.
   c. the government repairs his chair quickly with no questions asked.
6. Callahan believes that compared to the average "able-bodied person," he has
   a. half the amount of drive, or energy.
   b. the same amount of drive.
   c. twice as much drive.
7. In the end of Callahan's essay, an Oregon state senator asks him
   a. to replace Suzanne as a welfare caseworker.
   b. to draw him a cartoon.
   c. to join an advisory board studying welfare problems.
8. In "Blind Commuter," Albert Torres lost his vision as a result of
   a. cancer.
   b. retinal disease.
   c. inflammation of the optic nerve.
9. Albert Torres commutes to work by
   a. bus.
   b. van.
   c. train.
10. In his job at the Bronx Municipal Health Center, Torres
    a. develops X-ray film.
    b. counsels other blind people.
    c. makes mops.

_____ **CORRECT** × **10** = _____ %

ACTIVITY: EVALUATING YOUR GOALS

In your reading journal, write brief answers to the following questions:

1. The most important skills I used in reading and responding to the readings in

   this chapter were _____ .

2. The most valuable information I gained from this chapter was _____

   _____ .

Reading Further

With a partner, go to the local library and find one newspaper or magazine article that deals with physical disabilities.

Using the following outline as a guide, present a short oral report with your partner about the article. Take turns presenting different parts of the report, and be sure to ask your classmates for questions at the end of the presentation.

   I. Introduction
     A. Present title of article. (Also give author, newspaper or magazine title, publication date)
     B. Briefly summarize the main idea of the article.
  II. One Interesting Part of the Article
     A. Introduce and explain the main idea of this part of the article.
 III. Your Opinion
     A. Conclude by giving your opinion of the article.

Relationships

ACTIVITY: SETTING PERSONAL GOALS

As in the previous chapters, list in order of importance (with 1 as "most valuable") the learning objectives that are significant to you. Add personal learning objectives to the list if you wish.

GOAL   **RANK**

1. To increase comprehension of readings   _____
2. To expand vocabulary   _____
3. To increase reading speed   _____
4. To improve study skills   _____
5. To learn more about the subjects of this chapter   _____
6. _____   _____
7. _____   _____

The patterns of personal relationships are changing across the globe. Traditional families and friendships are giving way to more modern interrelationships. In the following articles, the writers present a range of practices that characterize this period of relational and familial change: living alone, homosexuality, and polygamy.

"One's Company: Is There Something Unnatural about Living Alone?" from *One's Company* by Barbara Holland

"We Are Family: Why Gays and Lesbians Form Strong Bonds" by Laura Markowitz

"My Husband's Nine Wives" by Elizabeth Joseph

ACTIVITY: PREDICTING CONTENT

Discuss these questions with some of your classmates.

1. Think about the topics in Chapter 6: living alone, homosexuality, and polygamy. Considering the titles of the readings, what do you predict the writers will say about each of these topics?
2. Look ahead at the photographs and other graphic material in the unit. Read the accompanying captions. What do they suggest about the content of the unit?
3. Which of the three topics in this chapter interests you the most? Make a list of your questions about this topic.

ACTIVITY: LISTENING FOR IDEAS

Prepare for the topic of interrelationships by viewing a television series that presents the lives of a family or a group of friends. You could choose either an old or a new television series, such as "Seinfeld," "Sisters," "Family Matters," "Love and War" or "Mad about You." Copy the following form into your reading journal. View a program from the series and then complete the form.

1. Title of Television Series: _____

   Time/Date: _____   Channel: _____

2. Main Characters in the Series:

   _____

   _____

3. Brief Summary of Episode You Viewed:

   _____

   _____

   _____

4. Your Impression of the Relationships of the Characters in the Series:

   _____

   _____

IT WORKS!
Learning Strategy:
Listening

ACTIVITY: SHARING IMPRESSIONS

With a small group of classmates, present your report and share your impressions of the television series you viewed. Discuss the following questions before you make your presentation: (Follow the outline of the report to organize your talk.)

1. Did you enjoy the television series? Why or why not?
2. What was your reaction to the program?
3. Were the relationships between any of the characters in the program surprising to you? If so, explain it to your group and ask for their reactions.

ACTIVITY: PREVIEWING

The title of the first reading is "One's Company: Is There Something Unnatural about Living Alone?" Discuss the question raised in the title with a partner. Share your ideas with the class.

ACTIVITIES

A. "One's Company: Is There Something Unnatural about Living Alone?" contains many references to people who enjoyed living alone. Without a knowledge of these references, you may have trouble completely understanding the writer's points.

With a partner, go to the library and consult the biographical entries section of an unabridged dictionary (for example, *The American Heritage Dictionary*), a specialized dictionary such as Longman's *Dictionary of English Language and Culture,* or an encyclopedia to find a brief description/definition of the following people mentioned in the article. (Record your definitions in your reading journal.)

1. Samuel Johnson
2. Henry Thoreau
3. William Wordsworth
4. John Milton
5. Greta Garbo
6. Emily Dickinson

B. Read the glossary below. Discuss with a partner which of the terms listed here contain cultural references. Add any words with cultural references to your journal or cards.

ACTIVITY: READING IN "CHUNKS"

Since Reading 1 is a lengthy text, divide your reading assignment into manageable "chunks," or sections. Consider your reading deadline; then, divide "One's Company: Is There Something Unnatural about Living Alone?" into three or four chunks, and read one at a time. As you did in previous chapters, try to find logical places to break up your reading, or ask your instructor to help you determine the "chunks."

Reading 1

Glossary
corporate ladder   corporate advancement
darlings   preferred persons
junk mail   unsolicited advertisement mail
crazies   crazy people
ears-to-heels   crowded
Happy-ever-after   referring to the happy endings of fairy tales
in a double bind   in trouble
like the tree falling in the empty forest   referring to the philosophical question:
   If a tree falls in a forest and no one hears it, does it make a sound?
Argyle   patterned knitted cloth
Chinese take-out   Chinese food to go

ONE'S COMPANY: IS THERE SOMETHING UNNATURAL ABOUT LIVING ALONE?

by Barbara Holland

1   Here we are, all by ourselves, all 22 million of us, by recent count, alone in our rooms, some of us liking it that way and some of us not. Some divorced, some widowed, some never yet committed.

2   If we're young and attractive and urban, the magazines call us "singles." Singles are said to live in a joyful flurry of other singles, racing each other through the surf, rising on the corporate ladder, and waking up in the penthouses of singles of the other sex. The darlings of a consumer society, they spend their incomes not on mortgages and disposable diapers but on electronic entertainment, clothes, and exciting cars. Singles rejoice in their freedom up until quite an advanced age, or so they keep telling us, the women until their childbearing years start narrowing down and the men often forever—only 5 percent of bachelors over 40 will ever marry.

3   Still, even the busiest of these merrymakers have moments, small but ominous cracks and leaks in the good life: evenings in June when the late sun slants into the apartment and the silence ticks like a bomb, Saturdays in October when the wind creaks down the street and the light chills and sharpens and the skin prickles restlessly.

4   Others are alone but not singles, just solitary. They're too old or too shy or too poor to be singles, or they were recently members of families and are still unadjusted and confused, or they live in the wrong sort of place. They buy a half loaf of bread and a can of tuna and let themselves into their apartments at the end of the day calling wistfully for the cat, check the unblinking light on the answering machine, and sit down to read through the junk mail, absorbing messages about carpet sales and grocery coupons sent in from the great busy world.

5   There are crazies among us, too—women with 17 parrots, and thin old men mumbling to themselves on the bus. People we have met by accident camp out in lofts or deserted offices and come to our house to shower and wash their hair, bringing a whiff of life's precariousness. Without the ballast of families, lone acquaintances call us at four in the morning to tell us they've just seen God or Elvis Presley, or they've invented a petroleum substitute or written an epic poem or had a strange dream. No one was home to tell them to shut up and go back to sleep, so the strange dream took root and grew.

6   Samuel Johnson, the eighteenth-century curmudgeon and author, said, "The solitary mortal is certainly luxurious, probably superstitious, and possibly mad."

7   The anarchy of life alone, sometimes called freedom, threatens us with chaos. Fear of chaos can lead to rigidity and tidiness and the multiplication of lists, schedules, and routines, since we have no one but ourselves to bind our lives together. We keep checking ourselves for signs of disintegration; it's important to stay, at the very least, sane.

8   In more primitive societies all over the world, nobody lives alone, and families accrete in generational layers to the toppling point. There are villages where people may know solitude for only a few hours to days in a lifetime, maybe in a hut on the outskirts, as part of a coming-of-age ritual; the rest of their lives they sleep ears-to-heels with all their relations and apparently like it that way.

9   Loneliness is peculiarly prevalent in America, built into our foundations somehow, maybe an outgrowth of our newness here and our mixed origins. In older places, the citizens say, "I'm French" or "I'm Korean" with an obvious sense of belonging to an extended family, but we seem to have left this consolation behind when we immigrated. A community is a firmer anchor than even the most loyal group of friends, but we have lost the sense of being fastened to a broader group instead of free-falling through a void.

10 Loneliness may be a sort of national disease here, and certainly it's a shameful one, more embarrassing for us to admit than any of the deadly sins.

Happy-ever-after has rejected us. The fairy story spits us out as unworthy, and sometimes we think we are.

11   On the other hand, to be alone but not lonely, alone on purpose, having rejected company rather than been cast out by it, is the hallmark of an American hero. The lone hunter, explorer, cowboy, needing no one. Thoreau, snug and smug in his cabin on the pond, his back deliberately turned to the town. Now, that's character for you.

12   This leaves us in a double bind. Here we are, alone because nobody wants us, and lonely because we're so spineless and empty-headed we can't find inspiration in our solitude.

13   Inspiration in solitude is a major commodity for poets and philosophers. They're all for it. They all speak highly of themselves for seeking it out, at least for an hour or even two before they hurry home for tea.

14   Consider Dorothy Wordsworth, for instance, wrapping the muffler around her brother William's neck, finding his notebook and pencil for him, and waving as he sets forth to look at daffodils all by himself. "How gracious, how benign, is solitude," he wrote, rudely.

15   No doubt about it, solitude is improved by being voluntary.

16   Look at Milton's daughters arranging his cushions and shawls before they tiptoe off, so he can mutter, "And Wisdom's self/Oft seeks to sweet retired solitude/Where, with her best nurse Contemplation,/She plumes her feathers and lets grow her wings." Then he calls the girls to come back and write it down while he dictates.

17   You may have noticed that most of these rapturous types went outdoors to be alone. The indoors was full of loved ones keeping the kettle warm till they came home.

18   The American high priest of solitude was Thoreau. We admire him, not for his self-reliance and his conceited musings, but because he was all by himself out there at Walden Pond, and he *wanted* to be. All alone in the woods.

19   Actually, he lived a mile, or 20 minutes' walk, from his nearest neighbor; half a mile from the railroad; three hundred yards from a busy road. He had streams of company in and out of the hut all day, asking him how he could possibly be so noble. Apparently the main point of his nobility was that he had neither wife nor servants, and washed his own dish. I don't know who did his laundry; he doesn't say, but he certainly doesn't mention doing his own, either.

20   Listen to him: "I find it wholesome to be alone the greater part of the time. To be in company, even with the best, is soon wearisome and dissipating. I love to be alone. I never found the companion that was so companionable as solitude."

21   Thoreau had his own self-importance for company. Thoreau alone with Thoreau was a crowd. Perhaps there's a message here. The larger the ego, the less the need for other egos around. The more modest, humble, and self-effacing we feel, the more we suffer from solitude, feeling ourselves inadequate company.

22   The only woman of record who spoke well of solitude was Greta Garbo. I don't count Emily Dickinson; all she had to do was unlock her bedroom door and go downstairs. She's one of the voluntaries, like Wordsworth out for a walk. She had a family; she just preferred to lurk upstairs. But for many of us, there's nobody in our living room to escape from.

23   If you live with other people, their temporary absence can be refreshing. Solitude will end on Thursday, or next month when the children come home from camp, and in the meantime you can stretch out your soul until it fills up the whole room, and squander your freedom, coming and going as you please without apology, staying up late to read, eating only when you're hungry, moving at your own pace. Those absent will be back. Their winter clothes are in the cedar closet and their dog keeps watching for them at the window.

24   But when you live alone, the temporary absence of your friends and acquaintances leaves a black hole; *they* may never come back. They've left nothing behind; perhaps they never existed at all. Perhaps you dreamed them. Perhaps they've moved to Seattle.

Threads

The number of persons living alone in the U.S. increased from 10,851 to 23,590 from 1970 to 1991.

The World Almanac and Book of Facts, 1994

25   Solitude strikes hardest at those who are suddenly alone after a death or a divorce or the departure of children. We may waste long hours of our new freedom just sitting there, hands folded patiently, waiting for someone to need us, someone to say, "When's dinner?" or "Where's my math book?" so we can return to our skins and be us again.

26   The Chinese have a ritual for calling your spirit back to you when it drifts away, in madness or nightmares: You recite a litany of all your ancestors and relatives, place names and former street addresses, as landmarks so your wandering spirit can find you again.

27   For ages past, women were defined only in relation to other people, and the definition lingers; a woman may be called a wife and mother for most of her life, while a man is called a husband and father only at his funeral. Even today, a solitary woman may feel like the tree falling in the empty forest; alone in a room, nobody's daughter, wife, lover, mother, or executive assistant. When she is alone, with no one to remind her of her self, a woman's spirit can detach itself and float loose, producing a weird sense of third-personness. With no one to watch her, she starts watching herself, from a slight distance, like a woman in a movie, so as not to disappear. This separation from self feels like a kind of madness, and probably is; all over the country, women peering closely at themselves as they feed the cat.

28   Meanwhile, recently divorced, widowed, or abandoned men are walking back and forth on the sidewalks in front of their homes. Sitting on porches and in bars and movie theaters and on the front steps. Without another person, they can neither concentrate nor sleep, and no one tells them they're wearing one black sock and one Argyle. No one reminds them to turn the clock ahead in April, and their refrigerators hold nothing but a withered half a lemon.

29   Most men find it hard to work up a meaningful relationship with an empty room, and a room with nobody else in it is empty, no matter how much furniture a girlfriend has helped them buy and arrange. One man I know, abandoned by his wife, keeps toothbrushes. He keeps a fresh, boxed-and-wrapped toothbrush in the medicine cabinet, of course, because he read an article recommending it in case some lovely young thing decides to sleep over, but he also keeps a plastic cup full of unwrapped, used-looking toothbrushes on the windowsill. They represent a houseful of loving family, and cheer him slightly, briefly when he sees them in the morning; a single toothbrush can be a terrible sight.

30   Men find it sadder to take care of themselves, and they feel peculiarly trapped by their dwellings. You meet them wandering, and they say, "My apartment was driving me crazy" or "I couldn't stand the empty house," as if the very walls had turned savage. For a man who has had a family and lost it, home seems an unnatural place to be. He may make gastronomical delights for his friends, but alone he drinks instant coffee at dawn and by night eats Chinese take-out from the carton, watching television.

31   He stays out later and later, postponing the dry click of the latchkey. He uses the phone in the bar to call a dozen people he doesn't really want to see. He looks in the phone book for people he knew in college. He goes back to his wife, or even back to his mother. Or, of course, he marries again, often an easier, swifter cure for men than for women.

32   For a woman, at first the condition of being alone seems temporary—surely the door will open, someone will walk in, and life will become magically normal any minute now. Then it begins to stretch out and feel, if not permanent, at least longer.

33   It's inconvenient, this solitary life. Nobody lends a hand. We can't say, "Would you get the door for me?—hand me the towel?—hold up the other end?—go see what's making that funny noise?—grab the cat while I shove the pill down her?—answer the phone?—mail a letter?—put your finger on this knot?" Hanging a picture, we punch a dozen holes in the wall because no one will stand across the room and decide where the nail should go. We do it ourselves or not at all, and

when we have clothes to drop off at the cleaners, we drive around and around looking for a parking space because there's no one to wait in the car. Only we will carry out the trash and carry in the groceries and cope with the IRS and confirm the plane reservation and open the mayonnaise and take the car to the shop and try to explain to the scornful mechanic about the way it wobbles. If the couch is too heavy for one person to move it, it stays where it is, waiting for the next strong guest. And only we will answer when we speak.

34 The condition of loneliness ebbs and flows, influenced by body chemistry and the weather, but the need to talk goes on forever. It's more basic than needing to listen. Oh, we all have friends we can tell important things to, people we can call to say our daughter got into Harvard or we lost our job or broke our arm. It's the daily small change of complaints and observations and opinions that backs up and chokes us. We can't really call a friend to say we got our feet wet walking home, or it's getting dark earlier now, or we don't trust that new Supreme Court justice.

35 Some people can, of course. I have a friend who does. She called me last week just to say she'd thought she'd lost her car keys, but then they turned up in the pocket of her coat, the gray coat she hardly ever wears because the shoulders are too tight.

36 I know how she feels. We all know. Solemn scientific surveys show that all us solitaries talk at length to ourselves and our pets and the television. We ask the cat whether we should wear the blue suit or the yellow dress, and does it think we'll need an umbrella. There's nothing wrong with this. It's good for us, and a lot less embarrassing than the woman in front of us in the checkout line who's telling the cashier that her niece Melissa may be coming to visit on Saturday, and Melissa is very fond of hot chocolate with marshmallows, which is why she bought the marshmallows though she never eats them herself.

37 It's important, as I said, to stay sane.

38 It's important to stop waiting and settle down and make ourselves comfortable, at least temporarily, in this moonscape, and find some grace and pleasure in our condition, not smugly like a British poet but like a patient, enchanted princess in a tower, learning to wring honey from a stone.

39 After all, here we are. It may not be where we expected to be, but for the time being we might as well call it home.

Comprehension

Without looking back at "One's Company: Is There Something Unnatural about Living Alone?" mark the following statements "True" or "False." Check your comprehension with the answer key on page 203 of Appendix II. Record your score and your reading speed in the chart on page 200 of Appendix I.

Page 129

_____ **1.** About 22 million Americans live alone, according to the article.

_____ **2.** The writer says "singles" are believed to live sorrowful lives.

_____ **3.** "Solitary" people are too old, shy, or poor to be "singles."

Pages 129–130

_____ **4.** One of the dangers of living alone is going crazy, the article says.

_____ **5.** Being alone on purpose means you don't want to be by yourself.

_____ **6.** Those who are suddenly alone usually have no trouble adapting to solitude.

Page 131

———— **7.** Men who live alone like to spend most of their time away from their homes or apartments, the writer says.

———— **8.** Divorced men often remarry to combat loneliness, the article says.

Pages 131–132

———— **9.** At first, women who are alone think their condition will be temporary.

———— **10.** Talking to yourself is healthy, according to the writer.

———— **CORRECT** × **10** = ———— %

LANGUAGE STUDY

ACTIVITY: IDENTIFYING THE ORGANIZATION

"One's Company: Is There Something Unnatural about Living Alone?" is organized into the cause-and-effect pattern that you studied in Chapter 5. Parts of the article discuss the *causes* of living alone; other parts describe its *effects*. With a classmate, find <u>at least two</u> paragraphs that present a *cause* (or causes) and <u>two</u> paragraphs that show an *effect* (or effects). Be prepared to explain briefly the main ideas in the paragraph(s) using this organization pattern.

LIVING ALONE

Organization Pattern	Paragraph Number(s)	Explain Cause(s) Effects
Cause(s)	———————— ————————	———————— ————————
Effect(s)	———————— ————————	———————— ————————

Many of the vocabulary items in "One's Company: Is There Something Unnatural about Living Alone?" contain common word parts. For example, these words from the article contain common suffixes (endings) that indicate adjectives and nouns:

IT WORKS!
Learning Strategy:
Word Parts

joy<u>ful</u>   lonel<u>iness</u>
dispos<u>able</u>   inspir<u>ation</u>

Which of the words listed are adjectives? Which are nouns?
Can you define the words by looking at the suffix meanings in the chart that follows?

ACTIVITY

Study the list of common suffixes that follows. In your reading journal, copy the chart and find at least <u>two</u> words from the reading that contain each suffix.

NOTE Some of the words may contain more than one suffix.

COMMON ADJECTIVE SUFFIXES

Suffix	Definition	Sample Word	Definition
ful	full of	joyful	_____
		_____	_____
ous, ious	referring to a condition	_____	_____
		_____	_____
al	relating to	_____	_____
		_____	_____

COMMON NOUN SUFFIXES

Suffix	Sample Word	Definition
ness	loneliness	_____
	_____	_____
ation	inspiration	_____
	_____	_____
ty, y	_____	_____
	_____	_____

REACTIONS

LEARNING STRATEGY

Forming Concepts: Some learners find that by listing, they clarify ideas in their minds.

ACTIVITY: SHARING IMPRESSIONS

Barbara Holland's article, taken from her book *One's Company,* presents mixed opinions on living alone. In examining the *effects* of this style of living, you probably found both advantages and disadvantages.

In a small group, discuss your reactions to each of the author's points about the effects of living alone. Make a list of your own opinions in support of or counter to living alone. Then decide whether you think it is better to live alone or with a group of family members or friends.

Share your impressions with the group and the class.

PREPARING TO READ

ACTIVITY: PREVIEWING

A. The second reading is entitled "We Are Family: Why Gays and Lesbians Form Strong Bonds." What is the difference between the two terms "gays" and "lesbians"? Why do you think gays and lesbians "form strong bonds"? With whom do you think they form these bonds?

A wedding of gay partners.

B. With a partner, discuss the following terms and expressions related to the subject of gays and lesbians. Use the context of the article to help you define the terms (paragraph numbers are in parentheses), and copy them into your reading journal. (Meanings are provided in the glossary below.)

homophobia (2)   AIDS (3)
coming out (2)   straights (7)

C. With a partner, read the poll results in the box that follows. Discuss the opinions and share with your class whether you agree or disagree with the majority view.

In a 1994 poll, 800 adult Americans gave the following response to the question:

"How do you feel about homosexual relationships?"

Acceptable for others but not self	52%
Acceptable for others and self	6%
Not acceptable at all	31%

Time magazine, June 27, 1994.

Reading 2

Glossary
pitch in   help
homophobia   the fear of homosexuals
coming out   telling others of one's homosexuality
AIDS   Acquired Immune Deficiency Syndrome
driving force   impetus; main force
straights   heterosexuals; nonhomosexuals

WE ARE FAMILY: WHY GAYS AND LESBIANS FORM STRONG BONDS

by Laura Markowitz

1   In her book *Families We Choose* (Columbia University Press 1991), anthropologist Kath Weston describes "a conviction widely shared by lesbians and gay men of all ages" that gays and lesbians have closer, more sustaining friendships than heterosexuals. It is common to hear gays and lesbians talk about their "families of choice," by which they mean an intimate circle of close friends, lovers, children, and even former lovers who celebrate holidays and successes together, pitch in during crises, create their own rituals and inside jokes, and enjoy a sense of ease and acceptance they all take for granted.

2   The most natural explanation for the phenomenon is that gays and lesbians who are alienated or estranged from their families of origin because of homophobia create a substitute family for themselves. Consider Ralph's case: After he came out to his parents and brother when he was 29, they cut him off. Although they relented a few years later and accepted him back into the fold, Ralph says he now feels more loyalty and connection to a close group of friends he has been a part of for more than a decade. "There are a group of eight of us—gay and lesbian—who have spent every Thanksgiving, Christmas, and Fourth of July together for the past 11 years," says Ralph, now 44. While he was growing up, he assumed his family would always be more important to him than friends, but when they shunned him he realized that family ties can be broken. Weston points out that this realization is common to nearly every gay and lesbian who even considers coming out as they anticipate the shock, anger, and rejection of family members that might follow such a revelation.

3   Ralph says his family of choice is very much like "an ideal family": They borrow money from one another, take care of one another's children, show up for dinner unannounced, look after one another's pets, and cared for two in the group who became sick with AIDS. "We nursed them in their home, supported them when their money ran out, were there when they died, even arranged their funerals," Ralph says. "Their parents were not nearly as [present] as we were in their lives and their deaths."

4   Contrary to popular belief, however, rejection by one's family of origin may not be the driving force behind these family bonds among friends. If this were the case, Weston says, then one would expect that those who aren't rejected by their families would have no interest in being part of such an intense friendship network—but the networks contain many such "accepted" gays.

5   More evidence to refute the theory comes from a pilot study comparing 500 straight people to 500 gays and lesbians. Preliminary data from the study, conducted by New York's Ackerman Institute for Family Therapy, seems to show that gays and lesbians aren't estranged from their families any more than straight people are. "These days, most gays and lesbians I know are connected to their original families," says John Patten, co-director of the Gay and Lesbian Families Project and a family therapist in New York City. "The friendships formed by heterosexual men and women in a large urban area like New York are not that [different] from those of gays and lesbians," says Patten. The dislocation of the modern family leaves gaps in straight people's lives, too, causing them to rely heavily on their friends, he says.

6   Gays and lesbians often differentiate between people in their lives who are just friends and friends who are also family, says Weston. Lesbians, for example, often consider ex-lovers to be family. "It doesn't seem at all strange to me that Diane and I continue to celebrate holidays together, even though we broke up five years ago and have both been in stable relationships since we separated,"

Threads

Light is the task when many share the toil.

Homer

says Delia, a 43-year-old massage therapist. "We also share custody of our two dogs and talk on the phone regularly. Diane and I know each other more intimately than friends. She's more like a sister."

7   The intensity and quality of friendship is difficult to measure, but many gays and lesbians say their friendships deepened when they came out. Weston believes there might be a connection between homophobia and straight people's inhibitions about forging bonds with friends of the same sex. "The dominant society tends to suspect you of being a 'fag' or a 'dyke' if you have a close, intimate friendship with someone of the same sex," she points out. "Straights may be intimidated by this and so back off from their same-sex friends, whereas gays and lesbians may be less controlled by that fear."

8   Disillusionment with the so-called gay and lesbian community may be another factor that led to the rather recent phenomenon of gays and lesbians defining their friendship networks as family, Weston says. "You've never met a gay community, but you imagine it in your head," she says—it's "a fantasy of a connection with others who share this same orientation. But then we realized we were a diverse group and didn't necessarily get along." Chosen families are a smaller community of like-minded people.

9   "We all need to feel at home somewhere," says Ralph. "My friends are the home of my heart."

Comprehension

Use the information in "We Are Family: Why Gays and Lesbians Form Strong Bonds" to mark the following statements "True" or "False." Check your comprehension with the answer key on page 203 of Appendix II. Record your score and your reading speed in the chart on page 200 of Appendix I.

_____ **1.** The anthropologist Kath Weston says lesbians and gay men believe they have closer friends than heterosexuals.

_____ **2.** "Families of choice" means one's families of origin.

_____ **3.** Many lesbians and gay men may create substitute families because their original families alienate them.

_____ **4.** Ralph, a gay man, gained immediate acceptance from his family of origin when he told them he was gay.

_____ **5.** In a survey of 500 gays and lesbians, researchers found that most of them are not connected to their original families.

_____ **6.** In large cities like New York, gay and lesbian friendships are very different from those of heterosexual men and women.

_____ **7.** Gays and lesbians rarely keep up friendships with ex-lovers, according to the article.

_____ **8.** The gay community is a diverse group, according to anthropologist Weston.

_____ **CORRECT** × 12.5 = _____ %

The roots of words are another important word part to recognize. Roots can occur in the middle, at the beginning, or even at the end of words.

The reading "We Are Family: Why Gays and Lesbians Form Strong Bonds" contains an important term—*homophobia*—that consists of two root parts. The root *homo* means *man* (as in human), *same*, or *like;* the root *phobia* means *fear.* Remembering the glossary definition of this term, notice how the root parts assist you in determining the word's meaning.

IT WORKS!
Learning Strategy:
Word Parts

LEARNING STRATEGY

Testing Hypotheses: Test your understanding of new words by making associations with words you already know.

ACTIVITY

With a partner, use an English language dictionary to find the definitions of the following terms, which are related to the reading. Record the words and their definitions in your journal.

1. homophile
2. homosexual
3. homosexuality

LEARNING STRATEGY

Testing Hypotheses: Guess the meaning of an unfamiliar word by replacing it with a familiar word that logically fits the context.

ACTIVITY

With a partner, use the contexts of surrounding words to guess a synonym for each of the following words, found in "We Are Family: Why Gays and Lesbians Form Strong Bonds." (Paragraph numbers are in parentheses.) Replace each word with a possible synonym. Complete the form below, writing your "synonym" for each word. Then check the definition of each of the text's words in the dictionary. If your "synonym" was correct, simply put a checkmark under "dictionary definition." Write the words and definitions in your reading journal.

	Your "Synonym"	Dictionary Definition
1. conviction (1)	_____	_____
2. estranged (2)	_____	_____
3. relented (2)	_____	_____
4. disillusionment (8)	_____	_____

ACTIVITY: DRAMATIZING

"We Are Family: Why Gays and Lesbians Form Strong Bonds" depicts the emotional experiences that gays and lesbians experience when they "come out" to their families.

Dramatize a situation in which a gay or a lesbian informs his or her parents of his or her sexual orientation. Imagine how that person might feel, as well as how the parents might react. Act out two scenes: In the first, the parents reject the homosexual son or daughter; in the second, the parents accept the son's or daughter's choice.

Share your dramatization with the class.

PREPARING TO READ

ACTIVITY: PREVIEWING

A. "My Husband's Nine Wives" is an intriguing title because it may make you wonder what society might have such a marriage system. Read the first three lines of the story. What is your reaction to this type of marriage? Do you think the writer favors—or opposes—polygamy?

B. Before you read, consult a partner and your dictionary to learn the meanings of these key terms:

polygamy   the Old Testament   monogamy

ACTIVITY: READING FASTER

Use the "key word" technique that you practiced in Chapter 5 in reading "My Husband's Nine Wives." Then check your comprehension. If you find your comprehension score is low, reread the essay and check your reading rate and comprehension again.

IT WORKS!
Learning Strategy:
Reading Faster

Reading 3

Glossary
at first blush   at the first moment of embarrassment
trade-offs   taking disadvantages along with advantages of a certain action
"booked"   busy

MY HUSBAND'S NINE WIVES

by Elizabeth Joseph

I married a married man. (1)

In fact, he had six wives when I married him 17 years ago. Today, he has nine. (2)

In March, the Utah Supreme Court struck down a trial court's ruling that a polygamist couple could not adopt a child because of their marital style. Last month, the national board of the American Civil Liberties Union, in response to a request from its Utah chapter, adopted a new policy calling for the legalization of polygamy. (3)

Polygamy, or plural marriage, as practiced by my family is a paradox. At first blush, it sounds like the ideal situation for the man and an oppressive one for the women. For me, the opposite is true. While polygamists believe that the Old Testament mandates the practice of plural marriage, compelling social reasons make the life style attractive to the modern career woman. (4)

Pick up any women's magazine and you will find article after article about the problems of successfully juggling career, motherhood, and marriage. It is a complex act that many women struggle to manage daily; their frustrations fill up the pages of those magazines and consume the hours of afternoon talk shows. (5)

In a monogamous context, the only solutions are compromises. The kids need to learn to fix their own breakfast, your husband needs to get used to occasional microwave dinners, you need to divert more of your income to insure that your pre-schooler is in a good day-care environment. (6)

I am sure that in the challenge of working through these compromises, satisfaction and success can be realized. But why must women only embrace a marital arrangement that requires so many trade-offs? (7)

When I leave for the 60-mile commute to court at 7 A.M., my 2-year-old daughter, London, is happily asleep in the bed of my husband's wife, Diane. London adores Diane. When London awakes, about the time I'm arriving at the courthouse, she is surrounded by family members who are as familiar to her as the toys in her nursery. (8)

My husband, Alex, who writes at night, gets up much later. While most of his wives are already at work, pursuing their careers, he can almost always find one who's willing to chat over coffee. (9)

I share a home with Delinda, another wife, who works in town government. Most nights, we agree we'll just have a simple dinner with our three kids. We'd rather relax and commiserate over the pressures of our work day than chew up our energy cooking and doing a ton of dishes. (10)

Mondays, however, are different. That's the night Alex eats with us. The kids, excited that their father is coming to dinner, are on their best behavior. We often invite another wife or one of his children. It's a special event because it only happens once a week. (11)

Tuesday night, it's back to simplicity for us. But for Alex and the household he's dining with that night, it's their special time. (12)

The same system with some variation governs our private time with him. While spontaneity is by no means ruled out, we basically use an appointment system. If I want to spend Friday evening at his house, I make an appointment. If he's already "booked," I either request another night, or if my schedule is inflexible, I talk to the other wife and we work out an arrangement. One thing we've all learned is that there's always another night. (13)

Most evenings, with the demands of career and the literal chasing after the needs of a toddler, all I want to do is collapse into bed and sleep. But there is also the longing for intimacy and comfort that only he can provide, and when those feelings surface, I ask to be with him. (14)

Plural marriage is not for everyone. But it is the life style for me. It offers men the chance to escape from the traditional, confining roles that often isolate them from the surrounding world. More important, it enables women, who live in a society full of obstacles, to fully meet their career, mothering, and marriage obligations. Polygamy provides a whole solution. I believe American women would have invented it if it didn't already exist. (15)

Comprehension

After reading "My Husband's Nine Wives," mark the following statements "True" or "False." Check your comprehension with the answer key on page 203 of Appendix II. Record your score and your reading speed in the chart on page 200 of Appendix I.

_____ **1.** The author's husband had eight wives when they got married.

_____ **2.** The author lives in Saudi Arabia.

_____ **3.** According to the author, the Old Testament condemns polygamy.

_____ **4.** In monogamy, women must juggle career, motherhood, and marriage, the writer says.

_____ **5.** The author works in a courthouse.

_____ **6.** She lives with another of her husband's wives and their three kids.

_____ **7.** Mondays are special because Alex, the author's husband, comes to dinner at her house.

_____ **8.** When the author wants to spend an evening at her husband's home, she drops by anytime she likes.

_____ **9.** The author spends most of her evenings with her husband.

_____ **10.** Polygamy enables women to fully meet their job and family obligations, according to the writer.

_____ **CORRECT** × **10** = _____ %

LANGUAGE STUDY

ACTIVITY: IDENTIFYING THE ORGANIZATION

Comparison and Contrast

In Reading 3, "My Husband's Nine Wives," the writer uses the organizational pattern of **comparison and contrast** to describe polygamy versus monogamy. In some cases, the writer describes both types of marriage; in others, she simply explains how her marriage situation works, assuming the reader knows how monogamous marriages operate.

Using the chart that follows, make a list of five major differences that exist between Elizabeth Joseph's polygamous marriage situation and that of a monogamous couple. Briefly describe each characteristic that Joseph presents. Write the paragraph number in which the information appears. If the writer doesn't present "the other side" of the comparison, simply fill in the characteristics with your own knowledge.

Be prepared to explain briefly the main ideas in the paragraphs using these organization patterns.

Polygamy versus Monogamy: Contrasts/Comparisons

Paragraph Number	Contrasts/Comparisons
_____	_____
_____	_____
_____	_____
_____	_____
_____	_____

ACTIVITY

IT WORKS!
Learning Strategy:
Word Parts

Using your knowledge of **prefixes** and **suffixes,** examine the following terms from "My Husband's Nine Wives," all of which contain the root word part "gam," which means "marriage." With a partner, discuss the prefix, suffix, and word meanings. (The word parts are underlined after each word.) In your reading journal, make a chart containing the word parts and their definitions, and the sample words and their definitions. Indicate the part of speech of each sample word.

Sample Word	Word Parts
polygamist	poly, gam, ist
polygamy	poly, gam, y
monogamous	mono, gam, ous

REACTIONS

LEARNING STRATEGY

Forming Concepts: When you argue for an opinion that you do *not* agree with, you sharpen your ability to formulate your *own* opinions.

ACTIVITY: DEBATING AN ISSUE

In a small group, discuss the advantages and disadvantages of polygamy versus monogamy. Your instructor will assign your group to argue in favor of one of the forms of marriage over the other. You will argue in favor of polygamy, for instance, while another group in your class will argue for monogamy.

Even if you disagree with the position you are asked to support in debate with another group, write down a list of points that you could present in support of your position. Make notes about each point. Discuss with your group members what the other group might argue in response to each of your points.

Divide your arguments among the group members so that each presents one major point. In a panel discussion, present your arguments to the class. An opposing group will then argue its position. In the end, each group must be prepared to respond to comments and questions from the audience.

ACTIVITY: TAKING NOTES

As each group presents its points, take notes. Use the form provided. Decide which group is the winner of the panel discussion.

LEARNING STRATEGY

Remembering New Material: Taking notes when you listen or read forces you to concentrate on essential ideas.

Panel Discussion Notes and Evaluation

Group A	Group B
Main Points: 1. _____ 2. _____ 3. _____ 4. _____ **COMMENTS:**	Main Points: 1. _____ 2. _____ 3. _____ 4. _____ Winning Group (circle one): **A** or **B**

LEARNING STRATEGY

Managing Your Learning: Make learning fun by playing games, and you accomplish two goals: you learn new ideas, *and* you have a good time.

Word puzzles are a favorite pastime, not only because they are amusing but also because they improve your knowledge of words and facts. One popular type of puzzle is the "secret word" puzzle. In this puzzle, you complete sentences with key words. Then, using one circled letter from each key word, you can discover another "secret word."

ACTIVITY

Working alone or with a partner, complete the puzzle, using the clues provided. All the key words in the puzzle appear in the Chapter 6 readings. The number of blank spaces indicates the number of letters in each key word needed to complete each sentence.

To get you started, the first key word is provided. Use the circled letters, <u>in numerical order</u>, to spell the "secret word," which is also a vocabulary term from Chapter 6.

HINT To find the key words, check the vocabulary lists in your reading journals, the comprehension check exercises after each reading, and the readings themselves.

1. About 22 million Americans live __ Ⓞ __ __ __, according to "One's
    1
    Company: Is There Something Unnatural about Living Alone?"

2. According to this article, those who are suddenly alone have trouble
    adapting to __ Ⓞ __ __ __ __ __ __.
                 2

3. The article "We Are Family: Why Gays and Lesbians Form Strong Bonds"
    suggests that homosexuals may become __ __ __ __ Ⓞ __ __ __ __
                                                          3
    from their families of origin after they "come out."

4. __ __ __ __ __ __ ◯ __ men often remarry to combat loneliness, says
                4
the author of "One's Company: Is There Something Unnatural about Living
Alone?"

5. "Lesbian" is another word for __ __ __ __ __ __ __ __ __ ◯.
                                         5

6. The fear of homosexuality is called __ __ __ __ __ __ __ __ ◯ __.
                                    6

7. The author of "My Husband's Nine Wives" believes that women must juggle
career, motherhood and marriage in __ __ ◯ __ __ __ __ __ __
                                  7
marriages.

8. Polygamy means plural __ __ __ __ __ __ __ ◯.
                              8

9. If a person who lives alone is young, attractive, and urban, the magazines
call them "__ __ __ __ __ __ ◯," according to the first reading in the
                            9
chapter.

10. The word "__ __ __ ◯" means homosexual men or women.
                    10

Secret Word:

In a variety of interrelationships, people may feel either closeness or

__ __ __ __ __ __ __ __ __ __.

EVALUATION

ACTIVITY: CHAPTER SELF-TEST

Assess your general understanding of the readings in Chapter 6 by taking the
following chapter self-examination. The day before you take this test, select ten
vocabulary items from your cards or your reading journal exercises on cultural
references, word parts, and personal vocabulary. Write them on a separate piece
of paper, and hand them in to your instructor. Then quickly review your reading
journal notes about the chapter and the readings.

On the test day, ask your instructor for your word list. Fill in the definitions and parts of speech of your ten personal vocabulary words in Part 1. Circle the appropriate completion of each statement in Part 2. Check your answers to Part 1 in your reading journal or on your cards, and score your test. See page 203 in Appendix II for the answers to Part 2.

Part 1: Vocabulary

Vocabulary Word	Definition	Part of Speech
1. _____	_____	_____
2. _____	_____	_____
3. _____	_____	_____
4. _____	_____	_____
5. _____	_____	_____
6. _____	_____	_____
7. _____	_____	_____
8. _____	_____	_____
9. _____	_____	_____
10. _____	_____	_____

_____ CORRECT × 10 = _____ %

Part 2: Comprehension

1. In "One's Company: Is There Something Unnatural about Living Alone?" the writer says that singles enjoy living alone until
   a. the women's childbearing years start narrowing down.
   b. the men feel the need to settle down and have a family.

2. The author says that loneliness is prevalent in America because
   a. it is built into this country's foundations.
   b. this country is new.
   c. Americans have mixed origins.
   d. all of the above

3. Three examples of famous writers that preferred solitude are
   a. William Wordsworth and Henry Thoreau.
   b. John Milton and Emily Dickinson.
   c. Barbara Holland and Elizabeth Joseph.
   d. a and b

4. One disadvantage of solitary life, according to the author, is
   a. high rent.
   b. inconvenience.
   c. difficulty in getting a dinner reservation.

5. According to the author of "We Are Family: Why Gays and Lesbians Form Strong Bonds," many gays and lesbians are rejected by their families when
   a. they borrow money from them.
   b. they tell their families they are homosexual.
   c. they don't communicate with their families.

6. The author says gays and lesbians may have stronger friendship ties because of
   a. rejection by their families of origin.
   b. homophobia and straight people's inhibitions about making friends of the same sex.
   c. disillusionment with the "gay community."
   d. all of the above

7. According to the author of "My Husband's Nine Wives," the American Civil Liberties Union adopted a policy calling for
   a. the legalization of polygamy.
   b. the prohibition of polygamy.

8. For the author, polygamy is
   a. an oppressive situation.
   b. an ideal situation.

9. According to Joseph, the "trade-offs" in a monogamous relationship are
   a. microwave dinners for the husband.
   b. kids fixing their own breakfasts.
   c. extra money spent on day care for preschoolers.
   d. all of the above

10. When the author says that a monogamous marriage isolates a woman from the outside world, while a polygamous marriage allows her to escape, the organizational pattern being used is
    a. cause and effect.
    b. narration.
    c. comparison and contrast.

ACTIVITY: EVALUATING YOUR GOALS

In your reading journal, write brief answers to the following questions:

1. The most important skills I used in reading and responding to the readings in this chapter were _____ .

2. The most valuable information I gained from this chapter was _____

_____ .

ACTIVITY: WRITING

In your reading journal, write a short composition in response to one of the following questions.

IT WORKS!
Learning Strategy:
Responding
in Writing

1. Should families reject their homosexual children? Give arguments to support your opinion.
2. Compare and contrast friendship in your native culture with friendship in U.S. society.
3. Would you rather be single or married? Give reasons for your opinion.

Reading Further

Find a reading that deals with some aspect of friendship or marriage. Find a magazine or newspaper article, or read part of a book. In your reading journal, write a brief summary and commentary on the reading. Give the name, author, publisher, and publication date of your reading.

Information

LEARNING GOALS

ACTIVITY: SETTING PERSONAL GOALS

As in previous chapters, list in order of importance (with 1 as "most valuable") the learning objectives that are significant to you. Add personal learning objectives to the list if you wish.

GOAL	RANK
1. To increase comprehension of readings	———
2. To expand vocabulary	———
3. To increase reading speed	———
4. To improve study skills	———
5. To learn more about the subjects of this chapter	———
6. _____	———
7. _____	———

PREPARING TO READ

In Chapter 7, you will examine the emerging world of information and technology, which is changing the face of the world. The first two readings explore the effects on the information revolution on countries throughout the world; the third reading suggests how future technologies impact individual lifestyles. The readings are:

"Who Will Own the Information Highway?" by Kevin Cooke and Dan Lehrer
"Third World Leapfrog," by Pete Engardio
"Computers Know a Lot about You," by Jennifer Vogel

ACTIVITY: PREDICTING CONTENT

Discuss the following questions in small groups.

1. What is the *information highway*?
2. Considering the titles of the readings in Chapter 7, what particular aspects of information technology do you think the authors will explore?
3. Which of the titles interests you the most? Why?
4. Look ahead at the photographs and other graphic material in the chapter. Read the accompanying captions. What do they suggest about the content?

ACTIVITY

In your reading journal, write for five minutes in answer to this question: "What aspect of the information revolution is having the greatest effect on my life?"

LEARNING STRATEGY

Overcoming Limitations: Understanding specialized vocabulary makes reading about technical fields or disciplines easier.

When you read, you will often need to understand **technical or specialized vocabulary.** Each field of discipline has its own particular set of technical or specialized words and expressions.

The readings in this chapter pertain to the field of computer science. Since you need to understand these terms to grasp the overall meaning of the reading, it's useful to define technical terms *before* you read. In a textbook with a glossary, look up and learn the meanings of these terms before reading so that you can focus on larger ideas when you read.

IT WORKS!
Learning Strategy:
Using Prior
Knowledge

ACTIVITIES

A. Chapter 7 contains many technical terms that deal with information technology, communications, and computers. With a group of two or three classmates, discuss the following italicized terms and define as many as you can.

Then, to define the remaining terms, find someone at your school or in your community who is knowledgeable in computer and information technology. You might consult an instructor or a student in a computer science department of a college or university, or you might ask a friend or family member who has experience in technology.

Copy the following key term chart into your reading journal, writing the definition for each term and identifying the source (i.e., group discussion, computer expert) of the definition. The reading and the number of the paragraph containing each term are listed after each key term in the chart.

Chapter 7: Computer/Information Technical Terms

Term	Meaning	Source of Definition
information highway (Reading 1, title)	_____	_____
cyberspace (Reading 1, para. 2)	_____	_____
modem (Reading 1, para. 2)	_____	_____
electronic bulletin board (Reading 1, para. 2)	_____	_____
electronic mail (e-mail) (Reading 1, para. 3)	_____	_____
Silicon Valley (Reading 1, para. 4)	_____	_____
log on (Reading 1, para. 12)	_____	_____
computer networks (Reading 1, para. 12)	_____	_____
hacker (Reading 1, para. 20)	_____	_____
digital communications (Reading 2, para. 2)	_____	_____
optical fiber (Reading 2, para. 3)	_____	_____
analog phones (Reading 2, para. 14)	_____	_____
database (Reading 3, para. 3)	_____	_____

B. In your group, report to the class the definitions that you found. Identify the source of your information, and explain how the expert presented the definition.

ACTIVITY: PREVIEWING

Before you read "Who Will Own the Information Highway?" discuss the question raised in the title with a partner and then with your class.

Reading 1

Glossary
Al Gore   a former U.S. senator who was elected U.S. Vice President in 1992
AT&T   American Telephone and Telegraph
Time Warner   a media communications/entertainment group of companies
Prodigy   a private network that provides services such as on-line shopping and air travel reservations to users
Orwellian   referring to George Orwell's 1949 novel, *1984,* which forecasted government interference in citizens' private lives

National Security Agency   a U.S. government "spy" agency
specter   a threatening possibility
adage   a wise saying

WHO WILL OWN THE INFORMATION HIGHWAY?

by Kevin Cooke and Dan Lehrer

1   Halfway around the world, Wam Kat files daily reports on life in Zagreb, Croatia. "I just stood about half an hour in the supermarket downstairs watching a firmly built man. . . . He was shouting at everybody in the shop," Kat wrote on May 24, 1993. "From what I could understand, he said that when Croatia was under the Serbs [in former Yugoslavia], the price of bread was at least half of what it is now. Just a few days ago I heard somebody say that under the communists we had our problems, but now under the capitalists we have our problems too. What is the difference if you work for the communist or capitalist elite?"

2   Kat's bulletins, which he calls "Zagreb Diary," don't appear in Croatian papers or on television. They exist in cyberspace. Kat types them on his computer in Zagreb and sends them by modem to an electronic bulletin board in Germany. From there, they are relayed to computers around the world via the global information stream called the Internet.

3   "Electronic mail is the only link between me and the outside world," says Kat, writing by E-mail. The Croatian government owns all the major media in the country and is prosecuting a group of journalists for treason.

4   Kat is only one of the millions of people participating in this community without walls. During other recent cataclysms, the Internet provided an instant, unfiltered link to the world. "In Russia, during the [1991] coup attempt, people were providing live reports on Russian Internet about what was really going on. They were widely circulated on the Net," says Mitchell Kapor, founder of Lotus Development Corporation and now chairman of the Electronic Frontier Foundation, a group advocating "electronic civil liberties," primarily freedom of speech and privacy. "During Tiananmen Square, students were getting the news out and were fund-raising through Internet," adds Tom Mandel, a futurist with SRI International, a Silicon Valley–based consulting firm. "A bunch of us were hungrily reading newsgroups, stuff we weren't getting from reporters."

5   The Internet is the most powerful computer network on the planet simply because it's the biggest. It encompasses 1.3 million computers with Internet addresses that are used by up to 30 million people in more than 40 countries. The number of computers linked to the Internet doubled every year between 1988 and 1992; in 1993 the rate of increase slowed slightly to 80 percent. To reach the Net, you need only a computer, a modem, and a password. Dan Van Belleghem, who helps connect organizations to the Internet for the National Science Foundation, says, "Nobody has ever dropped off the network. Once they get on they get hooked. It's like selling drugs."

6   Addictive as it is, it's not all smooth sailing on the sea of information. On most computers, the Internet is hard to use; the arcane commands make little sense to many average users. "The Internet today is still for computer weenies," says Kapor, "but the problem will take care of itself": Easier-to-use software tools will appear as the Net grows.

7   And as it gets easier to enter the Net, more and more people will experience the power that comes with the knowledge. Howard Rheingold, whose book *The Virtual Community* was published last fall by Addison-Wesley, says, "If you have a computer, you have the power to broadcast. It gives the power to individuals that used to be only that of the privileged few." And, he adds, the direct access to information that the Internet provides is "inherently politically subversive."

8   Internet activists want to make sure that the power stays with individuals. A debate is raging in Washington on how to transform the Internet into a faster, bigger network: the National Research and Education Network (NREN).

> ## Threads
>
> Today, literacy can refer to computer knowledge. Are you "computer literate" or "illiterate"?

Funding for NREN began with then-senator Al Gore in 1991. In 1993, Rep. Rick Boucher, D-Va., sponsored legislation called the National Information Infrastructure Act to add on to Gore's brainchild, providing $1.5 billion in funding to hook libraries, schools, and medical facilities to new high-speed computers. Telecommunications and computer companies, including NYNEX and Cray Research, have lined up in favor, and a Clinton administration spokesperson has said that the president is prepared to sign the legislation, which was passed by Congress in the summer of 1993 (a companion bill is expected to be before the Senate in January 1994).

9   Boucher's bill alarmed many longtime Net users because it encourages the NREN computers to use private networks instead of publicly subsidized ones. Boucher, chairman of the House Science Subcommittee, has suggested that the government should turn over areas of the Internet to private corporations whenever possible. "The Internet has grown without a clear plan or organization," he says. "There's no government for the Internet. One of the great challenges is to establish some means of providing order and giving markers along the way."

10   By itself, the first move toward privatization means little. Another Boucher-sponsored bill would grant antitrust exemptions for telephone companies, allowing a single company to own both phone and cable lines. Boucher thinks this will provide the financial incentive for the private sector to upgrade the communications links between the Internet and private homes. Critics fear that the end result could be the expansion of local cable and telephone monopolies into monopolies controlling all electronic access into the home.

11   By giving the private sector unregulated and monopolistic control over the Net's electronic connections, the government would in effect allow megacorporations like AT&T and Time Warner, who own the cable lines and manage what flows through them, to call the shots in the future. They could determine how much anyone, from a single individual to a university, will have to pay for access. Some phone companies are already discussing charging users either by the amount of time they log on to the Internet or by the amount of data they send over it—despite the fact that their network operating costs are fixed, no matter how many people use it or how much data flows through it. Changing the funding structure means the eventual extinction of the small, mom-and-pop computer networks, which could find themselves victims of predictable market forces. And that means that isolated users and cash-strapped colleges could be cut off from their virtual communities.

12   Net users have reacted fiercely to Boucher's proposals. The specter of censorship—as on commercial systems like Prodigy, where system administrators routinely delete "objectionable" messages—looms. "Communities, whether virtual or physical, should be self-determining, rather than determined by megacorporations," says the Electronic Frontier Foundation's Kapor. "The users of the Net should determine its uses and content." In a worst-case scenario, Rheingold says, corporations would not only monitor what's on the Internet, they would monitor you. If, as some predict, the information superhighway becomes primarily a conduit for watching movies, banking at home, and shopping, the Net could be used by marketing wizards—the same ones who flood us with annoying junk mail—to keep tabs on us all in Orwellian fashion, automatically recording our interests and habits.

13   Hackers have already developed a few defenses, which could be the seeds for preserving the right to free communication. Free software to encode all electronic transmissions is now widely available, with codes that even the fastest supercomputers would have a tough time cracking. This encoding, or encryption, means that nobody but the person you send something to—whether it's an E-mail note or a piece of software—can read it.

14   And anonymity is also possible. Networks have been set up in such disparate places as Helsinki and San Diego to enable completely anonymous speech. The

Finnish operator declared that he will never allow anyone to find out the true names of his users without a court order.

15   Nor are Internet activists happy with the Clinton administration's effort to impose a standard encoding scheme for data from E-mail to movies that only the government can break. "The machinery of oppression has weak spots," Rheingold says, noting the spread of encryption techniques that even the National Security Agency may not be able to crack.

16   Whether it's the government or private corporations, what everyone wants is control of a new form of communication. Given the stakes and the power of the interests now seeking to shape and profit from this new technology, the end result may not be a happy one for the average citizen-user: "The key questions of access, pricing, censorship, and redress of grievances will be answered in practice, in law, in executive order, or legislative action, over the next five years," Rheingold writes, "and will thus determine the political and economic structure of the Net for decades to come."

17   For the time being, the activities of people like Wam Kat seem to prove an old hacker adage: All information wants to be free.

Comprehension

Without looking back at the text, mark the following statements "True" or "False," based on information from "Who Will Own the Info Highway?" Check your answers on page 203 of Appendix II.

_____   **1.** Wam Kat is a Croatian government official.

_____   **2.** Kat's news bulletins about events in Croatia are published in newspapers and aired on television.

_____   **3.** The Internet is a global information system relayed via computers.

_____   **4.** During the 1991 Russian coup attempt, live reports were circulated on the Internet.

_____   **5.** About 30 million people in 40 countries use the Internet.

_____   **6.** To reach the Internet, you need a computer, a modem, and a password.

_____   **7.** U.S. political leaders, such as Al Gore, want Internet to remain free of controls.

_____   **8.** NREN stands for National Research and Education Network.

_____   **9.** Large corporations like AT&T could raise the cost of Internet membership.

_____ **10.** Some Internet users relay messages from faraway locations and use codes to keep their identities unknown.

_____ **CORRECT** × **10** = _____ %

ACTIVITIES: IDENTIFYING THE ORGANIZATION

A. In Chapter 4, you found that the main idea sentence, the *thesis statement*, often appears in the *introduction*—the first paragraph(s) of a reading. With a partner, quickly reread the beginning paragraph(s) of "Who Will Own the Information Highway?" and answer these questions:

1. Which paragraph(s) make up the introduction?
2. Which sentence is the thesis statement?

B. Reread paragraphs 8–12, the section of the reading that suggests what will happen if government or business takes over the Internet. With your partner, decide which of the following is the main organizational pattern used here:

Narration
Comparison and contrast
Cause and effect

Discuss the dominant organization pattern with the class. Then, in your reading journal, create a graphic organizer to restate the most important ideas in this section. Use the sample graphic organizers on page 82 in Chapter 4 as guides.

ACTIVITY

IT WORKS!
Learning Strategy:
Guessing
Meaning

As you did in previous chapters, use the surrounding contexts and word parts to guess the meanings of the italicized words.

The underlined prefixes and suffixes in the following words may help you with the definitions. With a partner, consult a dictionary to find the meanings of these word parts. Also, reread the sentences in which the words appear to get clues from surrounding words. Then guess the meaning of each word. Check your guesses in the dictionary, then record the words' meanings and their parts of speech in your reading journal or on cards.

1. treason (para. 3)
2. cataclysms (para. 4)
3. futur<u>ist</u> (para. 4)
4. arcane (para. 6)
5. <u>sub</u>versive (para. 7)
6. brainchild (para. 8)
7. publicly <u>sub</u>sidized (para. 9)
8. <u>mono</u>polies (para. 10)
9. call the shots (para. 11)
10. looms (para. 14)
11. <u>en</u>coding *or* <u>en</u>cryption (para. 16)

ACTIVITY: PREVIEWING

The title of the second reading is "Third World Leapfrog." What does "leapfrog" mean? Which countries are doing the "leapfrogging"? Considering the topic of Reading 1, what type of "leapfrogging" might these countries be doing? Why?

ACTIVITY

Before you read "Third World Leapfrog," work with a group of classmates to define the following terms. Use your own knowledge, consult a dictionary, and/or ask an expert in computers, communications, or business to help you define the following terms found in the reading: (Refer to the paragraph given if you wish to examine the context in which the word is used.)

1. fax lines (para. 1)
2. floppy disks (para. 1)
3. digital-communications circuits (para. 2)
4. (to) output (para. 2)
5. specs (para. 2)
6. digital switches (para. 3)
7. videoconferencing (para. 3)
8. multinationals (para. 4)
9. infrastructure (para. 4)

Write the words and definitions in your reading journal or on vocabulary cards. Then compare your definitions with some of your classmates'.

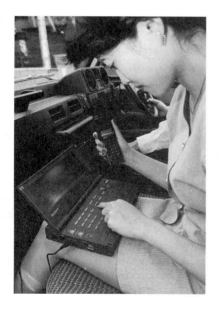

IT WORKS!
Learning Strategy:
Technical
Terms

Reading 2

Glossary
laggards   lazy persons
proverbial   related to a proverb or wise saying

THIRD WORLD LEAPFROG

by Pete Engardio

For seven years, Japan's Seiko Epson Corp. has found South China to be a fine source of low-cost labor. But for Shinpei Misawa, Epson's Hong Kong–based manager of information systems, it has also meant "many, many headaches." Shuttling troubleshooters from Hong Kong into Epson's two factories, where 5,000 workers churn out 100,000 printers monthly and more than 100 models of Seiko watches, involves scrambling for tickets on constantly overbooked trains. Fax lines often produce illegible copies or go dead in tropical storms. A simple change in manufacturing specifications can mean putting floppy disks on the next delivery truck bound for China. (1)

Misawa's headaches are about to go into remission, however. Thanks to high-speed digital-communications circuits that will be installed by year-end, both plants will be connected to Epson's regional electronic flow of up-to-the-minute inventory, delivery, and output data that make possible just-in-time production. And engineers in Japan will be able to transmit specs for new products to the factory floor in seconds. (2)

Epson is just one example of a transformation that should greatly boost living standards in the developing world. Places that until recently were incommunicado are rapidly acquiring state-of-the-art telecommunications that will let them foster both internal and foreign investment. It may take a decade for many countries in Asia, Latin America, and Eastern Europe to unclog bottlenecks in transportation and power supplies. But by installing optical fiber, digital switches, and the latest wireless transmission systems, urban centers and industrial zones from Beijing to Budapest are stepping into the Information Age. Videoconferencing, electronic data interchange, and digital mobile-phone services already are reaching most of Asia and parts of Eastern Europe. And in Latin America, where only 7% of the population has access to a phone, the demand for communications has created the fastest-growing cellular market in the world. (3)

All these developing regions see advanced communications as a way to leapfrog stages of economic development. Widespread access to information technologies, for example, promises to speed the transition from labor-intensive assembly work to "value-added" industries that involve engineering, marketing, and design. "Multinationals want to set up where the infrastructure is the best it can be," says Lloyd Kubis, Motorola Inc.'s regional director of telecommunications government relations for the Asia/Pacific region. Modern communications "will give countries like China and Vietnam a huge advantage over countries stuck with outmoded technology." (4)

How fast these nations should push ahead is a matter of debate. Many analysts think Hanoi is overdoing it by requiring that all mobile phones be expensive digital models, when Vietnam is desperate for any phones, period. "These countries lack the expertise in weighing costs and choosing between technologies," says John Ure, director of telecommunications research at the University of Hong Kong. (5)

Still, there's little dispute that communications will be a key factor separating the star performers from the laggards. Consider Russia. Because of its strong educational system in mathematics and science, it should thrive in the Information Age. Problem is, its national phone system dates from the 1930s. Russia is starting to install fiber optics and has a grand plan to pump $40 billion into various communications projects. But it's too broke to do so rapidly. (6)

Compare that with China. Over the next decade, it plans to pour some $100 billion into telecom equipment, adding 80 million phone lines by the year 2000, four times the number it has now. In a way, China's backwardness is a blessing, because the expansion occurs just as new technologies are becoming more cost-effective than copper wire and analog systems. By the end of 1995, each of China's 26 provincial capitals except Lhasa in Tibet will have digital switches and high-capacity optical fiber links to Hong Kong, Singapore, Taiwan, and Thailand. This means that major cities such as Beijing, Shanghai, and Guangzhou are getting the basic broadband infrastructure to become interchanges on the Information Superhighway. "When a country goes from no infrastructure to the latest, it will leapfrog entire rungs of development," says John J. Legere, AT&T's managing director of consumer services for Asia. (7)

Telecommunications is also a key to Shanghai's dream of again becoming a premier financial center. Citibank, Merrill Lynch, and Morgan Stanley already have offices in the city, the hub of China's fast-growing stock and bond markets. To offer the razzle-dazzle electronic data and paperless trading global investors expect, Shanghai plans broadband networks as powerful as those in Manhattan. (8)

In Eastern Europe, meanwhile, Hungary also hopes to vault into the modern world. Currently, 700,000 Hungarians are waiting for phones, and businesspeople regularly rank poor phone links as a chief headache. So for the past three years, the country has been laying optical fiber. To speed the import of Western technology, in December Hungary sold a 30% stake in its national phone company to Deutsche Bundespost Telekom and Ameritech International Inc. To further whittle the waiting list, Hungary has granted a license to Pannon, a Dutch-Scandinavian consortium, to build what it says will be one of the most advanced cellular digital communications systems in the world. (9)

In fact, cellular is one of the most popular ways to get a phone system up fast in developing countries. It's cheaper to build radio towers than string lines across a country, and businesses eager for reliable service are willing to cough up the significantly higher tolls for a cellular call—typically two to four times as much as for calls made over fixed lines. Look at Latin America where cellular demand and usage have exploded in every country. (10)

For cellular providers, in fact, a LatAm franchise is the proverbial license to print money. BellSouth Corp., with operations in four Latin wireless markets, estimates its annual revenue per average subscriber at about $2,000, vs. $860 in the United States. That's partly because LatAm cellular customers talk two to four times as long on the phone as their North American counterparts. (11)

Thailand is also turning to cellular, as a way to allow Thais to make better use of all the time they spend on the road. A lack of planning despite years of more than 8 percent growth has left Bangkok virtually paralyzed in traffic, discouraging foreign investors. And it isn't that easy to call from the office: The waiting list for phones has from one to two million names on it. So cellular phones have become the rage among businesspeople, who can remain in contact despite the logjams. The result: There are nearly 500,000 cellular subscribers in Thailand, the most in any Southeast Asian country. (12)

Vietnam is making one of the boldest leaps. Currently, it has one phone for every 435 people. But despite per capita income of just $220 a year, Hanoi wants the best. All of the 300,000 lines it plans to add annually will be optical fiber with digital switching, rather than cheaper analog systems. By going for next-generation technology now, Vietnamese telecom officials say they'll be able to keep pace with anyone in Asia for decades. "Vietnam will be capable of carrying any network services a global company could want," says James R. Long, president of Northern Telecom Ltd.'s World Trade Div. (13)

Still, many believe Vietnam is going overboard—and point to its experience with cellular phones as proof. After Ho Chi Minh City awarded two licenses for analog cellular systems, Hanoi mandated that all networks elsewhere in the country be digital. The result: Thousands of analog phones have been sold, compared with fewer than 200 digital phones, which cost twice as much. Plus, the digital phones won't work on analog systems, so if you travel between the two systems you need two phones. (14)

Still, for countries that have played catch-up for so long, the temptation to do so in one jump is hard to resist. And despite the mistakes they'll make, they'll persist—so that one day they can cruise alongside Americans and Western Europeans on the Information Superhighway. (15)

ENDING TIME: _____ : _____
TOTAL TIME: _____
1301 WORDS ÷ _____ MIN = _____ WORDS/MIN

Comprehension

Without looking back at the text, mark the following statements "True" or "False," based on information from "Third World Leapfrog." Check your answers on page 203 of Appendix II. Record your reading speed and comprehension score on page 200 of Appendix I.

_____ **1.** Japan's Seiko Epson Corporation operates two factories in South China.

_____ **2.** A Seiko Epson manager reports there are no problems with transportation or communication between South China and Hong Kong or Japan.

_____ **3.** Many Third World countries are upgrading their telecommunications systems.

_____ **4.** The fastest growing cellular phone market in the world is Eastern Europe.

_____ **5.** China and Vietnam have advantages over other Third World countries because they are installing new systems rather than upgrading old ones.

_____ **6.** Russia has immediate plans to spend $40 billion on communications projects.

_____ **7.** Hungary has sold shares and issued licenses to Western companies to speed up its import of Western technology.

_____ **8.** In Thailand, businesspeople use cellular phones while stuck in traffic.

_____ **9.** At present, most Vietnamese homes have telephones.

_____ **10.** Vietnam is planning to add 300,000 optical fiber phone lines annually.

_____ **CORRECT** × **10** = _____ **%**

LANGUAGE STUDY

LEARNING STRATEGY

Managing Your Learning: To interpret numeric information in a chart or graph, try to find meaningful relationships among the numbers you read.

ACTIVITY

Read the chart on page 162 entitled "The Developing World Gets Wired" to find the following information:

A. The top five countries in terms of percentage increase in telecommunications lines are (in order):

1. China   19.3%

2. _____   _____

3. _____   _____

4. _____   _____

5. _____   _____

B. The top five countries in terms of billions of dollars spent on telecommunications are (in order):

1. China $53.5 billion

2. _____   _____

3. _____   _____

4. _____   _____

5. _____   _____

C. The country in the chart that has spent the least amount on telecommunications projects is _____, which has spent _____ billion to add _____ million lines, a _____ percent increase in its present number of lines.

THE DEVELOPING WORLD GETS WIRED			
	Millions of Phone Lines Added, 1993–2000	**Percent Increase in Lines**	**Investment $ Billions**
China	35.5	19.3%	$53.3
Russia	15.5	6.7	23.3
India	9.1	11.2	13.7
Brazil	6.8	6.4	10.2
Mexico	6.3	8.5	9.4
Thailand	4.3	16.7	6.6
Malaysia	3.1	11.9	4.6
Poland	2.7	6.7	4.0
Indonesia	2.6	13.6	3.9

Data: International Telecommunication Union

ACTIVITY: PERSONAL VOCABULARY

Find ten vocabulary words from "Third World Leapfrog" that you would like to learn. Define each word and identify its part of speech. Write your definitions in your reading journal or on vocabulary cards.

IT WORKS!
Learning Strategy:
Choosing What
to Learn

ACTIVITY: PREVIEWING

Consider the title of Reading 3. What do you think computers know about you? How do you think computers get this information? What is done with the information?

Reading 3

Glossary

memory chip   a unit of a computer that stores data for retrieval

bar-hopping   going from one bar to another in a single evening

piggyback   (to function) as if carried on the shoulders or back of another

FBI   U.S. Federal Bureau of Investigation

moochers   ones who obtain things free of charge through trickery

thugs   hoodlums; criminals

credit bureaus   private companies that collect data and report people's financial histories

Big Brother   In George Orwell's *1984,* the name referred to the government, which kept a close watch on citizens.

COMPUTERS KNOW A LOT ABOUT YOU

by Jennifer Vogel

1   Imagine a small plastic card that holds all manner of information about you on a tiny memory chip: your date of birth, Social Security number, credit and medical histories. And suppose the same card lets you drive a car, fill prescriptions, get cash from machines, pay parking tickets, and collect government benefits.

2   One incarnation of this so-called smart card is already in use. Some insurance companies issue medical history cards of policyholders, who need them to get prescriptions filled. This type of technology evolves out of convenience, says Evan Hendricks, editor of *Privacy Times* newsletter, but "the dark side is that landlords, employers, and insurance companies could say we won't do business with you unless you show us your card."

3   Personal information gets harder to protect as more companies and government agencies build computerized databases that are easily linked. "You can go database-hopping the way people go bar-hopping," says Hendricks. "The information superhighway will probably be developed by corporations, but the government is always willing to piggyback on these things. Companies develop databases for direct marketing and then the FBI uses them for investigative purposes."

4   According to Simson L. Garfinkel, writing in *Wired* (February 1994), the database craze started with Ronald Reagan's fables of welfare queens bilking taxpayers. "It was called Operation Match," says a privacy expert quoted by Garfinkel, "and it matched databases of people who owed money to

the government with other databases of people who got money from the government. Match went after government employees who had defaulted on student loans and welfare recipients with large unearned and unreported incomes."

5   Saving the public from moochers and thugs has been an effective excuse for whittling away everyone's personal privacy. The White House has been pressing for computer makers to incorporate "clipper chips" in their machines to allow law enforcement agencies to eavesdrop on electronic communications. The administration claims that failing to do so would be begging terrorists and criminals to collude in cyberspace.

6   That may still seem like James Bond stuff; more troubling is the growing accessibility of everyday information. Take the computerization of medical records—which promises to be fast-forwarded by the Clinton health plan. As Mubarak S. Dahir points out in *Philadelphia City Paper* (May 28, 1993), "your video renting habits are better protected by law than your medical records." That's because there's more money in your medical records. A privacy expert quoted by Dahir says insurance companies generate "lists of individuals with certain kinds of medical problems and then turn around and sell those lists to pharmaceutical companies [and] other businesses."

7   Medical records are used to make a whole host of decisions about you that aren't related to your health. According to a 1991 government report, writes Dahir, "50 percent of employers regularly use medical records information for hiring and promotion purposes. Of those who do, nearly 20 percent . . . do not inform their employees that their medical records have been used for such purposes." Turner Broadcasting System won't hire smokers, notes Dahir, and Best Lock Corporation of Indianapolis fired an employee after finding out he was a social drinker.

8   Employers and landlords often buy this information from companies that are in the business of creating data profiles. Besides criminal history, workers' compensation claims, and civil court records, one of their mainstays is credit information, which isn't always accurate. One of the country's largest credit bureaus, TRW, paid out big bucks a few years ago after settling a case filed by 19 states claiming the company's reports were full of errors.

9   But the Big Brother information gatherer of them all is the Department of Motor Vehicles, according to Garfinkel. "The DMV is a one-stop shop for state agencies that want to reach out and affect our lives," he writes. Given the existing system, which links together all 51 U.S. motor vehicle agencies, "no other state agency tracks the movement of people more accurately."

10   Nor is DMV data used solely for matters related to driving. "Oregon has 109 different offenses that can result in the temporary suspension of a driver's license; 50 of them have nothing at all to do with driving," writes Garfinkel. Wisconsin residents, he notes, can lose their license for not paying library fines, neglecting to shovel the sidewalk, or failing to trim a tree that overhangs a neighbor's property. In Kentucky, students who drop out of school, have nine or more unexcused absences, or become "academically deficient" lose their driving privileges "unless they can prove family hardship."

11   It's hard to avoid being a blip on the DMV computer screens, but there are ways to keep a low profile in other areas. Dahir quotes a health official who recommends that when you sign an authorization form you amend it to make it clear "that you do not consent to having information re-released or sold to a second party without your express, written consent."

12   Lots of other advice is available in publications listed in the *Whole Earth Review* (Fall 1993). Two of the most intriguing books on the list are *Privacy for Sale* by Jeffrey Rothfeder and *Your Right to Privacy* by Evan Hendricks of *Privacy Times* newsletter. Another well known and useful periodical is the monthly *Privacy Journal*.

INLAND BANK

BANK STATEMENT

TO:
MARY LENDER
4115 N. LINCOLN
INLAND, IN 47304

ACCOUNT NUMBER:
75–197–66

DATE	YOUR BALANCE WAS	WE SUBTRACTED		SERVICE CHARGE	WE ADDED		MAKING YOUR PRESENT BALANCE
		NO.	CHECKS		NO.	DEPOSITS	
8/31/––	186.43	14	586.65	1.90	2	706.09	303.97

DATE	CHECKS			DEPOSITS	BALANCE
					186.43
8/2				286.75	473.18
8/6	125.00				348.18
8/9	23.46	40.00			284.72
8/10	9.45	15.00			260.27
8/12	15.74	139.00			105.53
8/15	34.10				71.43
8/16				419.34	490.77
8/17	21.19				469.58
8/19	8.00				461.58
8/22	14.86	10.00	45.00		391.72
8/27	85.85				305.87
8/31	1.90SC				303.97

Please notify bank immediately of any change of address. The account will be considered correct if errors are not reported immediately.

Symbol code:
SC   Service Charge
OD   Overdrawn Account
SP   Stop Payment
ER   Error Correction

Comprehension

Mark the following statements "True" or "False," without referring to "Computers Know a Lot about You." Check your answers on page 203 of Appendix II.

_____ **1.** A "smart card" is a card that makes its holder intelligent.

_____ **2.** Insurance companies may one day compile policyholders' medical histories on "smart cards."

_____ **3.** Government agencies and companies presently link computerized databases that contain information about individuals.

_____ **4.** Employers must inform a person before they use that person's medical records to decide whether to hire or promote him or her.

_____ **5.** The largest information gatherer is the TRW credit bureau.

_____ **6.** In Kentucky, students with excessive unexcused absences can lose their driving privileges.

_____ **7.** One health official recommends that people should demand that companies and agencies not release their data to others.

_____ **8.** No magazines exist to inform people about computers and privacy.

_____ **CORRECT** × **12.5** = _____ %

Managing Your Learning: Reading to learn and remember detailed information requires you to read carefully and slowly.

ACTIVITY: IDENTIFYING THE ORGANIZATION

When you read for details, you read to identify and remember specific pieces of information. Because you must stop and think about these smaller units of ideas, you must read the material thoroughly, perhaps several times. Details are specific pieces of information that are generally considered less important than main ideas; they can include facts, numbers, dates, proper names, examples, narrative details (specific events told in a story), or descriptive words.

In "Computers Know a Lot about You," the writer includes many details about specific agencies, companies, and other organizations that have specific information about individuals. Likewise in "Third World Leapfrog," you find many specific details about particular countries and their technological advances in specific areas.

Reading material for detail takes extra time, since your mind (and your eyes!) stop to examine small bits of information. Furthermore, if the information contains technical details that are unfamiliar to you, you may need to read still more slowly and even reread a passage several times.

ACTIVITIES

A. With a partner, practice your ability to distinguish between main ideas and details in the following passages. After each passage, write a sentence in your words to explain the main idea. Circle the detail words. Discuss your ideas with some of your classmates.

   1. From "Third World Leapfrog":

> For seven years, Japan's Seiko Epson Corp. has found South China to be a fine source of low-cost labor. But for Shinpei Misawa, Epson's Hong Kong–based manager of information systems, it has also meant "many, many headaches." Shuttling troubleshooters from Hong Kong into Epson's two factories, where 5,000 workers churn out 100,000 printers monthly and more than 100 models of Seiko watches, involves scrambling for tickets on constantly overbooked trains. Fax lines often produce illegible copies or go dead in tropical storms. A simple change in manufacturing specifications can mean putting floppy disks on the next delivery truck bound for China.

Main Idea:

_____

_____

_____

2. From "Computers Know a Lot about You":

Medical records are used to make a whole host of decisions about you that aren't related to your health. According to a 1991 government report, writes Dahir, "50 percent of employers regularly use medical records information for hiring and promotion purposes. Of those who do, nearly 20 percent . . . do not inform their employees that their medical records have been used for such purposes." Turner Broadcasting System won't hire smokers, notes Dahir, and Best Lock Corporation of Indianapolis fired an employee after finding out he was a social drinker.

Main Idea:

_____

_____

_____

B. Reread the following paragraphs from "Third World Leapfrog." With a partner, write down details in your journal about the communications systems or changes occurring in each of the countries listed. Compare your details with some of your classmates'.

1. Russia (para. 6)
2. China (para. 7)
3. Hungary (para. 9)
4. Thailand (para. 12)
5. Vietnam (para. 13)

ACTIVITY: PERSONAL VOCABULARY

IT WORKS!
Learning Strategy:
Choosing What
to Learn

Choose ten vocabulary words from the text "Computers Know a Lot about You" that you would like to learn. Write each word, its definition, and its part of speech in your reading journal or on a vocabulary card. Then, in your journal or on each card, write an original sentence in which you use each word. Check your sentences with your instructor.

REACTIONS

ACTIVITY

IT WORKS!
Learning Strategy:
Making
Connections

Refer to the three readings in Chapter 7. Each of these articles describes certain changes taking place in the world due to technological advances. Which of the changes do you view as positive? Which do you view as negative? Why?

Discuss your opinions in a small group; then share your views with the class.

REVIEWING

LEARNING STRATEGY

Remembering New Material: Check your understanding and recall of reading material by "talking through" important ideas with another person.

Good students often use study groups as a way to better understand and remember material learned in classes. Especially in classes in which technical, detailed reading material is taught, students find collaborating on their learning to be productive and effective.

A technique called a **"talk-through"** is commonly used by study group members. One or more group members will orally "test" group members on new material by asking them to recite the information. In other words, the student being tested "talks through" important ideas from a reading or lecture. Then the listeners "correct" the student doing the talking by supplying him or her with more accurate information. In this way, both the speakers and the listeners learn and remember material.

ACTIVITY: TALK-THROUGH

In a small group, take turns asking each other for the main ideas in the three readings in Chapter 7. Your instructor will help by modeling the activity. For example, in a group of three or four, one student can "talk through" the ideas in "Who Will Own the Information Highway?" while the other group members ask him or her questions.

Use the following questions as guides for important ideas to ask each other about:

1. What does the title of the reading mean?
2. What is the main idea of the reading?

3. Define _____ (an important vocabulary word from the reading).

EVALUATION

ACTIVITY: CHAPTER SELF-TEST

Assess your general understanding of the readings in Chapter 7 by taking the following chapter self-examination. The day before you take this test, select ten vocabulary items from your journal or cards (technical terms, personal vocabulary, and other vocabulary from exercises) that you would like to learn. Write them on a separate piece of paper. Then review your reading journal notes about the chapter and the readings.

167

168

On the test day, fill in the definitions and parts of speech of your ten vocabulary words in Part 1. Circle the appropriate completion of each statement in Part 2. Check your answers to Part 1 in your reading journal or cards, and score your test. See page 203 in Appendix II for the answers to Part 2.

Part 1: Vocabulary

Vocabulary Word	Definition	Part of Speech
1.		
2.		
3.		
4.		
5.		
6.		
7.		
8.		
9.		
10.		

_____ **CORRECT** × **10** = _____ %

Part 2: Comprehension

1. For Wam Kat, the Croatian author of the "Zagreb Diary" mentioned in "Who Will Own the Information Highway?" the only link to the outside world is
   a. E-mail.
   b. newspapers.
   c. television.
   d. radio.
2. The author says that "electronic civil liberties" means
   a. a free computer.
   b. free Internet membership.
   c. freedom of speech and privacy.
   d. all of the above.
3. In recent years, the number of computers linked to the Internet worldwide
   a. has increased.
   b. has declined.
4. U.S. government leaders like Rep. Rich Roucher want to regulate the Internet because
   a. the Internet has no clear organization.
   b. the Internet has no government.
   c. both a and b

5. In "Third World Leapfrog," the writer says the Third World countries that are "stepping into the Information Age" include
   a. Latin America and Russia.
   b. most of Asia and Eastern Europe.
   c. most of Asia and Russia.
   d. Latin America and Eastern Europe.

6. The writer says Latin America has become a large cellular phone market because
   a. it's cheaper to build towers than string phone lines across a country.
   b. stringing phone lines is impossible due to weather conditions.
   c. Latin Americans prefer cellular phones to noncellular phones.

7. Vietnam is facing one key problem in building its new telecommunications system:
   a. its national phone system dates from the 1930s.
   b. digital systems are used in Hanoi and analog systems in Ho Chi Minh City.
   c. foreign companies are competing to gain licenses to operate its system.

8. In the chart, "The Developing World Gets Wired," the number one country in telecommunications spending and growth is
   a. Russia.
   b. India.
   c. China.
   d. Brazil.

9. According to the author of "Computers Know a Lot about You," computerized databases containing information about individuals are being used by
   a. employers.
   b. pharmaceutical companies.
   c. landlords.
   d. all of the above

10. In the future, the author says, U.S. government officials would like to
    a. install chips that would allow law enforcement agencies to monitor individuals.
    b. impose an additional federal tax on all computer purchases.

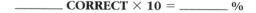

_____ CORRECT × 10 = _____ %

ACTIVITY

Answer the following questions in your reading journal to help you self-assess your reading habits and adjust your goals accordingly. Consult your instructor for suggestions.

1. Has your reading rate increased since you began this course?
2. If so, identify one technique that you have used that you believe helps you read faster. Explain how you are using the technique.
3. If not, identify one technique that you will use in the future to help you read faster. Explain how you will use this technique.

IT WORKS!
Learning Strategy:
Evaluating
Your Progress

ACTIVITY: EVALUATING YOUR GOALS

In your reading journal, write briefly in answer to the following questions:

1. The most important skills I used in reading and responding to the readings in this chapter were _____.

2. The most valuable information I gained from this chapter was _____

_____.

EXPANSION

Reading Further

Read about one particular advancement in information, communications, or computer technology occurring in one country of the world. Find an article from a magazine or newspaper, or read part of a book. In your reading journal, write a brief summary and commentary on the reading. Give the name, author, publisher, and publication date of your reading.

ACTIVITY: WRITING

IT WORKS!
Learning Strategy:
Responding
in Writing

In your reading journal, write a brief composition in answer to this question: What aspect of the information revolution will have the greatest effect on my community in the future? (You may define your community as the country in which you live, the country in which you were born, your city, or your neighborhood.)

Government

ACTIVITY: SETTING PERSONAL GOALS

As in the previous chapters, list in order of importance (with 1 as "most valuable") the learning objectives that are significant to you. Add personal learning objectives to the list if you wish.

GOAL	RANK
1. To increase comprehension of readings	_____
2. To expand vocabulary	_____
3. To increase reading speed	_____
4. To improve study skills	_____
5. To learn more about the subjects of this chapter	_____
6. _____	_____
7. _____	_____

PREPARING TO READ

In Chapter 8, you will examine the governments of two countries on two continents, and you will consider the political and economic future of the world as a whole. South Africa and China exemplify many other developing countries that are moving in new political directions. The evolution of these and other developing countries—as well as major changes in the developed world—will amplify the political and economic activity of the coming decades. The following readings raise many thought-provoking questions:

"Free at Last: South Africa's Election Ratifies a Political Miracle for the Ages" by Jerelyn Eddings and Eric Ransdell
"The Chinese: Will They Be Capitalists?" by Brenda Dalglish
"How the World Will Look in 50 Years" by Bruce W. Nelan

ACTIVITY: PREDICTING CONTENT

Discuss these questions in a small group:

1. Considering the titles of the readings in Chapter 8, what topics do you predict will be covered?
2. Look ahead at the photographs and other graphic material in the unit. Read the accompanying captions. What do they suggest about the content of the chapter?
3. Which of these readings interests you the most? Why? Make a list of questions you have about this topic.

ACTIVITY: LISTENING FOR IDEAS

In a small group, prepare yourself for the topic of government by viewing a television news broadcast about a timely international political issue such as overpopulation, famine, communications, education, women's rights, or minority rights. You might listen to a ABC, CBS, NBC, or public television nightly news show. Listen for a segment of the program that deals with the politics or economics of one country.

Take notes on the information you hear. Copy the following form into your journal or onto a separate piece of paper. View the program and then fill out the report.

IT WORKS!
Learning Strategy:
Listening

1. Title of News Program: _____

Time/Date: _____   Channel: _____

2. Country(ies) Named in the News Segment:

_____

_____

3. Brief Summary of the Segment:

_____

_____

4. Brief Description of Photographs Shown during News Report:

_____

_____

5. Your Reaction to the News Segment:

_____

_____

ACTIVITY: SHARING IMPRESSIONS

Share your report on your news segment with a group of classmates. Listen to your classmates' reports; then discuss the issues presented in the reports.

ACTIVITY: PREVIEWING

Reading 1 is entitled "Free at Last: South Africa's Election Ratifies a Political Miracle for the Ages." What do you know about South Africa's 1994 election? Why is it called "a political miracle"?

ACTIVITY

As you did in Chapter 4, use the headings in the following reading to write questions about each section of the reading. Then, as you read, try to answer the questions you wrote.

You may want to construct your questions using one of these word groups (or others):

Why is (are) . . .?
How do (did) . . .?
When did . . .?
Why did . . .?
What is (are) . . .?
What does (do) . . .?

Reading 1

Glossary
apartheid   the policy of separation of population based on race
Afrikaans   a dialect of Dutch spoken by white South Africans
eclipses   overshadows
Berlin Wall   the wall in the German city of Berlin that formerly divided Eastern and Western Europe
queues   lines
squatter camp   a temporary town
left-leaning   politically liberal
neo-Nazi   a post-Nazi political group that shares the beliefs of Adolf Hitler's Nazi movement
right-wingers   politically conservative people

FREE AT LAST: SOUTH AFRICA'S ELECTION RATIFIES A POLITICAL MIRACLE FOR THE AGES

by Jerelyn Eddings and Eric Ransdell

Freedom finally arrived in South Africa at 7 A.M. on April 26 [1994]. At Sefikeng Church in the black township of Soweto outside Johannesburg, the old women arrived a few minutes earlier, just before the polls opened for the first multiracial elections in the nation's history. They came with their heads wrapped in traditional style and with checkered wool blankets covering their shoulders, moving slowly, some with the aid of walking sticks. In deference to their ages and their years of suffering, first under white domination and then, since 1948, under the racist policy of apartheid, an election monitor ushered them carefully to the front of the already long line. Four decades ago, they had watched as their homes in Johannesburg's vibrant, multiracial community of Sophiatown were bull-dozed. Then they were herded onto Army trucks, which carried them to the stark little houses in this part of Soweto known as Meadowlands. Their old neighborhood gave way to a new working-class suburb named Triomf, which means triumph in Afrikaans, the language of their oppressors. (1)

Last week, however, triumph belonged to apartheid's victims, to the disenfranchised and the dispossessed who lost their homes, their loved ones, and their friends to a system that measured a person's worth by the color of his skin and the curl of his hair. They came by the millions to cast their votes for a new South Africa, lining up for hours in queues that stretched for miles through busy cities on the rich gold reef, through quaint towns in the farming heartland, and through dusty villages in the poor homelands once assigned to blacks. "I didn't think I would ever see this day," said Hanna Kotana, 75, who leaned on a cane and squinted through thick, dark-rimmed spectacles. "I feel happy and energetic. I think I could throw this cane away. The way I feel I have no words to say." (2)

Starting over

In many ways, the spectacle is a political and human "miracle." As other nations in Europe, Africa, and elsewhere are torn limb from limb by old grievances, new greed and ethnic hatred, the most deeply and bitterly divided country in the world, a nation long ruled by racist laws and consumed throughout its history by racial, tribal, and ethnic hostilities, is poised to bind its wounds and start over. Four years of difficult, multiparty negotiations have produced one of history's great moments, one that rivals and perhaps even eclipses the fall of the Berlin Wall and the collapse of the Soviet Union. (3)

Communism, tired, corrupt, and bankrupt, imploded with a whimper. South Africa's transition from tyranny to democracy is an act of enormous courage and monumental statesmanship, both by those who are gaining power and by those who are giving it up. State President F. W. de Klerk has done what Mikhail Gorbachev lacked both the vision and the courage to do—willingly dismantle the monopoly on power held at gunpoint by his privileged elite. And in Nelson Mandela, the "old man" of the African National Congress, South Africa and the world have found a leader who possessed both the steel to win the long war against apartheid and the grace to face the future without bitterness or recrimination. (4)

The fear of chaos that had prompted some whites to stock up on supplies and ammunition before Election Day dissolved in the warm glow of reconciliation during and after the four days of voting. Said Mandela: "I think every one of us will agree that the people of South Africa have been victorious. They have won." (5)

Flag of Hope

A spate of right-wing bombings early in the week, which most South Africans hope were the death rattle of white extremism, failed to derail, or even overshadow, the elections. As the voting got underway, a new flag was hoisted, a new interim Constitution took effect, and a new national anthem, "God Bless Africa," was raised. Blacks and whites lined up together, patiently sharing soft drinks as hundreds of polling stations around the country ran out of ballot papers. Wealthy white matrons and their black maids, equals for the first time in their lives, embraced in the queues. Whites brought water to blacks who came to voting stations in their tree-lined neighborhoods. Black squatter-camp residents warmly greeted whites who came to vote under tents in their desolate settlements. In parts of the country, conservative whites and left-leaning blacks stood side by side all day, as did political rivals from Mandela's African National Congress and Mangosuthu Buthelezi's Inkatha Freedom Party. (6)

The balloting was not without its problems: Millions of ballots were inexplicably lost, leading to accusations of theft and vote rigging. A rush to print 9.3 million new ballots averted a threatened pullout by Buthelezi, the combative Zulu leader and Inkatha president who entered the election at the last minute and hinted that he might yet reject the results. (7)

But such problems were addressed quickly, and the balloting went off smoothly enough that the election is bound to be pronounced free and fair by South Africa's Independent Electoral Commission. Though final results were not expected until early this week, the ANC vote should be sufficient to ensure that Mandela is sworn in May 10 [1994] as the country's first black president. De Klerk's National Party is expected to be the second biggest vote-getter, which would give him a place in the government of national unity that will govern South Africa for the next five years. (8)

Beyond the euphoria awaits the tough job of putting South Africa right and building it into a strong, unified nation. In addition to the obvious economic and social challenges arising from apartheid, the new government faces threats from the neo-Nazi fringe responsible for last week's bombings and from Buthelezi, whose followers have fought a bitter war with the ANC since 1984. (9)

The black-led government could face a longer-term political threat if it fails to meet the high expectations of South Africa's long suffering black majority. Soon after Mandela names a new cabinet, he intends to embark on a program of building homes, electrifying townships, improving schools, and constructing clinics for black communities that were grossly underserved by previous regimes. (10)

Daily Elections?

In many areas, however, the first priority will be to bring peace. Last week's polls have put the country off to a good start. In [the northern Zulu town of] Natal and on Johannesburg's East Rand, torn by the feud between the ANC and the Inkatha, political violence dropped off to nothing during the polls. "We ought to have an election every day," one man told a visiting U.S. observer team led by Jesse Jackson. (11)

At week's end, Jackson told reporters: "The transfer of power is legitimated." Despite its flaws, the election remains a landmark victory for negotiation over confrontation. Unlike in Namibia, Zimbabwe, Angola, and other nations, South Africa's "negotiated revolution" was carried out by its own people without any foreign assistance or intervention. In Africa, where democracy has so often faltered or failed, and beyond, South Africa could become a model for overcoming ethnic strife and political upheaval. (12)

Last week's elections demonstrated the country's uncanny ability to pull itself back from the brink of disaster. Throughout the four-year transition from apartheid to majority rule, South Africa has teetered between racial reconciliation and civil war. As recently as two weeks ago, most analysts were predicting low-level war in Natal and a bloody uprising by white right-wingers. (13)

Yet the elections many thought would blow the long-divided country apart have served to bring it together. Like many South Africans, Johannesburg artist Reshada Crowse feared the worst. But after last week's polls she, too, was caught up in the tide of relief and elation: "It's like a completely unique revolution, something not seen in the history of the world. There was so much bitterness, it could have been so awful, and yet it wasn't." (14)

ENDING TIME: _____ : _____
TOTAL TIME: _____
1312 WORDS ÷ _____ MIN = _____ WORDS/MIN

Comprehension

Without looking back at the text, mark the following statements "True" or "False," based on information from "Free at Last: South Africa's Election Ratifies a Political Miracle for the Ages." Check your answers on page 203 of Appendix II. Record your reading rate and comprehension score on page 200 of Appendix I.

_____ **1.** Freedom arrived in South Africa in 1994 with national elections.

_____ **2.** Old black women who arrived at the voting polls were escorted to the end of the line.

_____ **3.** Nelson Mandela, the "old man" of the African National Congress, is South Africa's new leader.

_____ **4.** Because of lost ballots, Mandela threatened to pull out of the election.

_____ **5.** The new South Africa government faces threats from the forces of Zulu leader Mangosuthu Buthelezi.

_____ **6.** South Africa's "negotiated revolution" was carried out by foreign countries.

_____ **7.** It took South Africa four years to move from apartheid to majority rule.

_____ **8.** The elections in South Africa blew the country apart.

_____ **CORRECT** × **12.5** = _____ %

LANGUAGE STUDY

LEARNING STRATEGY

Managing Your Learning: Scanning is beneficial any time you must read quickly to find specific information.

In many settings—academic and nonacademic alike—you need to read and process information quickly in order to identify and isolate specific ideas. For example, when you read a television listing, searching for a favorite program, you find the program by scanning (or reading quickly) the words in the television guide, then focusing in on a familiar name or time included in the program title you are looking for.

Similarly, when you read an academic text, you can scan for specific information by searching for a key word or phrase that is related to the information you are seeking; then you can locate the target information nearby.

Scanning can serve you well as a study tool, too. For instance, you can reread a history text more carefully, searching for names and dates if you know that you may be tested on this material.

ACTIVITY: SCANNING

With a partner, scan the preceding article to find specific information from the story. Look for key words in the sentences to help you locate the answers. Complete the sentences that follow, and write them in your reading journal for future study.

1. Freedom arrived in South Africa on _____.

2. Mangosuthu Buthelezi is _____

_____

3. Buthelezi almost pulled out of the election because of _____

_____

4. South Africa's "negotiated revolution" was carried out _____.

5. The elections have not blown the country apart; in fact, they have served

_____

ACTIVITIES: ANNOTATING A TEXT

IT WORKS!
Learning Strategy:
Scanning

A. Mark the sections of the text that contain the ideas stated in the previous five sentences. You may want to underline or highlight words or sentences within the text. Then write key words or phrases in the margins of the reading so that you can refer to them later. Compare your annotations with some of your classmates'.

B. Next, mark the sections of the text that contain the answers to the questions you listed in the predicting activity before you read the article. Use the same method of annotation you previously employed, comparing your textual and margin notes with those of your classmates.

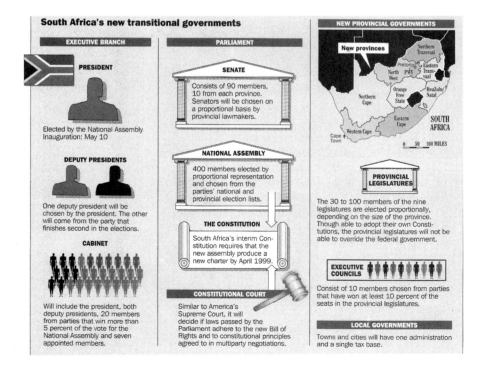

ACTIVITY: SCANNING

Scan the chart, "South Africa's New Transitional Governments," to answer the questions on the next page.

1. Who selects the deputy presidents?
2. Who will be members of the cabinet?
3. How many senators will South Africa have?
4. How many national assembly members will there be?
5. What is the constitutional court?

ACTIVITY

Work with a partner to guess the meanings of the following words taken from the first five paragraphs of "Free at Last: South Africa's Election Ratifies a Political Miracle for the Ages" (paragraph numbers are in parentheses). Use the surrounding words and phrases as well as your knowledge of word parts to help you. Check your guesses in a dictionary. If they are accurate, simply put a check under "Dictionary Definition." Write the words and their definitions in your reading journal.

IT WORKS!
Learning Strategy:
Guessing
Meaning

	Your Definition	Dictionary Definition
1. herded (1)	_____	_____
2. stark (1)	_____	_____
3. disenfranchised (2)	_____	_____
4. dispossessed (2)	_____	_____
5. eclipses (3)	_____	_____
6. imploded (4)	_____	_____
7. dismantle (4)	_____	_____
8. steel (4)	_____	_____
9. recrimination (4)	_____	_____
10. reconciliation (5)	_____	_____

ACTIVITY: PERSONAL VOCABULARY

Choose ten vocabulary words that you would like to learn from paragraphs 6–14 of "Free at Last: South Africa's Election Ratifies a Political Miracle for the Ages." Write each word, its definition, and its part of speech in your reading journal or on a vocabulary card. Then, in your journal or on each card, write an original sentence in which you use each word. Check your sentences with your instructor.

IT WORKS!
Learning Strategy:
Choosing What
to Learn

ACTIVITY

IT WORKS!
Learning Strategy:
Making
Connections

Look back at "I Leave South Africa," the story of a young student's journey from his homeland to America (page 11, Chapter 1). Skim the story quickly.

In your reading journal, write a one-paragraph composition in which you compare how the lives of South Africans as described by the author of "I Leave South Africa" are changing due to the elimination of apartheid, the racist policy that separated whites and blacks in that country.

ACTIVITY: SHARING IMPRESSIONS

In a small group, answer the questions below, which relate to the racial policies of countries other than South Africa.

1. In your native country, are any racial or ethnic groups discriminated against in any way, such as not being allowed to vote, being forced to live in separate communities, or having a lower social status than other groups?
2. Are any racial or ethnic groups discriminated against in the United States or other countries (besides your native country) in which you have lived? In what ways?
3. In any of the countries where you have witnessed racial discrimination, what changes need to take place?

PREPARING TO READ

ACTIVITY: PREVIEWING

What do you know about the political system of the People's Republic of China? Consider the question the author raises in her title in the following reading. *Will* the Chinese become capitalists? What is a capitalist?

Reading 2

Glossary

Tiananmen Square   the Beijing square in which students protested Chinese government policy

gold rush   referring to the rush to prospect for gold in the western United States and Canada in the late nineteenth century

Maclean's   a Canadian business magazine

THE CHINESE: WILL THEY BE CAPITALISTS?

by Brenda Dalglish

1   The rich, black earth of the Pearl River Delta in southeast China's Guangdong province is some of the most fertile in the country. But this spring, the delta is sprouting almost as many construction sites as it is rice shoots. Farmers wearing straw coolie hats bend over in ankle-deep water planting rice seedlings. They carry out their timeless labor apparently oblivious to the disappearance of neighboring rice paddies, just an irrigation ditch away, under six feet of landfill and a five-story building. To meet the demand for even more flat land, bulldozers are chewing down the gentle green mountains that edge the delta. The half-demolished slopes look lopsided and vulnerable with their dense tropical foliage ripped away to expose the red earth below. An old Chinese proverb says that it is easier to move a mountain than to change a man's nature. But along the Pearl River Delta, the topographical changes are less revolutionary than the philosophical ones. The very nature of China is being reinvented. Across the province, colorful government billboards echo a new motivational message from Chinese leader Deng Xiaoping: "Time is money. Efficiency is life."

2   Just 20 years ago, during the Cultural Revolution, capitalism and foreigners, particularly foreign businessmen, were considered enemies of the Chinese state. Now, Communist party officials are some of China's most aggressive entrepreneurs. Businessmen are responding to the changes with a degree of enthusiasm reminiscent of the gold-rush fever that opened up the West Coast of North America in the 1800s. And nowhere is China's new wealth more apparent than in the Pearl River Delta. Although few Chinese are allowed to own cars, every day hundreds of Mercedes, belonging to rich businessmen or party cadres, vie for space with the transport trucks and commercial vans that jam the congested highway between Guangzhou, better known to Westerners as Canton, and Macau, the Portuguese gambling colony.

3   In booming Guangzhou, the principal city of Guangdong province, long lines of people queue for the opportunity to buy their first apartment. China has averaged an enviable economic growth rate of 10 percent a year for the last decade. Guangdong, the province just across the border from Hong Kong that is serving as the economic development model for China, has averaged an astonishing annual growth rate of 25 percent for each of the last five years. But China's economic transformation is fragile. With its massive population, it is in danger of running out of natural resources as it industrializes. And it also faces such manmade problems as inflation and corruption.

4   Deng began China's transformation in 1979 and, with the exception of the sudden disillusioning regression in 1989 after the army used guns and tanks to smash the students' democracy protest in Beijing's Tiananmen Square, the economic reforms gradually gathered speed. Now, China's so-called socialist-market economy is the fastest-growing in the world. If the pace continues, by the end of the century China will not only have one-quarter of the world's population, it will have the world's third largest economy, after the United States and Japan.

5   Led by overseas Chinese investors, manufacturers have flooded into Guangdong, first to take advantage of cheap labor and land, but also with the greater hope of getting a foot in the door of what is potentially the biggest consumer market in the world—1.2 billion Chinese eager for material goods. Avon, the American door-to-door cosmetics company, for example, has 15,000 saleswomen in the city of Guangzhou and, by the year 2000, it expects to have a quarter of a million Avon ladies ringing doorbells, or their Chinese equivalent, across the country. But perhaps the ultimate demonstration of the economic changes in China is a plan by Manufacturers Life Insurance Co. of Toronto. Manulife, which is Hong Kong's third-largest life insurer, plans to open its first representative office in mainland China this week. Said Victor Apps, vice president and general manager of Manulife Hong Kong: "Insurance is a product for the middle class. We think China is ready for it."

6   For his part, Canadian businessman James Ting, who is one of the more aggressive entrepreneurs leading the way into the Chinese consumer market, says that the opening of China's economy is a once-in-a-lifetime business opportunity. Ting, based in Markham, Ont., north of Toronto, says that he bought the Singer sewing machine franchise five years ago because he envisaged a huge potential demand for that type of consumer product in rapidly developing countries like China. The soft-spoken engineer-turned-businessman is operating six joint ventures in China, including a first for China, a consumer credit system that will allow Chinese customers to buy consumer goods now and pay later. China's economic boom "is a modern gold rush," said Ting. "Everyone is rushing in hoping to strike it rich."

7   More than a decade of steady economic growth combined with the Chinese government's escalating pro-business rhetoric have persuaded many investors that China is irrevocably committed to economic reform. Hong Kong businessmen led the way during the 1980s by gradually moving their light manufacturing operations, including garment and consumer electronic factories, over the border into Guangdong. Now, Hong Kong manufacturers employ three million workers in China, or the equivalent of more than half of Hong Kong's total population of 5.8 million.

8   The early entrepreneurs' experience, and especially their profits, soon convinced others that the risk of doing business in an officially Communist country was not an insurmountable obstacle. Northern Telecom Ltd., the Mississauga, Ont.–based telephone equipment manufacturer and marketer, views China as a prime market. The reason: the government plans to increase the number of telephones to 65 million by the end of the century from about 20 million now. The Canadian company opened a joint-venture manufacturing plant four years ago in the new city of Shekou, in the first special economic zone of Shenzhen, along the border between China and Hong Kong. Ming Li, senior managing director of North Telecom (Asia) Ltd. in Hong Kong, expressed agreement with Ting's gold-rush image. "It's true—it's just like the Wild West over there," said Ming with a laugh. "The taxation laws are not complete, actually none of the laws are finished, so you can make lots of money and not pay tax. Lots of people are getting rich."

9   But not all that glitters is gold. China faces huge obstacles in its single-minded push to join the industrialized world. Its shortage of resources and its environmental problems are growing as fast as its population. Despite China's draconian efforts to enforce its rule of one child per family, the World Bank estimates that China's population will grow to 1.9 billion from the current 1.2 billion before stabilizing in the mid-twenty-first century. Said Vaclav Smil, a professor of geography at the University of Manitoba: "China has immense environmental problems that are going to get much worse as it industrializes." Added Smil, author of *China's Environmental Crisis,* which is to be published this month: "To feed its people, it now uses even more fertilizer per hectare than Japan, which uses five times more than Canada. [The Chinese] have less arable land per capita than Bangladesh." The Chinese consume only about four

percent as much wood per capita as Canadians use, but even at that low level, said Smil, China "will run out of trees by the end of the century."

10   As well, the fast economic growth of the last decade is producing inflation, now running at a rate of 15 percent in urban areas. The costs of some products, especially those used in construction, are soaring. The price of cement has risen by 70 percent in a year. And in addition to inflation, the scourge that has killed economic growth in other less-developed countries, China faces the problem of widespread corruption among government officials and other people in positions of power. Foreign businessmen say that such corruption could ultimately undermine confidence in the system.

11   And concerns remain about possible political instability. Despite China's open-door economic reforms, its rulers continue to pursue a repressive policy of even tighter control over political issues. Asia Watch, a United States–based human rights organization, says that at least 40 political dissidents were arrested in China last year and are still being held. And Deng continues to take a hard-line position against demands for greater political freedom. "Once the factors of turmoil reappear in the future," he said in March [1993], "we will, if required, not hesitate to use any means to eliminate them as soon as possible."

12   Some observers say that even the pragmatic Chinese will not be able to sustain their unlikely marriage of convenience between capitalism and communism for long. The only questions are whether the breakup will be gradual and amiable, or messy and violent, and who will win the family assets. Meanwhile, as eager businessmen are quick to point out, China's one-party authoritarian government is the main reason China has been so successful at implementing its economic reforms. Authoritarianism efficiently eliminates the kind of opposition that can make a democracy unwieldy and resistant to change. The businessmen do not mention, however, that the same centralized government structure could also make it easy for China to reverse course. China's history has been marked by swift mood swings; it would not be the first time that the government has led the way on a mad dash to one economic extreme, only to turn and start a mad scramble back to the other.

13   Still, the dominant spirit among most Westerners doing business in China remains optimistic. Matthew Barrett, chairman of the Bank of Montreal, toured the Pearl River Delta, Hong Kong, and Taiwan last month sounding out the depth of the changes that have taken place. The bank, which already has operations in several Asian centers, including Hong Kong, is about to open its second office in China, in Guangzhou. Barrett expressed enthusiasm. "The rest of the world needs to understand the magnitude of the development taking place," he told *Maclean's*. "Even if you don't do a dollar's worth of business in China, you have to know what's happening here because it's going to change the world."

14   More ominous is the fact that China appears to have the potential to overwhelm the rest of the developing world. "It's a little unnerving," said Barrett. "China has a seemingly limitless supply of human capital with such a strong work ethic and an inherent entrepreneurial drive that you have to wonder whether there will be any low-value-added jobs left in the rest of the world." He added, "It is certainly a major competitive threat to Mexico and the other Latin American countries." The differences between the two regions are striking. Many officials of foreign-owned light manufacturing plants in Mexico complain of an annual turnover rate among their low-skilled workers of almost 100 percent. But in Guangdong, plant managers looked puzzled at questions about employee turnover. They say that less than 10 percent of their workers leave each year.

15   Given China's enormous potential and Canada's good relationship with the country, Barrett says that he is perplexed that there are not more Canadian companies helping to develop China's outdated, inadequate transportation and communications infrastructure. "Canada is good at just about everything China needs," said Barrett, "and, yet, we are noticeable by our absence." Other Canadian businessmen in China—and even government officials—expressed similar opinions. Lu Jinhan, vice-chairman of the Guangzhou Municipal

Commission of Foreign Economic Relations and Trade, said that he would like to see more Canadian entrepreneurs at work in his province. "There are many, many business opportunities here," said Lu, "and the Chinese in Canada can play the role of a bridge between us."

16   But even the Bank of Montreal's Barrett is cautious. He has still not decided whether to rent or buy space for the Guangzhou office. He cited the costly example of his bank's lending in the 1970s to economically promising less-developed countries including Brazil, Argentina, and Mexico, which led to massive loan losses in the 1980s. "There is always the danger," he said, "that if it grows like a weed, it could be a weed."

17   China is trying to allay such concerns. Lu, the Guangzhou foreign relations official, cites the major improvements in people's living standards as the best reason why the policy of economic reform will continue. Indeed, the narrow aisles of Guangzhou's new department stores are crammed with people buying everything from cosmetics and Disney toys to washing machines and air conditioners. Said Lu: "From the government to the people, everyone believes that the reforms have been good for the country."

18   Lu's conviction carries weight because of his own experiences. He graduated from high school in 1966, at the height of Mao Tse-tung's

Cultural Revolution, which created chaos in the country as the masses were encouraged to challenge and overthrow all forms of traditional authority. Lu said that because his parents had been well educated, government officials sent him to the country to work as a factory laborer for ten years. He was allowed to return in 1978. That was the year that Deng, who was accused of being a "capitalist roader" during the Cultural Revolution and imprisoned, announced the Four Modernizations program. Lu was then allowed to go abroad to university. Said Lu, without a flicker of doubt: "There will be no turning back."

Comprehension

Without looking back at the text, mark the following statements "True" or "False," based on information from "The Chinese: Will They Be Capitalists?" Check your answers on page 203 of Appendix II.

_____ 1. China's Guangdong province is located in northeast China.

_____ 2. "Time is money" is a new message from Chinese leader Deng Xiaoping.

_____ 3. The Cultural Revolution occurred 20 years before this article was published.

_____ 4. Now, the greatest wealth in China lies in Guangzhou, capital of the Pearl River delta.

_____ 5. The average economic growth rate for Guangzhou over the past five years has been 10 percent.

_____ 6. If China's growth rate continues, by 1999 it will be the world's third largest economy.

_____ 7. One Canadian company that already does business in China is Manulife, a life insurance firm.

_____ 8. James Ting, the Canadian engineer-businessman, purchased a Coca-Cola franchise in China.

———— **9.** One negative aspect about China's economic future is its environmental problems.

———— **10.** Mexico poses a competitive threat to China because its workers have a lower job turnover rate and strong work ethic.

———— **CORRECT** × 10 = ———— %

LANGUAGE STUDY

ACTIVITIES: IDENTIFYING THE ORGANIZATION

A. In previous chapters, you learned that a reading contains an **introduction** that varies in length from one to several paragraphs. The introduction introduces the topic and often contains the thesis statement (main idea sentence) of the reading. With a partner, quickly reread the beginning paragraph(s) of "The Chinese: Will They Be Capitalists?" and answer these questions:

  1. Identify the paragraph(s) that make up the introduction.
  2. Find the thesis statement.

B. With your partner, reread each remaining paragraph of the story and identify its main idea sentence. Underline or highlight that sentence.

ACTIVITIES

A. Some of the topic sentences that you identified in the previous exercise may contain vocabulary and grammatical constructions that make them difficult to understand. Look at this topic sentence from paragraph 12, for example:

> Some observers say that even the <u>pragmatic</u> Chinese will not be able <u>to sustain</u> their unlikely <u>marriage of convenience</u> between capitalism and communism for long.

Comprehending this sentence may seem difficult because of the high-level vocabulary words, which are underlined. In addition, the length of the sentence and its noun clause (beginning with "that even . . . ") further complicates the message.

Guessing the meaning of complex sentences such as these becomes easier if you divide the sentence into understandable parts. Then you can "translate" each part into a simple idea that you will be able to understand.

Here's a way you might divide the sentence:

> [Some observers say] that [even the <u>pragmatic</u> Chinese] [will not be able <u>to sustain</u>] [their unlikely <u>marriage of convenience</u>] [between capitalism and communism] [for long].

Reading each part individually and thinking about it (or even making simple notes about its meaning) will help you understand such sentences more easily. Here's a simplified version of the main idea of the preceding sentence:

> China might not be able to be both a capitalist and communist country for a long time.

IT WORKS!
Learning Strategy:
Guessing
Meaning

B. With a partner, read over the main idea sentences you identified in the previous exercise. Discuss the meaning of each sentence, and be prepared to explain it in simple words. Take notes to express the main idea of each sentence.

PREPARING TO READ

ACTIVITY: PREVIEWING

The stimulating title of the third reading is "How the World Will Look in 50 Years." How do you think your part of the world will look in 50 years? Are you optimistic or pessimistic about the future?

ACTIVITY: PREDICTING CONTENT

With a partner, read the first paragraph of the reading "How the World Will Look in 50 Years." Read the questions raised in the first paragraph. Go over any unfamiliar vocabulary words, and then discuss your opinions on the answers to the questions. Record your ideas in your reading journal.

Reading 3

Glossary
trade bloc   a group of trade-aligned nations
centrifugal forces   forces that direct movement towards a center
Pacific Rim   countries located on the edge of the Pacific Ocean
Rand Corp., Brookings Institution   research organizations

HOW THE WORLD WILL LOOK IN 50 YEARS
by Bruce W. Nelan

1   Just as wars—two World Wars and, equally important, the cold war—dominated the geopolitical map of the twentieth century, economics will rule over the 21st. All the big questions confronting the world in the century ahead are basically economic. Is the United States in an irreversible decline as the world's premier power? Will Japan continue its competitive conquest of international markets? Can Europe manage to hold together as the world's largest trade bloc in the face of strong centrifugal forces? And does the future hold any hope at all for the poverty-stricken Third World?

2   This concentration on economics will be made possible by the prospect of general peace in the twenty-first century, heralded by the lifting of the nuclear arms threat in the 1990s. In the century ahead, the world will contain more democracies than ever before, and they will dominate in Europe, the Americas, and the countries of the Pacific Rim. Since it is a truism that democratic states do not make war on one another, warfare should become essentially irrelevant for these nations, most of which will reduce their armed forces to the minimum necessary for individual or collective defense. "We're not going to see nation-states bullying one another as they have in the past," predicts senior analyst Carl Builder of the Rand Corp.

3   New realities will also curb the old acquisitive impetus toward imperialism. Raw materials of all sorts, for example, will lose much of their importance because the manufacture of twenty-first century products will use fewer and fewer of them. Even the need for oil, now the most vital of interests in the West, will fall from the strategic agenda as it is replaced by solar power and controlled nuclear fusion. The end of the petroleum age will make the Arab states of the Middle East poorer and less stable but of declining interest to the West. The Islamic world, powerfully resistant to modernization, will tend to isolate itself.

4   Unfortunately, the lifting of the nuclear threat in the 1990s will continue to create opportunities for mischief among some nationalist ideologues and local despots. In the decades ahead, the major powers will ignore most petty tyrants and the brutal but small-bore wars that they foment—unless they seriously endanger their neighbors or threaten their own people with genocide. When that occurs, the United Nations will, in most cases, authorize joint armed intervention. When it does not, the United States and other states that share its views will act on their own.

5   But cooperation with the U.N. will be the norm, in both warlike and peaceful pursuits. The world will have to utilize the powers of the U.N. to solve other overreaching problems, such as environmental pollution, global warming and damage to the ozone layer, that cannot be approached piecemeal. John Steinbruner, director of foreign policy studies at the Brookings Institution in Washington, foresees "a much more advanced form of international politics, involving more sophisticated coordination and more consequential decisions made at the international level."

6   The United States will remain the one reigning military superpower in this less heavily armed world. Its forces will shrink considerably to enable it to concentrate more of its energies on economic and social advances, but it will continue to provide global outreach with state-of-the-art weapons and an invulnerable nuclear arsenal. The United States will have to preserve this role because the technical know-how to build nuclear weapons cannot be abolished no matter how carefully arms-control treaties are drafted. Truly determined governments, among them many smaller nations that covet prestige and power, cannot be prevented from buying or building nuclear arms. The United States will have to be prepared against them if necessary, in order to protect its friends and head off nuclear blackmail.

7   The competition that is normal and inevitable among nations will increasingly be played out in the twenty-first century not in aggression or war but in the economic sphere. The weapons used will be those of commerce: growth rates, investments, trade blocs, imports, and exports. "The move to multinational trade blocs around the world has suppressed nationalism," says Gregory Schmidt of the Institute for the Future in Menlo Park, California. "Economics will eventually win out in the twenty-first century."

8   In his new best-seller *Head to Head,* M.I.T. economist Lester Thurow writes, "World trade in the next half-century is apt to grow even faster than it did in the last half-century. Any decline in trade between the blocks will be more than offset by more trade within the blocks."

9   The big winner will be Europe. At the opening of the twenty-first century, the European Community will comprise an integrated market of 20 countries, newly including such advanced economies as Switzerland, Sweden, Norway, Finland, and Austria. By the middle of the century, it will have added the Czech republic, Hungary, and Poland, and its members' population will total more than 400 million. By then, Ukraine, Russia and most of the rest of Eastern Europe will have achieved associate membership in the Community.

10   That last stage of Europe's growth will demand a lot of work. Eastern Europe's conversion from communist central planning to democratic market economies is one of the most difficult undertakings imaginable. As the Carnegie Endowment's National Commission referred to it in a report last July [1992], "You can make fish soup out of an aquarium, but you can't make an aquarium out of fish soup."

11   What exists in Eastern Europe—mostly antiquated factories, worthless currency, and a socialist hangover—will have to be replaced. What does not exist—a commercial banking system, marketing networks, cost accounting—will have to be created from scratch. The biggest hope for the future of the old socialist world is its very well-educated work force and a high level of science and technology.

12   Another major plus for the emergent democracies will be the eagerness of governments in the West to do everything necessary to build prosperity in the East in order to keep waves of economic migrants from rolling over Germany, Italy, France, and their neighbors. As Western investments and technical assistance take hold, the East will forge ahead. East Europeans will drop their most extreme nationalist and ethnic preoccupations in order to qualify for the economic payoffs they expect from association with the E.C. Of course, some countries, including Romania, Bulgaria, and Albania, will simply not be able to transform themselves.

13   On the other side of the world, the astonishing Asians will continue their success story, but with more diversity and less coordination than Europeans. Japan will not have things so much its own way in the next century. Its ultramodern and finely calibrated economy will not falter, but several factors will impose limits on its once seemingly boundless growth.

14   To begin with, Japan's special sort of samurai work ethic will be under assault. Coming generations of young "salary-men" will be less willing to work such grueling hours. They will want more leisure time, larger apartments, shorter commutes. Japanese men and women alike, no longer content to be poor people in a rich country, as they describe themselves, will demand a larger share of the national wealth they create. The resulting higher consumption at home will inevitably mean more imports and a reduction in Japan's trade surpluses.

15   Problems for Japan are already building up in the Pacific Rim and are bound to intensify. Tokyo's long-range plan for growth is to bring in the raw materials it needs from Russia and steadily increase its sales of manufactured products to what it envisions as a vast market in China. But things will not work out quite that way. Communism will collapse in China, clearing the way for the powerhouse of Taiwan to join Hong Kong as a special economic zone of the Chinese motherland.

16   Even with their help, however, China cannot grow into an industrial giant in the twenty-first century. Its population is too large and its gross domestic product too small (it is expected to reach only $900 per capita by the year 2000). China's economy seems to be growing at 7 percent in 1992, but, as the former Soviet Union and East Germany once did, Beijing cranks out phony statistics. Moreover, China's growth projections are based essentially on light industry.

17   China will have a potential alternative supplier in Korea, where communism will be abolished in the North. The merged Koreas will prove to be a strong competitor to Japan. Right now, all Asia's "little tigers"—South Korea, Taiwan, Hong Kong, Singapore—run considerable deficits in their trade with Japan. In the twenty-first century, they will be as much Japan's rivals as its trading partners. Like the rest of the world, they will be less willing to buy from a Japan that does not buy much from them.

18   The hard laws of economic life also decree that in the twenty-first century, the rich will generally get richer and the poor poorer. In order to rise to a level of prosperity, a developing country must achieve decades of high growth rates while simultaneously holding its population stable. Few will be able to manage

that trick successfully. India in 2025, for example, will have 1.4 billion people. By 2050 the world's population is likely to have surged from the present 5.5 billion to 11 billion, and its production of goods and services will have quadrupled. But almost all the population increase is projected for the less-developed countries, while most of the increased output will occur in the industrial democracies.

19   Moreover, developed countries are already buying less from the Third World and more from one another. Even now, trading by the three main economic regions—Europe, North America, and the Pacific Rim—accounts for 75 percent of the world's total. Over the past decade, 20 of the world's 24 largest industrial powers have signed bilateral agreements that regulate their trade and set up new barriers to imports.

20   If the dynamics of the twenty-first century produce a gloomy outlook for the poorest countries, the most bothersome question facing much of the world is about the fate of the United States. There is no doubt, of course, that America will be a major player on the world scene. Its military power, its 20 percent share of the world's gross national product, and its mastery of such cutting-edge fields as biotechnology, microprocessors, and information technologies guarantee that. It will bestride the North American Free Trade Agreement like a colossus.

21   But serious worries shadow the U.S. future. The country has run a $1 trillion trade deficit over the past ten years, and its national debt is more than $4 trillion. One day the United States will have to pay those bills. And the only way it can do so is to stop devouring the products of other nations, put more of its wealth into investment at home, and greatly expand its exports.

22   Aside from the skewed balance sheets, there are serious doubts about the country's intrinsic health. Its educational system is in crisis, its industries faltering, its investment in itself too meager. "In a world whose workers require ever more basic education, technological savvy, and specialized skill," Marvin Cetron and Owen Davies write in their book *Crystal Globe,* "America's schools are the least successful in the Western world." Says Brookings' Steinbruner: "There's no way of overcoming the disparity in education." U.S. spending on civilian research and development is tenth in the world, a level that M.I.T.'s Thurow estimates will "eventually lead to a secondary position for American science and engineering and lower rates of growth in productivity."

23   Will the United States be able to diagnose its ills and swallow cures that are certain to be bitter? Probably. The country is good at rising to occasions, once it recognizes them. The end of the cold war has released immense resources and millions of talented people who can now turn to the repair of America's damage. Because the United States is, among other things, an even-handed superpower and a vast market, most of the world has a stake in its continued success. But if the United States is to be counted among the winners in the next century, it will have to make gravely important decisions—and act on them—before the end of this one.

Comprehension

Without looking back at the text, mark the following statements "True" or "False," based on information from "How the World Will Look in 50 Years." Check your answers on page 203 of Appendix II.

_____ **1.** Economics will dominate the political world map of the twenty-first century, the article says.

_____ **2.** In general, the twenty-first century will be warlike, according to the author.

_____ **3.** In the twenty-first century, the Islamic world will become poorer and more isolated.

_____ **4.** The number one military superpower of the next century will be Russia.

_____ **5.** Europe will be the economic winner of the twenty-first century, the author says.

_____ **6.** Japanese workers will continue to work long hours in the coming century, according to the author.

_____ **7.** The author predicts that Taiwan and Hong Kong will become economic zones of the Chinese motherland (China).

_____ **8.** The author believes the United States will probably not be able to repair its domestic damage.

_____ **CORRECT** × **12.5** = _____ %

LANGUAGE STUDY

ACTIVITY

IT WORKS!
Learning Strategy:
Key Terms

In "How the World Will Look in 50 Years," the main subject areas are political science and economics. With a partner, define the following key terms, and list them and their definitions in your reading journal or on vocabulary cards. (Paragraph numbers are in parentheses.)

1. geopolitical (1)   **5.** genocide (4)
2. trade bloc (1)   **6.** intervention (4)
3. imperialism (3)   **7.** arms-control treaties (6)
4. ideologues (4)   **8.** nationalism (8)

LEARNING STRATEGY

Forming Concepts: Distinguishing between facts and opinions in speech or writing enables you to make clearer judgments about the information you receive.

Bruce W. Nelan's article, "How the World Will Look in 50 Years," contains many predictions about the politics and economy of countries in the world. In addition, Nelan presents many facts about these countries.

Examine these two sentences from the final paragraph of Nelan's article, and decide which presents a *fact* and which presents the author's *opinion*:

The end of the cold war has released immense resources and millions of talented people who can now turn to the repair of America's damage. . . .

But <u>if</u> the United States is to be counted among the winners in the next century, it <u>will have to make gravely important decisions—and act on them—before the end of this one</u>.

The first sentence is a *fact* because the cold war *has* ended and the United States can (has the ability to) work on its domestic problems. The second sentence, on the other hand, contains an *opinion,* the writer's prediction that if the United States wants to continue to be a world power, it must make important decisions within a certain time limit. The parts of this sentence that show it reflects an opinion are underlined.

ACTIVITY: FACT OR OPINION

Mark the statements below as F (Fact) or O (Opinion). Compare your answers with those of a classmate and then with those of the class.

_____ **1.** This concentration on economics will be made possible by the prospect of general peace in the twenty-first century, heralded by the lifting of the nuclear arms threat in the 1990s.

_____ **2.** In the century ahead, the world will contain more democracies than ever before, and they will dominate in Europe, the Americas, and the countries of the Pacific Rim.

_____ **3.** Truly determined governments, among them many smaller nations that covet prestige and power, cannot be prevented from buying or building nuclear arms.

_____ **4.** The biggest hope for the future of the old socialist world is its very well-educated work force and a high level of science and technology.

_____ **5.** Japan will not have things so much its own way in the next century.

_____ **6.** Right now, all Asia's "little tigers"—South Korea, Taiwan, Hong Kong, Singapore—run considerable deficits in their trade with Japan.

_____ **7.** In order to rise to a level of prosperity, a developing country must achieve decades of high growth rates while simultaneously holding its population stable.

_____ **8.** "In a world whose workers require ever more basic education, technological savvy and specialized skill," Marvin Cetron and Owen Davies write in their book *Crystal Globe,* "America's schools are the least successful in the Western world."

REACTIONS

ACTIVITY: SHARING IMPRESSIONS

Nelan's article, "How the World Will Look in 50 Years," contains numerous facts and opinions about the future of the world.

In a small group, review the statements in the previous exercise on page 191 in which you distinguished facts from opinions. Discuss your reactions to each of the statements. Make a list of your own opinions in support of or counter to each of the author's points.

Share your group's impressions with the class.

EVALUATION

ACTIVITY: CHAPTER SELF-TEST

Assess your general understanding of the readings in Chapter 8 by taking the following chapter self-examination. The day before you take this test, select ten vocabulary items from your reading journal or cards (key terms, personal vocabulary, and other vocabulary from exercises) that you would like to learn. Write them on a separate piece of paper and turn them in to your instructor. Then review your reading journal notes about the chapter and the readings.

On the test day, your instructor will return your word list. Fill in the definitions and parts of speech of your ten personal vocabulary words in Part 1. Circle the appropriate completion of each statement in Part 2. Check your answers to Part 1 in your reading journal or cards, and score your test. See page 203 in Appendix II for the answers to Part 2.

Part 1: Personal Vocabulary

Vocabulary Word	Definition	Part of Speech
1.		
2.		
3.		
4.		
5.		
6.		
7.		
8.		
9.		
10.		

_____ CORRECT × 10 = _____ %

Part 2: Comprehension

1. In "Free at Last: South Africa's Election Ratifies a Political Miracle for the Ages," the authors report that South Africa has a history that includes
   a. racist laws.
   b. tribal hostilities.
   c. white domination.
   d. all of the above

2. Which of the following statements best describes the present state of the Neo-Nazi movement in South Africa?
   a. It has been completely eliminated.
   b. It still threatens the new government.

3. The chart "South Africa's New Transitional Government" reports that South Africa
   a. will have two deputy presidents.
   b. will have ten deputy presidents.
   c. will have one deputy president.

4. In "The Chinese: Will They Be Capitalists?" which of these statements best describes the current activity in China's Guangdong province?
   a. Farmers grow rice.
   b. Buildings are under construction.
   c. Life remains the same as 20 years ago.
   d. a and b

5. Businessmen compare China's economic growth to
   a. the Cold War of the 1960s.
   b. the Gold Rush of the 1800s.
   c. the Great Depression of the 1930s.

6. Many foreign investors are attracted to China due to
   a. more than a decade of steady growth.
   b. the Chinese government's pro-business attitude.
   c. early entrepreneur's profits.
   d. all of the above

7. Due to its large population, China
   a. now uses as much fertilizer as Canada.
   b. will run out of trees by the end of the year.
   c. has less arable land per capita than Bangladesh.
   d. all of the above

8. Asia Watch, a United States–based human rights organization, describes China's policies towards political dissidents as
   a. fair.
   b. unfair.

9. The Arab states will have less power in the twenty-first century because of
   a. lower demand for oil.
   b. increased reliance on solar power.
   c. increased use of controlled nuclear fission.
   d. all of the above

10. The author says United Nations' role in the twenty-first century will be
    a. ineffective.
    b. powerful.
    c. limited.

_____ CORRECT × 10 = _____ %

ACTIVITY

Answer the following questions in your reading journal to help you self-assess your reading habits and adjust your goals accordingly. Consult your instructor for suggestions.

IT WORKS!
Learning Strategy:
Evaluating Your
Progress

1. Has your reading ability improved since you began this course?
   a. If so, identify the strategies that you have used that you believe make you a better reader. Explain how you are using these strategies.
   b. If not, identify the strategies that you will use in the future to make you a better reader. Explain how you will use these strategies.

ACTIVITIES: EVALUATING YOUR GOALS

A. Re-evaluate the learning objectives that you identified in previous chapters as most significant to you. Change the ranks of goals that you now think are more valuable. Add new personal learning objectives to the list if you wish.

GOAL   **RANK**

   1. To increase comprehension of readings   _____

   2. To expand vocabulary   _____

   3. To increase reading speed   _____

   4. To improve study skills   _____

   5. To learn more about the subjects of this chapter _____

   6. _____   _____

   7. _____   _____

B. In your reading journal, write briefly in answer to the following questions:

   1. The most important skills I used in reading and responding to the readings in

   this chapter were _____.

   2. The most valuable information I gained from this chapter was _____

   _____.

EXPANSION

Reading Further

Read about one political or economic change that is occurring in one country of the world. Find an article from a magazine or newspaper, or read part of a book. In your reading journal, write a brief summary and commentary on the reading. Give the name, author, publisher, and publication date of your reading.

Suggested magazines and journals include *Time, Current, Newsweek, World Watch, U.S. News & World Report, Utne Reader, UN Chronicle,* and *The Futurist.*

Appendix I

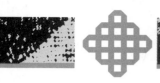

Two basic goals of reading are to understand and remember what you read. At times you also may need to understand, remember, and *read faster.* Realistically, if you want to read more, you will probably need to read faster. Your success in college, for instance, may require you to read a number of volumes in one short semester. In your everyday life, you may occasionally need to read a product warranty or a contract "on the spot" and make a quick decision. Thus, practice in increasing your reading speed, ideally to a rate of between 300 and 400 words per minute, is a key part of this course. Reading at that speed takes work, but it is achievable if you use tested and proven strategies. A few basic techniques are presented in "How to Read Faster," a practice timed reading included in this appendix. A comprehension test follows it.

In addition, each chapter includes timed readings. You can record your reading speed and self-monitor your comprehension by taking the comprehension tests following each reading. A chart on page 200 allows you to record your reading rates and comprehension scores as you work through the textbook. To begin, time yourself as you read the following text, which explains three simple steps for reading faster.

Timed Reading

Author Notes: Bill Cosby is a well-known American television and film actor. He starred in "The Cosby Show," a comedy about a black American family, during the 1980s, and has appeared in many feature films. In 1994, he began a television series entitled "The Cosby Mysteries." In addition, Cosby, who holds a doctorate in education, promotes literacy and donates millions of dollars to educational institutions.

HOW TO READ FASTER
by Bill Cosby

When I was a kid in Philadelphia, I must have read every comic book ever published. (There were fewer of them then than there are now.)

I zipped through all of them in a couple of days, then reread the good ones until the next issues arrived.

Yes indeed, when I was a kid, the reading game was a snap.

But as I got older, my eyeballs must have slowed down or something! I mean, comic books started to pile up faster than my brother Russell and I could read them! It wasn't until much later, when I was getting my doctorate, I realized it wasn't my eyeballs that were to blame. Thank goodness. They're still moving as well as ever.

The problem is, there's too much to read these days, and too little time to read every word of it.

Now, mind you, I still read comic books. In addition to contracts, novels, and newspapers. Screenplays, tax returns, and correspondence. Even textbooks about how people read. And which techniques help people read more in less time.

I'll let you in on a little secret. There are hundreds of techniques you could learn to help you read faster. But I know of three that are especially good.

And if I can learn them, so can you—and you can put them to use *immediately.*

They are commonsense, practical ways to get the meaning from printed words quickly and efficiently. So you'll have time to enjoy your comic books, have a good laugh with Mark Twain, or a good cry with *War and Peace*. Ready?

Okay. The first two ways can help you get through tons of reading material—fast—*without reading every word*.

They'll give you the *overall meaning* of what you're reading. And let you cut out an awful lot of *unnecessary* reading.

1. Preview—If It's Long and Hard

Previewing is especially useful for getting a general idea of heavy reading like long magazine or newspaper articles, business reports, and nonfiction books.

It can give you as much as half the comprehension in as little as one tenth the time. For example, you should be able to preview eight or ten 100-page reports in an hour. After previewing, you'll be able to decide which reports (or which *parts* of which reports) are worth a closer look.

Here's how to preview: Read the entire first two paragraphs of whatever you've chosen. Next read only the *first sentence* of each successive paragraph. Then read the entire last two paragraphs.

Previewing doesn't give you all the details. But it does keep you from spending time on things you don't really want—or need—to read.

Notice that previewing gives you a quick, overall view of *long, unfamiliar* material. For short, light reading, there's a better technique.

2. Skim—If It's Short and Simple

Skimming is a good way to get a general idea of light reading—like popular magazines or the sports and entertainment sections of the paper.

You should be able to skim a weekly popular magazine or the second section of your daily paper in less than *half* the time it takes you to read it now.

Skimming is also a great way to review material you've read before.

Here's how to skim: Think of your eyes as magnets. Force them to move fast. Sweep them across each and every line of type. Pick up *only a few key words in each line*.

Everybody skims differently.

197

You and I may not pick up exactly the same words when we skim the same piece, but we'll both get a pretty similar idea of what it's all about.

To show you how it works, I circled the words I picked out when I skimmed the following story. Try it. It shouldn't take you more than 10 seconds.

My brother (Russell) (thinks monsters) (live) in our (bedroom closet at night). But I told him (he is crazy).

"Go and (check) it (then)," he said.

"(I didn't want) to." Russell said (I was chicken).

"(Am not)," I said.

"(Are so)," he said.

So (I told him) the monsters were going to (eat him) (at midnight). He started to cry. My (Dad came) in and (told) the monsters to (beat it). Then he told us to (go to sleep).

"(If I hear) any more about monsters," he said. "I'll spank (you.)"

We went to (sleep fast). And you (know something)? They (never did) (come back).

Skimming can give you a very good *idea* of this story in about half the words—and in less than half the time it'd take to read every word.

So far, you've seen that previewing and skimming can give you a *general idea* about content—fast. But neither technique can promise more than 50 percent comprehension, because you aren't reading all the words. (Nobody gets something for nothing in the reading game.)

To *read faster and understand most*—if not all—of what you read, you need to know a third technique.

3. Cluster—To Increase Speed and Comprehension

Most of us learned to read by looking at each word in a second—*one at a time.*

Like this:

My—brother—Russell—thinks— monsters . . .

You probably still read this way sometimes, especially when the words are difficult. Or when the words have an extra-special meaning—as in a poem, a Shakespearean play, or a contract. And that's OK.

But word-by-word reading is a rotten way to read faster. It actually *cuts down* on your speed.

Clustering trains you to look at *groups* of words instead of one at a time—to increase your speed enormously. For most of us, clustering is a *totally different way of seeing what we read.*

Here's how to cluster: Train your eyes to see all the words in clusters of up to three or four words at a glance:

Here's how I'd cluster the story we just skimmed:

(My brother Russell) (thinks monsters) (live in) (our bedroom closet) (at night.) (But I told him) (he is crazy.)

"(Go and) (check it then,)" (he said.) "(I didn't want to.)" (Russell said) (I was chicken.)

"(Am not,)" (I said.)

"(Are so,)" (he said.)

(So I told him) (the monsters) (were going to) (eat him) (at midnight.) (He started) (to cry.) (My Dad came in) (and told the monsters) (to beat it.) (Then he told us) (to go) (to sleep.)

"(If I hear) (any more about) monsters," he said. ("I'll spank you.")

(We went) (to sleep fast.) (And you) (know something?) (They never did) (come back.)

Learning to read clusters is not something your eyes do naturally. It takes constant practice.

Here's how to go about it: Pick something light to read. Read it as fast as you can. Concentrate on seeing three to four words at once rather than one word at a time. Then reread the piece at your normal speed to see what you missed the first time.

Try a second piece. First cluster, then reread to see what you missed in this one.

When you can read in clusters without missing much the first time, your speed has increased. Practice 15 minutes every day and you might pick up the technique in a week or so. (But don't be disappointed if it takes longer. Clustering *everything* takes time and practice.)

So now you have three ways to help you read faster. <u>Preview</u> to cut down on unnecessary heavy reading. <u>Skim</u> to get a quick, general idea of light reading. And <u>cluster</u> to increase your speed <u>and</u> comprehension.

With enough practice, you'll be able to handle *more* reading at school or work—and at home—*in less time.* You should even have enough time to read your favorite comic books—<u>and</u> *War and Peace*!

ENDING TIME: _____ : _____
MINUTES TO READ: _____
TOTAL NUMBER OF WORDS: _____ = _____ WORDS/MIN

Comprehension Check

ACTIVITY

Mark the following statements "True" or "False," based on information in the reading, "How to Read Faster." Then, check your answers on page 203 of Appendix II. Record your percentage as well as your reading rate in the Reading Rate and Comprehension Chart on page 200 of this appendix.

_____ 1. As people get older, they read more slowly, according to the writer.

_____ 2. Previewing lets you comprehend about 50 percent of a reading, the author says.

_____ 3. It's good to skim long, unfamiliar texts.

_____ 4. Skimming means reading only the key words in each line.

_____ 5. Clustering helps you increase reading speed and comprehension.

_____ 6. Clustering is a reading technique that comes naturally to most people.

_____ 7. Everyone can learn the clustering technique in about one week.

_____ 8. The author uses all three methods to reduce his reading time.

NUMBER CORRECT: _____ × **12.5** = _____ %

READING RATE AND COMPREHENSION CHART

Timed Reading	Speed	Comprehension	Timed Reading	Speed	Comprehension

Appendix II

Chapter 1, p. 7

1.	T	6.	T
2.	F	7.	T
3.	F	8.	T
4.	T	9.	T
5.	F	10.	F

Chapter 1, p. 15

1.	T	6.	T
2.	F	7.	F
3.	T	8.	T
4.	F	9.	F
5.	F	10.	T

Chapter 1, p. 21

1.	T	6.	F
2.	F	7.	T
3.	T	8.	F
4.	F	9.	F
5.	T	10.	T

Chapter 1, p. 23

1.	c	6.	e
2.	b	7.	d
3.	c	8.	c
4.	d	9.	c
5.	c	10.	a

Chapter 2, p. 33

1.	F	6.	F
2.	T	7.	T
3.	T	8.	F
4.	F	9.	T
5.	F	10.	T

Chapter 2, p. 41

1.	T	6.	T
2.	F	7.	F
3.	T	8.	T
4.	F	9.	F
5.	F	10.	T

Chapter 2, p. 45

1.	b	6.	b
2.	a	7.	a
3.	a	8.	b
4.	c	9.	a
5.	a	10.	c

Chapter 3, p. 54

1.	F	6.	F
2.	F	7.	T
3.	T	8.	T
4.	F	9.	F
5.	T	10.	T

Chapter 3, p. 59

1.	T	6.	F
2.	T	7.	F
3.	F	8.	F
4.	T		
5.	T		

Chapter 3, p. 65

1.	F	6.	F
2.	F	7.	T
3.	T	8.	F
4.	T	9.	F
5.	F	10.	T

Chapter 3, p. 69

1.	T	6.	T
2.	T	7.	T
3.	T	8.	T
4.	F	9.	F
5.	T	10.	T

Chapter 3, p. 71

1.	b	6.	d
2.	a	7.	b
3.	d	8.	a
4.	c	9.	b
5.	a	10.	c

Chapter 4, p. 80

1.	T	6.	T
2.	F	7.	F
3.	F	8.	T
4.	T	9.	F
5.	T	10.	T

Chapter 4, p. 88

1.	F	6.	T
2.	T	7.	T
3.	F	8.	T
4.	T	9.	F
5.	T	10.	T

Chapter 4, p. 93

1.	T	6.	T
2.	F	7.	T
3.	F	8.	T
4.	F		
5.	F		

Chapter 4, p. 95

1.	a	6.	a
2.	d	7.	c
3.	b	8.	b
4.	a	9.	d
5.	c	10.	a

Chapter 5, p. 107

1.	F	6.	T
2.	T	7.	F
3.	F	8.	F
4.	T	9.	F
5.	T	10.	T

Chapter 5, p. 114

1.	T	6.	T
2.	F	7.	T
3.	F	8.	T
4.	T	9.	T
5.	F	10.	F

Chapter 5, p. 119

1. F	**6.** T
2. T	**7.** F
3. T	**8.** T
4. F	**9.** F
5. T	**10.** T

Chapter 5, p. 122

1. b	**6.** c
2. c	**7.** c
3. a	**8.** c
4. d	**9.** c
5. b	**10.** a

Chapter 6, p. 132

1. T	**6.** F
2. F	**7.** T
3. T	**8.** T
4. T	**9.** T
5. F	**10.** T

Chapter 6, p. 137

1. T	**6.** F
2. F	**7.** F
3. T	**8.** T
4. F	
5. F	

Chapter 6, p. 141

1. F	**6.** T
2. F	**7.** T
3. F	**8.** F
4. T	**9.** F
5. T	**10.** T

Chapter 6, p. 146

1. a	**6.** d
2. d	**7.** a
3. d	**8.** b
4. b	**9.** d
5. b	**10.** c

Chapter 7, p. 155

1. F	**6.** T
2. F	**7.** F
3. T	**8.** T
4. T	**9.** T
5. T	**10.** T

Chapter 7, p. 160

1. T	**6.** F
2. F	**7.** T
3. T	**8.** T
4. F	**9.** F
5. T	**10.** T

Chapter 7, p. 165

1. F	**6.** T
2. T	**7.** T
3. T	**8.** F
4. F	
5. F	

Chapter 7, p. 169

1. a	**6.** a
2. c	**7.** b
3. a	**8.** c
4. c	**9.** d
5. b	**10.** a

Chapter 8, p. 177

1. T	**6.** F
2. F	**7.** T
3. T	**8.** F
4. F	
5. T	

Chapter 8, p. 184

1. F	**6.** T
2. T	**7.** T
3. T	**8.** F
4. T	**9.** T
5. T	**10.** F

Chapter 8, p. 190

1. T	**6.** F
2. F	**7.** T
3. T	**8.** F
4. F	
5. T	

Chapter 8, p. 192

1. d	**6.** d
2. b	**7.** d
3. a	**8.** b
4. d	**9.** a
5. b	**10.** b

Appendix I, p. 199

1. F	**5.** T
2. T	**6.** F
3. F	**7.** F
4. T	**8.** T